Historical Perspectives on Modern Economics

D0087333

The history of econometric ideas

Historical Perspectives on Modern Economics

General Editor: Professor Craufurd D. Goodwin, Duke University

This series contains original works that challenge and enlighten historians of economics. For the profession as a whole it promotes a better understanding of the origin and content of modern economics.

Other books in the series
Don Lavoie: *Rivalry and central planning: The socialist calculation debate reconsidered*
Takashi Negishi: *Economic theories in a non-Walrasian tradition*
E. Roy Weintraub: *General equilibrium analysis: Studies in appraisal*
William J. Barber: *From new era to New Deal: Herbert Hoover, the economists, and American economic policy, 1921–1933*
Gerard M. Koot: *English historical economics*
Kim Kyun: *Equilibrium business cycle theory in historical perspective*

The history of econometric ideas

MARY S. MORGAN
Department of Economic History,
London School of Economics

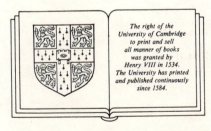

The right of the
University of Cambridge
to print and sell
all manner of books
was granted by
Henry VIII in 1534.
The University has printed
and published continuously
since 1584.

CAMBRIDGE UNIVERSITY PRESS

Cambridge

New York   Port Chester   Melbourne   Sydney

Published by the Press Syndicate of the University of Cambridge
The Pitt Building, Trumpington Street, Cambridge CB2 1RP
40 West 20th Street, New York, NY 10011, USA
10 Stamford Road, Oakleigh, Melbourne 3166, Australia

First published 1990

Printed and bound in Great Britain by
Redwood Burn Limited, Trowbridge, Wiltshire

British Library cataloguing in publication data

Morgan, Mary S.
The history of econometric ideas – (Historical perspectives on modern
economics).
1. Econometrics, history.
I. Title. II. Series.
330′.028

Library of Congress cataloguing in publication data

Morgan, Mary S.
The history of econometric ideas / Mary S. Morgan.
      p.   cm. – (Historical perspectives on modern economics)
Bibliography.
Includes index.
ISBN 0 521 37398 0
1. Econometrics. I. Title. II. Series.
HB139.M66   1990
330′.01′5195–dc20   89–9790 CIP

ISBN 0 521 37398 0

To Charles

Contents

Figures

Preface

When I first began to research the history of econometrics in 1979, it was a fairly common assumption amongst economists that econometrics had no past, no history, before the 1950s. I was glad to find this was not so, and my pages were not to remain blank. But, instead of the decorative collection of antique notions which might have been expected, I had the excitement of discovering that pre-1950 econometrics was bristling with interesting people and functional ideas. No wonder, for it was during this early period that the fundamental concepts and notions of the econometric approach were thought out. This book is the history of those ideas.

Since there was little in the way of existing literature on the development of econometrics, I have relied on the help of many people. First, I should like to thank those pioneer econometricians who patiently answered my questions about what they were doing and thinking anything up to 50 years, or even more, ago. Amongst the founding fathers of the subject, I was able to talk to Trygve Haavelmo, Herman Wold, Richard Stone, Jan Tinbergen, Olav Reiersøl, George Kuznets, and the late Tjalling Koopmans, Sewall Wright and Holbrook Working. All helped me in various ways: they corrected some of my misapprehensions and filled in the gaps in my understanding in the way that only those with personal experience of the events and their time could do. Their help gave me confidence that I was working along the right lines, particularly when it came to questions of interpretation and channels of influence which usually remain off the written record. The second generation of econometricians were equally generous with their time and amongst many, I would like to thank particularly Ted Anderson, Guy Orcutt, Lawrence Klein, Karl Fox, Arnold Zellner, Arthur Goldberger and Clive Granger.

David Hendry first introduced me to the history of econometrics and his enthusiasm for the subject has been the major stimulation to my work: he pointed out the paths to follow and guided me along them. I have gained greatly from his insights into the nature of econometrics, and his questions and arguments over the last 10 years have forced me to think more rigorously about the field's history than I otherwise would have done. John Aldrich too has been an influential and invaluable critic of my work. I have learnt much about the history of econometrics from John; nevertheless, we agree to differ on a number of issues and his history features different personnel and different ideas. Dudley Baines, Meghnad Desai and Steven Pudney were all at one time or another the supervisors (along with David Hendry) of my LSE doctoral thesis (1984), in which this book originated: each helped me in different ways. To all of these, I offer thanks, but especially to David Hendry and John Aldrich.

My approach to the history of econometrics was both sharpened and shaped by my experience of 1982–3, when I was lucky enough to join a large research group of historians and philosophers of science investigating the 'probabilistic revolution' in science and society since 1800. I would like to thank all the participants of that year, which was one of great intellectual stimulation and excitement for me as I was introduced to the great wide world of history of science. I have particularly benefited from the help, both then and since, in reading, in conversation and in comments on chapters from Nancy Cartwright, Raine Daston, Ted Porter, Gerd Gigerenzer, Norton Wise and Ian Hacking. I thank MIT Press for permission to use the material I contributed to *The Probabilistic Revolution* (edited by Lorenz Krüger *et al.*, 1987) in Chapter 8 of this book.

Three other colleagues who have provided criticism and intellectual encouragement at vital points are Margaret Schabas, Neil de Marchi and Jens Andvig. Margaret and Jens have been pursuing parallel projects on Jevons and Frisch respectively and both have proved great working allies. Neil's questions and queries have provoked me to express myself more accurately. Friends such as these should not be taken for granted and I thank them.

Numerous others have made helpful comments and offered insights, in correspondence or during the course of seminars on my work, for which I thank them all. Not the least of those who remain, I thank the publisher's referee for many pertinent comments; I hope the final product meets with approval. With so much help, it is impossible to acknowledge fully the individual contributions to the development of my ideas and this book. Grateful as I am, it is necessary to add that those who have helped me should not of course, be taken to agree with my reconstruction and interpretation of events. And, despite all the help I have received and my best efforts to be accurate, errors no doubt remain and for these I am responsible.

My research was made possible by the generosity of the ESRC (then the SSRC) in funding the original 'History of Econometric Thought' project at the LSE under David Hendry's direction (Grant HR6727), and the Volkswagen Foundation who supported my participation in the Probabilistic Revolution project directed by Lorenz Krüger. To both, I am very grateful. Thanks are also due to the Central Research Fund of the University of London and the Northern Studies Fund at the LSE for travel support. The Suntory-Toyoto International Centre for Economics and Related Disciplines at the LSE and the Centre for Interderdisciplinary Research at the University of Bielefeld kindly 'housed' me during the course of my research. I would also like to thank Anne Craiger of the Special Collections Library at UCLA for helping me with Marschak's papers, and Mr Gjönnes, the librarian at the University of Oslo, who helped me with Frisch's papers. In addition, I am indebted to James Heckman and the late Leif Johansen who helped me during my research visits to Chicago and Oslo respectively, and I especially thank Peter Phillips who arranged my access to the Cowles Commission archives and looked after me so well during my visit to the Cowles Foundation at Yale.

Mike Lail and William Corley checked all my bibliographical entries and Kealan Doyle the quoted material; Linda Sampson has provided secretarial support; and Patrick McCartan and Linda Randall of CUP and my father and Joan Cox helped with the final stages of the book's production, for which I thank them all.

Finally, I am grateful that my family and friends have borne with me sympathetically during the long process of writing this book. My deepest and most heartfelt thanks are to Charles Baden Fuller who most patiently read several drafts of each chapter, helping me to clarify my thoughts at each stage. It is truly the case that this book would never have been written without his constant help and encouragement.

Acknowledgements

The author thanks the following societies and publishers for their permission to reprint diagrams and other materials used in this book: Macmillan Press Ltd for Figure 1 (Plate XIV in W. S. Jevons, *Investigations in Currency and Finance* (1884)) and for Figure 2 (Figure 27 in H. L. Moore, *Economic Cycles – Their Law and Cause* (1914)); the National Bureau of Economic Research for Figure 4 (Chart 2, p. 35, in A. F. Burns and W. C. Mitchell, *Measuring Business Cycles*, Studies in Business Cycles, No. 2. New York: Columbia University Press (copyright 1946 by the National Bureau of Economic Research)); the President and Fellows of Harvard College for Figure 5 (the diagram on p. 112 of W. M. Persons, 'Indices of Business Conditions', *Review of Economic Statistics*, **1** (1919)); the Royal Statistical Society for Figure 6 (Figure 5 in G. U. Yule, 'Why Do We Sometimes Get Nonsense Correlations Between Time-Series?', *Journal of the Royal Statistical Society*, **89** (1926)); the Econometric Society for Figure 7 (Figure 3 in E. E. Slutsky, 'The Summation of Random Causes as the Source of Cyclic Processes', *Econometrica*, **5** (1937)) and the material quoted in Chapter 8 from T. Haavelmo, 'The Probability Approach in Econometrics', *Econometrica*, **12** (Supplement) (1944); the Royal Economic Society for Figure 12 (Graph 1 in J. Tinbergen, 'A Reply', *Economic Journal*, **50** (1940)); Generale de Droit et de Jurisprudence for Figure 13 (Figure 44 in M. Lenoir, *Etudes sur la formation et le mouvement des prix* (1913)) and for permission to translate and quote part of Lenoir's text in Chapter 6; the American Statistical Association for Figure 14 (Charts II and III in P. G. Wright's review of H. Schultz' *Statistical Laws of Demand and Supply*, *Journal of the American Statistical Association*, **24** (1929)). Figure 3 is reprinted from C. Juglar, *Des crises commerciales et de leur retour périodique en France, en Angleterre et aux Etats-Unis*, published by Guillaumin et Cie (1889), and reprinted by Augustus M. Kelly (1967). I also thank Jan Tinbergen for permission to reprint Figures 10–12 from his League of

Nations' work; and Trygve Haavelmo for permission to quote extensively from his 1944 paper 'The Probability Approach in Econometrics' and to use Figures 17 and 18 adapted from his joint 1941 paper with H. Staehle.

Introduction

Econometrics was regarded by its first practitioners as a creative synthesis of theory and evidence, with which almost anything and everything could, it seems, be achieved: new economic laws might be discovered and new economic theories developed, as well as old laws measured and existing theories put to the test. This optimism was based on an extraordinary faith in quantitative techniques and the belief that econometrics bore the hallmarks of a genuinely scientific form of applied economics.[1] In the first place, the econometric approach was not primarily an empirical one: econometricians firmly believed that economic theory played an essential part in finding out about the world. But to see how the world really worked, theory had to be applied; and their statistical evidence boasted all the right scientific credentials: the data were numerous, numerical and as near as possible objective. Finally, econometricians depended on an analytical method based on the latest advances in statistical techniques. These new statistical methods were particularly important for they gave economists of the early twentieth century ways of finding out about the world which had been unavailable to their nineteenth-century forebears, ways which, in themselves, seemed to guarantee scientific respectability for econometrics.

So, when econometrics emerged as a distinct activity at the beginning of the twentieth century, its use of statistical methods and data to measure and reveal the relationships of economic theory offered a form of investigation strikingly different from those of nineteenth-century economics, which ranged from the personal introspection and casual observation of classical economics to the detailed empiricism of historical economics. The applied economics of the twentieth century was to be based on a more modern technology: its tools were to be statistical methods, mathematical models and even mechanical calculators. With

---

[1] Moore (1911) (particularly pp. 4–6) provides an excellent example of the optimistic programme laid down in econometrics and its associated technology.

the appeal of this new technology, econometrics was to become firmly established by the 1940s, and the dominant form of applied economic science thereafter.

Those readers who know something of present-day econometrics may already suspect that the econometrics programme has changed in some respects from its original conception and practices. The most salient difference between early and modern econometrics is that the early econometricians consciously *conjoined* mathematical economics and statistical economics. Indeed the Econometric Society, founded in 1931, had as its main aim:

> to promote studies that aim at a unification of the theoretical-quantitative and the empirical-quantitative approach to economic problems and that are penetrated by constructive and rigorous thinking similar to that which has come to dominate in the natural sciences. Any activity which promises ultimately to further such unification of theoretical and factual studies in economics shall be within the sphere of interest of the Society.
>
> (Frisch (1933b), p.1)

For the econometricians of the first half of the twentieth century, the union of mathematics and statistics with economics was the ideal way of practising scientific economics.

Exactly how the econometric ideal, the union of mathematical and statistical economics, emerged in the early twentieth century is an interesting question. The obvious supposition is that the roots of econometrics lie in the mathematical and statistical economics of the nineteenth century. Yet, in the contemporary view of that time (as in economics today), mathematics and statistics were believed to operate in different spheres. Mathematics was thought essential to the further advancement of economics as a deductive scientific discipline.[2] It was believed that the use of mathematics, that is calculus and algebra, would lead to clarity and conciseness in the expression of theories (and of the assumptions these involved) and that the process of mathematical reasoning would make economic arguments more rigorous. The many virtues claimed for the mathematical method helped it to gain acceptance amongst a small group of analytical economists in the nineteenth century, with the result that mathematical economics was at the cutting edge of theoretical work from the 1880s. But, if one takes into account the full range of styles and methods in economics,

---

[2] See for example Schabas' papers (1984) on Jevons, and (1989) on Marshall. Of course, the desire for a scientific economics as opposed to a theological or historical economics was not shared by all nineteenth-century economists. Arguments about the validity of using mathematics and statistics in economics both pre-date and post-date the development of econometrics.

mathematical reasoning was used by only a handful of economists, albeit an influential one, in the last quarter of the nineteenth century. The method only really came into more common, though still not widespread, usage in the period after 1930. Numerical examples and geometric illustrations were sometimes introduced to help explain economic ideas before algebra and differential calculus were used in theory development, but even these were still comparatively rare before 1900.[3]

By comparison, the use of statistical data in economics has a long history going back to the political arithmetic school of Petty and Graunt in the late seventeenth century.[4] But there was no continuing tradition, not that is until the general rise of statistical thinking in the nineteenth century which was particularly associated with the emergent social sciences.[5] It was believed then that the application of statistical analysis would improve the inductive side of economics, and as the nineteenth century wore on, the casual and often indiscriminate use of statistical data in economics did begin to give way to a more careful usage. Statistical data proved helpful in establishing economic regularities, in presenting economic arguments and most effectively in taking measurements of economic variables (of which easily the most sophisticated was the construction of index numbers).

Jevons even hoped that statistics could be used to obtain the numerically precise (or 'concrete') laws thought to be typical of good physical science.

> I do not hesitate to say, too, that Political Economy might be gradually erected into an exact science, if only commercial statistics were far more complete and accurate than they are at present, so that the formulae could be endowed with exact meaning by the aid of numerical data.
>
> (Jevons (1871), p. 25)

Perhaps he had in mind the example of astronomy, generally regarded as the most perfect and advanced of the sciences, which had by the mid-nineteenth century already invoked the aid of both mathematics and statistics. Astronomers faced with several different measures of the path of a planet (believed to be of an exact mathematical form)

---

[3] The post 1930s timing is suggested by G. J. Stigler (1965) who analysed the proportion of journal articles using mathematical techniques of all sorts. The early uses of graphs in economics are surveyed by J. L. Klein (1987a).

[4] The political arithmetic school of late seventeenth-century Britain and the physiocrats of eighteenth-century France are covered at some length in Schumpeter's (1954) discussion of examples of statistics in economics. In passing he also mentions other economists who depended on statistical information in Spain (sixteenth century) and in Germany and Italy (eighteenth century).

[5] See the essays in the fourth section: 'Society' in Krüger et al. (1987, I), and Porter (1986), which I discuss later in this Introduction.

extracted the equation of the path, discarding the residuals as errors of measurement. Economists could look also to the field of psychology, where statistical techniques were first used in the 1860s to measure stimulus–response relationships in experimental circumstances (the Weber–Fechner law). These 'psychophysicists' adopted both the mathematical model and statistical methods of early nineteenth-century astronomy, thus effectively safeguarding both determinism in theories and objectivity in applied work, in order to gain scientific respectability for psychology.[6] It does not seem too far-fetched to imagine a polymath such as Jevons experimenting on himself to try and measure increments of utility, rather as Fechner measured his own ability to discriminate between differently weighted objects. Note, though, that the possibility of experiment was not a necessary pre-requisite to the use of statistics to measure economic relationships; after all, astronomers could not manipulate the planets and stars.

But these are speculations, for econometrics did not emerge in the nineteenth century. With hindsight, one can see a number of obstacles which precluded a unified scientific programme of mathematical and statistical economics of the sort which flowered in the first half of the twentieth century. One obvious problem was the lack of relevant economic data: not all theoretical variables had measurements or even observational counterparts (utility being only one example). Equally pertinent, statistical methods (discussed in more detail later in this introduction) were not sufficiently advanced to be able to assign numerical values to the complex causal laws of behaviour which featured in economic theories. Even in the late nineteenth century statistical methods could still do little more for the social sciences than establish descriptive regularities in single variables, like suicide, or provide comparisons of regularities in two variables. Even had data and appropriate methods been available, mathematical economists rarely framed their theories with an eye to making them amenable to statistical treatment. With some prescience, J. N Keynes (1891) noted that the geometric representations favoured by mathematical econo-mists 'lend themselves naturally to the registering of statistics', but geometric representations as I have noted already were still unusual. Last but not least, nineteenth-century economists believed that mathematics and statistics worked in different ways: mathematics as a tool of deduction and statistics as a tool of induction. Jevons, who pioneered the use of both mathematics and statistics in his work,

---

[6] See S. M. Stigler (1986) for a recent account of the nineteenth-century use of statistics in astronomy and psychophysics. Gigerenzer relates how the tactics of psychophysicists were followed by later generations of psychologists in essay 1 in Krüger *et al.* (1987, II).

expressed both the status quo of those aiming at a scientific economics and his own vision of econometrics when he wrote:

> The deductive science of Economy must be verified and rendered useful by the purely inductive science of Statistics. Theory must be invested with the reality and life of fact. But the difficulties of this union are immensely great. (Jevons (1871), p. 26)

It might be argued that we should look not to the history of economic methods but to the history of the people, the economists themselves, in order to understand where econometrics came from. Here, too, we can suggest possibilities rather than find definitive answers. In one of the few systematic descriptions of the rise of quantification in nineteenth- and early twentieth-century economics, Spengler (1961) discusses both national styles and schools of thought. He suggests that quantification flourished in the neoclassical school, and that Marshall and Edgeworth were particularly responsible for its success, for both believed in the complementarity of the deductive and inductive methods in economics. Yet Marshall did not have much time for statistical economics (and his strong influence on English economics perhaps accounts for the poor representation of Britain in early econometric work) and Edgeworth's peculiar brand of probability and economics did not turn into econometrics. That other great mathematical and neoclassical pioneer, Walras, like his compatriot Cournot, had no time for statistics (see Ménard (1980)). Jevons alone seems to fit the bill and the surprise is rather that despite his pronouncements he avoided the complementary use of mathematical models and statistical techniques in his applied work. Further, the most important pioneer American econometrician, Moore, embraced econometrics partly because he became disenchanted with the ideas and methods of the neoclassical school. Although econometricians of the 1930s were to refer to their tradition as that of Cournot, Walras and Marshall, any simple derivation of econometrics from the neoclassical programme is highly dubious, not least because it ignores the important inputs from empirical economics.

Late nineteenth-century economists of the historical and institutionalist schools tended to welcome the growing wealth of statistical facts without necessarily adopting statistical explanations. In Germany, the historical school of political economists formed the nucleus of a wider intellectual circle which warmly embraced statistical thinking.[7] This circle provided intimate links between statistical thinkers such as Lexis and Engel and historical economists such as Schmoller. Craver and

---

[7] See the three overlapping accounts by Porter, Hacking and Wise (essays 17–19) in Krüger *et al.* (1987, I).

Leijonhufvud (1987) trace both how this empirical statistical strand entered the American institutionalist school in the late nineteenth century (many of whose members had trained in Germany with economists of the historical school) and how this statistical approach was re-exported back to Europe in the 1920s. But the American economists who accepted statistical evidence were often those who most strongly rejected mathematical methods and models in economics. The USA apart,[8] the most fertile environments for the practical development of econometrics in the early twentieth century proved to be the Netherlands and Scandinavia, yet Spengler suggests that nineteenth-century Dutch economists had no particular strengths in mathematics or statistics and the Scandinavians were good in mathematics but had little in the way of statistical background. So, despite many interesting comments on mathematical and statistical economics separately, Spengler does not help us to gain a clearer idea about the personal process by which econometrics emerged.

This search for a pattern reaching back into nineteenth-century economics may well be doomed, for the econometricians of the early twentieth-century period were not wedded to any particular tradition. They were a determinedly international bunch, of diverse intellectual backgrounds, and eclectic in their economic beliefs.[9] National style and theoretical allegiance seemed to matter less than the enthusiasm econometricians generated for their common methodological programme. Frisch's memory of the First European Meeting of the Econometric Society in 1931 in Lausanne was vividly recalled in 1970:

> We, the Lausanne people, were indeed so enthusiastic all of us about the new venture, and so eager to give and take, that we had hardly time to eat when we sat together at lunch or at dinner with all our notes floating around on the table to the despair of the waiters.   (Frisch (1970), p. 152)

Tracing out the personal roots of this enthusiasm, and the links between econometricians and the wider scientific community of the twentieth century, remain important tasks for the future. The most fruitful place to start such a search might well prove to be amongst the statistical thinkers, for the content and evolution of the econometric programme in its formative years was much influenced by developments in statistics. And in the longer run, mathematical economics and

---

[8] Craver and Leijonhufvud (1987) also stress the importance of the intellectual migration from Europe in the later period (1930s and 1940s) to the econometric work done in the USA during the 1940s.

[9] That the econometricians believed in freedom of economic theory is borne out by a glance at the original Advisory Editorial Board of *Econometrica* which included economists from many different schools of thought.

statistical economics divided again, leaving econometrics firmly on the statistical side of the fence.[10]

When we look at the history of statistics we find that econometrics was far from an isolated development, for statistical methods and probabilistic thinking were widely introduced into nineteenth- and early twentieth-century science. Few scientific fields remained unaffected, although statistical thinking and probability did not always enter at the same level in each discipline, as I have helped to argue elsewhere.[11] The econometrics movement was paralleled in particular by biometrics in biology and psychometrics in psychology. As their names suggest, all three were concerned with measurement and inference, in particular with the use of statistical methods to reveal and to substantiate the laws of their subject matters; and all three developed at roughly the same time.

Two recent books on the history of statistics prior to 1900 set the scene for this explosion of statistical activity (of which econometrics was a small part) in the early twentieth century. T. M. Porter's (1986) excellent book illuminates the difficult terrain between statistical thinking (ways of analysing masses of events) and probabilistic thinking (where chance and randomness hold sway). This account is complemented by S. M. Stigler's (1986) equally interesting history of the techniques of statistical inference. Both authors stress the importance in the early nineteenth century of Quetelet's statistical characterisation of human behaviour: individuals behave in an unpredictable way, but taken together these apparently disorganised individuals obey the law of errors in deviating from the ideal 'average man'. This observation of statistical regularity in human affairs proved enormously influential. For example, Porter shows how such social statistics led physicists, by analogy, to statistical mechanics. For Stigler, on the other hand, Quetelet's notions created barriers to the transfer of

---

[10] Although the econometricians aimed to synthesise mathematical and statistical economics, it is not clear whether mathematical models were necessary for the successful application of statistics to economics. The material in the first two Parts of this book suggests only that mathematical economics was an important prerequisite for certain applications of statistics, but not all (see also Morgan (1988)). That there is no absolute necessity for the two methods to go together is evident when we remember that Galton required no mathematical law of inheritance to see the statistical regression relation in his data on the heights of fathers and sons. In psychometrics, we find mathematical models developed out of the statistical work rather than being an essential part of its development.

[11] The question of levels of entry is discussed in the introduction to Krüger *et al.* (1987, II), and the papers in that volume provide case studies of the use of statistics and probability in the sciences. These show that in some sciences, probability and statistics helped in measurement and data description; in others, the focus was on inference; and in others still, such ideas entered the theories themselves.

inference techniques from astronomy and geodesy to the emergent social sciences.

Quetelet's influence is reflected in the typical nineteenth-century interpretation of statistical regularity to be found in Mill's (1872) classic discussion of methods of scientific inference.[12] Thus: taking many observations together has the effect of eliminating those circumstances due to chance (i.e. the variable or individual causes), and the statistical regularity that emerges from the mass of data verifies that a causal law (or constant cause) is at work. This idea of individuals as subject to one constant cause and many small variable causes (obeying the law of errors) left the constant cause operating at, or through, the medium of 'society'. But statistical inference procedures were not adept at uncovering such a constant cause of the average man's tendency to suicide, or to murder, or whatever. A plurality of causes acting at the individual level might be more credible to our minds, but would be equally difficult to uncover, for, as Stigler points out, there were no natural or external (theoretically imposed) ways of categorising such social observations into the homogeneous groups necessary for the existing statistical analysis, and as yet no statistical methods to deal with the plurality of causes.

The resolution of these difficulties began in the late nineteenth century with the reinterpretation of people's behaviour not in terms of errors, but as natural or real variation due to the complex causes of human and moral affairs. Porter identifies this as the second breakthrough in statistical thinking, when the 'law of errors' became the 'normal distribution'. This led directly to the development of statistical laws of inheritance in genetics, namely regression (1877–86) and correlation (1889–96).[13] These law-like relations are important because they are, according to Hacking (1983a), the first genuinely 'autonomous statistical laws': laws which offer an effective explanation for phenomena without the need to refer back to previous causes. In Porter's account, the adoption of such statistical models freed the social and natural sciences from the determinism of nineteenth-century physical science, and led both to a flowering of statistical work in diverse applied fields and to the development of the theoretical field of

---

[12] The original edition of Mill's treatise was 1843. My account reflects the situation in the eighth edition (1872) (the last in his lifetime), by which time Mill had become acquainted with Quetelet's ideas on statistics via Buckle's popularising efforts. From the point of view of the interpretation of statistical regularities, the situation changed little between these editions, or until the end of the century, as is evident from Durkheim's (1895) treatise on sociological method.

[13] The span of these dates reflects the main development of the concepts and their mathematical expression, based on S. M. Stigler's (1986) and Porter's (1986) accounts.

mathematical statistics. For Stigler, it is Yule's (1897) contribution linking these new statistical laws to the old astronomical method of least squares which was the crucial step in making least squares regression a general tool for statistical analysis. This transformation opened up the development of multivariate analysis in which there was the possibility of statistically controlling (or categorising) one variable while investigating the behaviour of the remaining variables.

An account which aims at a more specialised history of the conceptual foundations of econometrics, from late seventeenth-century political arithmetic to 1920, is offered by J. L. Klein (1986). Although she draws on the same areas of applied statistics as both Porter and Stigler, she tells yet another story. Her argument is that both biometrics and econometrics were founded on the need to make temporal variation amenable to analysis. Thus, logical (or non-temporal) variation in human phenomena were given a statistical identity in terms of Quetelet's 'average man' and Pearson's normal distribution. In order to provide for the temporal variation between generations, biometricians developed the relationships of regression and correlation. Econometricians adopted these new biometric tools, along with some notions of stochastic processes from astronomy, to provide statistical ways of characterising economic relationships over time.

These three accounts of the history of statistics by Porter, Stigler and Klein are all very suggestive, but why should economists want to adopt the new statistical methods? What was it about the new methods that justified early twentieth-century econometricians' optimism about their approach? The answer lies in the ability of the new statistical methods to provide a substitute for the experimental method. The idea of a scientific or controlled experiment is to reproduce the conditions required by a theory and then to manipulate the relevant variables in order to take measurements of a particular scientific parameter or to test the theory. When the data are not collected under controlled conditions or are not from repeatable experiments, then the relationship between the data and the theoretical laws is likely to be neither direct nor clear-cut. This problem was not, of course, unique to economics; it arose in other social sciences and in natural sciences where controlled experiments were not possible. In order to see how statistics comes in here, we need to return just once more to the nineteenth century, when economists seeking a more scientific profile for economics regularly bewailed the fact that the experimental method available to the physical sciences was inapplicable to economics.

A statistical substitute for scientific experiment in the nineteenth century relied on the statistical method's ability to extract a regularity, or repeated pattern, or constant relationship, from a mass of data (instead of taking one observation from an individually manipulated or varied event). As Porter's account emphasises, the ability of statistics to discern order out of chaos was one of the crucial innovations in nineteenth-century social statistics. And, I have referred already to the example of astronomy, the paradigmatic example of nineteenth-century use of statistical methods in which an exact relationship was extracted from several varying measurements of the relationship. But such nineteenth-century statistical ideas and methods did not necessarily provide ready-made solutions to twentieth-century problems. Yule expressed this most neatly:

> The investigation of causal relations between economic phenomena presents many problems of peculiar difficulty, and offers many opportunities for fallacious conclusions. Since the statistician can seldom or never make experiments for himself, he has to accept the data of daily experience, and discuss as best he can the relations of a whole group of changes; he cannot, like the physicist, narrow down the issue to the effect of one variation at a time. The problems of statistics are in this sense far more complex than the problems of physics.   (Yule (1897), p. 812.)

The highly complex causal laws of the social and biological sciences required measurement methods designed to neutralise or allow for the effects of the variable (i.e. uncontrolled) circumstances under which data have been collected in place of the full control which defines the ideal case of the scientific experiment. These are precisely the characteristics which Stigler seizes upon in his account of the new statistical methods emanating from the biometric school; measurement methods which were to enable the twentieth-century scientist some degree of control over non-experimentally obtained data and which allowed them to deal with the plurality of causes.[14]

It does seem that the conditions necessary for the successful prosecution of a statistical economics were fulfilled in the early twentieth century, but we should beware, for there is no necessity about any field's adoption of new ways of statistical thinking as the variety of case studies in Krüger *et al.* (1987, II) makes clear. In addition, both Porter

---

[14] As support for my argument here, it is appropriate to note that many twentieth-century philosophers of science take it for granted that scientists use these statistical methods as a substitute for experiments they cannot conduct. Whether statistical methods are efficacious in uncovering causal laws continues, as in the nineteenth century, to be open to question. Of several recent contributions, Cartwright's (1989) treatment is particularly relevant for she discusses the case of econometrics. She argues that the statistical methods used in econometrics could in principle give knowledge of causal relationships, though very often the presuppositions of the method are not met, so that the causal inferences can not be made (see her Chapters 1 and 2).

and Stigler stress the difficulties of adapting statistical tools and ideas designed in one scientific arena for use in another. This problem did not simply disappear in 1900, as evidenced by the fact that biometrics, psychometrics and econometrics forged their own different versions of the new tools. In biometrics, R. A. Fisher designed techniques to randomise (and thus neutralise) the effects of non-controllable factors in agricultural experiments. Psychometricians such as Thurstone developed Spearman's factor analysis method to extract measurements of the apparently unobservable 'vectors of the mind' from data on observable characteristics in order to solve their own data-theory gap.[15] Neither technique was directly appropriate for economics. Provided with general tools, econometricians still had to develop their own statistical solutions to the problems of bridging the gap between conditions demanded by theory and the conditions under which data were collected. It would be wrong to suggest that, in doing so, econometricians were consciously making their own substitute for experiments, rather they responded to the particular problems of measurement and control, the particular mismatch between theory and data, which occurred in their applied work. Only later did they begin theoretical discussions and seek general solutions to their practical problems.

The structure of this book reflects the importance of applied work in the development of econometric ideas: applications formed the catalyst necessary for econometricians both to recognise their difficulties and to search for solutions. Parts I and II of the book trace the evolution of econometrics through the practical work on business cycles and on market demand analysis, which together constituted most of the applied econometrics of the period up to about 1950. The exploration of these fields reveals not only advances in understanding, but also confusion and dead ends. Part III of the book reconstructs the history of formal econometric models of the data-theory relationship. This final part draws on the applied econometric work discussed in the earlier sections and on the theoretical econometrics which began to develop during the 1930s. By the 1940s, theoretical discussions and applied practice had crystallised into a programme which is recognisable as modern econometrics.

[15] The different ways in which the new statistical methods were taken up by American psychologists are discussed by Danziger and Gigerenzer (essays 2 and 3 in Krüger *et al.* (1987, II)) who give considerable insight into the way data-theory problems were overcome in that field.

Part I

Business cycles

Introduction to business cycles

The nineteenth-century economists did not, for the most part, recognise the idea or existence of regular cycles in economic activity. Instead, they thought in terms of 'crises', a word implying an abnormal level of activity and used in several different ways: it could mean a financial panic (that is the peak turning point in a commercial or financial market) or it could mean the period of deepest depression when factories closed. A financial crisis was not necessarily followed by an economic depression, but might be a phenomenon solely of the financial markets.[1] There were a few exceptions amongst economists and industrial commentators who recognised a cyclical pattern in economic activity, including, for example, Marx.[2] In addition, there was no agreed theory about what caused a crisis, indeed it sometimes seemed that not only each economist but each person had their own pet theory of the cause of crises in the economy. One telling example, 'The First Annual Report of the Commissioner of Labor' in the USA in 1886 listed all the causes of depressions reported to the various committees of Congress. This list ran to four pages, from

> Administration, changes in the policies of
> Agitators, undue influence of

through various economic and institutional reasons to

> War, absorption of capital by destruction of
> property during
> Work, piece.[3]

---

[1] Kindleberger's recent analysis (1978) of 'crises' rather than cycles shows how varied the meaning of the term was in the nineteenth century and earlier.

[2] Schumpeter (1954) discusses the emergence of the business cycle as a unit of analysis in the nineteenth century and suggests that apart from Marx and Jevons, economists were not much interested in this field.

[3] The full list is quoted by Hull (1926), pp. 262–6.

There was not much chance of making sense of so many causes using the standard ways of gathering evidence in support of theories in nineteenth-century economics. Casual empiricism: the use of odd facts, a few numbers, or individual cases could not penetrate very deeply into the causes of complex macroeconomic behaviour over time. Full-blown empiricism, such as that of the German historical school, suffered from the inability to synthesise its masses of evidence into coherent theories. The third source of evidence for economists, introspection, was more suited to investigating microeconomic behaviour. It was against this background that serious quantitative study of business cycles began in the late nineteenth century. The development of a standard approach was not likely to be straightforward, for there was no agreed theory or even definition of the phenomena. Instead, there was a considerable amount of blundering about in the dark looking for the business cycle. Did it exist or was it just a tendency; was it a fixed recurring cycle; was each cycle different; was it predictable? Econometricians tried to discover the answers to their questions directly from the evidence; but there were many different ways of choosing data, of analysing them and of exploring the relationships of interest. As for the evidence itself, although standard national income accounts did not exist, there was a considerable body of data available on prices, output, financial markets and so on, which was suitable for business cycle analysis.

The development of the econometric analysis of business cycles is described in four chapters. Chapters 1 and 2 discuss the histories of two different approaches to statistical study of the business cycle. These approaches were associated with different notions of the business cycle and employed different methodologies, which together implied different analytical techniques. The first chapter deals with the early attempts to confirm clearly defined theories in which economic cycles were assumed to be regular standard events subject to statistical analysis. In contrast, Chapter 2 covers the work of those who rejected a strong theoretical input in their quantitative study and who regarded each observed cycle as a different individual event. These economists used statistical evidence and techniques to enrich a descriptive approach which was in some cases theory-seeking and in others blatantly empirical in outlook; questions of measurement and definition dominated their work. The methods used by both groups did not go uncriticised. Chapter 3 shows how statistical discussions on time-series issues led to an understanding of the design features required to make economic theories of the business cycle amenable to econometric study. Chapter 4 describes how a fully-fledged econometric approach to business cycle measurement and testing emerged, dependent on both mathematically expressed theory and statistical understanding.

CHAPTER 1

Sunspot and Venus theories of the business cycle

Wiliam Stanley Jevons was one of the first economists to break away from the casual tradition of applied work which prevailed in the nineteenth century and combine theory with statistical data on many events to produce a general account of the business cycle. Then, in the early twentieth century when statistical work was still uncommon, Henry Ludwell Moore adopted more sophisticated techniques to develop an alternative theory of the cycle. This chapter relates how Jevons and Moore set about building their theories. Both of them relied heavily on statistical regularities in the formation of their hypotheses, which featured periodic economic cycles caused by exogenous changes in heavenly bodies. The development of the econometric approach to business cycle analysis between the 1870s and the 1920s is shown in their work, and in its changing reception from reviewers. Jevons' and Moore's cycle work deserves to be taken seriously as pioneering econometrics, yet the periodic cycle programme they initiated did not prove to be very influential. The last section of this chapter explores why this was so.

1.1   Jevons' sunspot theory

Jevons' sunspot theory of the cycle has always been the object of mirth to his fellow economists, despite the fact that by the time he began to work on the subject in the 1870s he was already well known and distinguished for his contributions to mainstream economics.[1] He was also renowned for statistical analyses of various problems, particularly the problem of index numbers. This statistical work included some fine studies of economic fluctuations, for example, on the seasonal

---

[1] William Stanley Jevons (1835–82) was best known during his life for his writings on practical economic and policy issues. His theoretical contributions and his role in developing marginal analysis were not recognised till later. He was a keen advocate and user of statistics and mathematics in economics, on which see S. M. Stigler (1982) and Schabas (1984).

variations in money markets. In contrast, his empirical work in a series of papers from 1875 to 1882 on solar periods and economic cycles won him little praise.[2]

The initial hypothesis of Jevons' first paper on trade cycles was that the sunspot cycle led to a weather cycle which in turn caused a harvest cycle and thence a price cycle (Jevons, 1875: see (1884), Paper VI). The problem was that there was little evidence to back up his hypothesis: there was no obvious cycle in grain prices to match the 11.1-year sunspot cycle. He thought that this was probably because there were many other influences on the harvest besides the sun, and that grain prices were also influenced by social, political and economic factors. In other words, the sun's effect on the harvest cycle, and thus the price cycle, was overshadowed by these other disturbing factors for which his methods could not control.

Encouraged by the fact that Schuster had already found a cycle in German wine vintages that matched the sunspot cycle in length, Jevons decided to use agricultural data from the thirteenth and fourteenth centuries (collected by Rogers (1866)) to test his hypothesis. He felt that using data from these earlier centuries would lessen the problem of interference from other factors and consequently that agricultural price data would show clear cycles. Jevons did not even have sunspot data for this early period; he simply assumed that the length of the sunspot cycle had been the same in the thirteenth and fourteenth centuries as it was in the nineteenth century.

Jevons' analysis of the price data was interesting. His method was to lay out the data, for a number of price series for different crops over a 140-year period, on a grid representing 11 years. Analysis of the grid semed to show a similar pattern of variation in the prices of each of the crops. In addition the variation in the aggregate figures seemed to Jevons to be greater than that which would be expected by the impact of purely accidental causes such as wars, plagues and so forth (even after omitting outlying observations). He also checked the number of maxima and minima of crop prices occurring in any given year of the 11-year grid and found that their distribution looked distinctly

---

[2] Jevons' interest in time-series fluctuations may have grown out of his earlier work on meteorology, in which area he first published. His work on sunspot cycles was made known in papers given at meetings of the British Association (Section F) and in contributions to *The Times* and to *Nature*. These appear, together with much of his other statistical work, in the collection *Investigations in Currency and Finance* published posthumously in 1884. Other items and letters can be found in Jevons' *Papers*, published recently under the editorship of R. D. Collison Black (see Vols. IV and V, 1977, and Vol. VII, 1981). These include a previously unpublished but very interesting unfinished piece on cycles which Jevons wrote for the *Princeton Review*.

non-uniform.[3] The evidence of the variation in prices revealed by the grid convinced Jevons of the existence of an 11-year cycle in crop prices. He admitted that his results would be more persuasive if the price series on different crops were independent sets of observations, which of course they were not. But Jevons did not assert positive proof based on his analysis, which was just as well because he soon discovered that if he analysed the prices on a grid of 3, 5, 7, 9 or 13 years the results were just as good![4]

Returning to the nineteenth century in his search for evidence, Jevons began to look at cycles in commercial credit instead of in agricultural prices. His analysis of the dates of nineteenth-century financial crises produced an average cycle length of 10.8 years, a little less than the sunspot cycle of 11.1 years. He tried to get around this slight difference by suggesting that his sunspot theory, combined with the theory of the credit cycle as a mental or psychological phenomenon, would produce such an observed average cycle length. He wrote:

> It may be that the commercial classes of the English nation, as at present constituted, form a body, suited by mental and other conditions, to go through a complete oscillation in a period nearly corresponding to that of the sun-spots. In such conditions a comparatively slight variation of the prices of food, repeated in a similar manner, at corresponding points of the oscillation, would suffice to produce violent effects. A ship rolls badly at sea, when its period of vibration corresponds nearly with that of the waves which strike it, so that similar impulses are received at similar positions. A glass is sometimes broken by a musical sound of the same tone as that which the glass produces when struck. A child's swing is set and kept in motion by a very small push, given each time that it returns to the same place. If, then, the English money market is naturally fitted to swing or roll in periods of ten or eleven years, comparatively slight variations in the goodness of harvests repeated at like intervals would suffice to produce those alternations of depression, activity, excitement, and collapse which undoubtedly recur in well-marked succession ... I am aware that speculations of this kind may seem somewhat far-fetched and finely-wrought; but financial collapses have recurred with such approach to regularity in the last fifty years, that either this or some other explanation is needed.   (Jevons, 1875: see (1884), pp. 184–5)

So in this combined theory, the sunspot cycle caused a harvest cycle which in turn maintained or intensified the natural cyclical motion of

---

[3] Probability held an important place in Jevons' philosophy of science, but he rarely, as in this example, used probability ideas in conjunction with statistical evidence (but see Aldrich (1987)).

[4] Jevons did not immediately publish his 1875 paper because of this discovery, which he noted in a letter to J. Mills in 1877 (1977, IV, letter 482). The paper was prepared by Jevons for publication in the *Investigations* (1884).

the economy. This idea of a combination of endogenous and exogenous causes turned out to be an important element in econometric models of the business cycle in the 1930s.

Convinced that sunspot cycles and business cycles were of the same length, Jevons resolved early in 1878

> to prove the matter empirically, by actual history of last century occurrences.   (Jevons (1977), IV, letter 511)

This work was mainly concerned with dating the various commercial crises of the previous 150 years or so going back to the South Sea Bubble. Aware that his commitment to the theory clouded his judgement, Jevons wrote at this point:

> I am free to confess that in this search I have been thoroughly biased in favour of a theory, and that the evidence which I have so far found would have no weight, if standing by itself.   (Jevons, 1878: see (1884), p. 208)

He used the cycle dates of other commentators to buttress his case wherever possible. He searched avidly for evidence of crises where there appeared to be ones missing in the sequence and even for evidence which would make the cycles come at exactly equal intervals by suggesting reasons why crises had been either accelerated or retarded by a few months from their due date.

The evidence of regular credit cycles did not, according to Jevons, stand by itself: there was also the coincidence of cycle lengths. The extended series of commercial crises gave him an average cycle length of somewhere between 10.3 and 10.46 years. Luckily, this corresponded with a new estimate of the sunspot cycle length, which was now put at 10.45 years. Jevons argued:

> Judging this close coincidence of results according to the theories of probabilities, it becomes highly probable that two periodic phenomena, varying so nearly in the same mean period, are connected as cause and effect.
> (Jevons, 1878: see (1884), p. 195)

His theory was based on a 'perfect coincidence' which

> is by itself strong evidence that the phenomena are causally connected.
> (Jevons, 1878: see (1884), p. 210)

The recalculation of the sunspot cycle length so close to that of the average interval between commercial crises enabled Jevons to disown his earlier 'fanciful' explanation of the difference between them. He now described the idea of a mental cycle pushed at regular intervals by a harvest cycle as merely a construct to explain that difference.

Despite the coincidence of cycle lengths, Jevons was aware that there

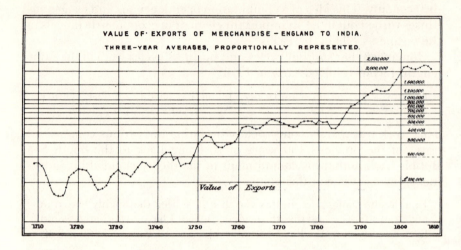

Figure 1   Jevons' trade cycle graph
Source: Jevons (1884), Plate XIV

was still no evidence of how the sunspots caused the commercial cycle since there was no obvious cycle in the intermediary of agricultural prices. He thought he could see a way round this difficulty when he observed that famines in India appeared to have a cyclical pattern similar to the sunspot cycle. Jevons believed that he would be able to observe the causal relationship between sunspots and agricultural output directly by studying events in the tropical and subtropical regions (e.g. India), where other disturbing factors affecting crop prices were likely to be less important than in the industrialised zones such as Britain. He theorised that when agricultural output was low and food prices were high in India, the Indian peasant had no money left over to buy British cotton textiles, thus Britain's exports fell and a commercial cycle was induced in the economic affairs of Britain. He did not regard this theory as being incompatible with the presence of other, more immediate, causes of crises such as bank failures (which could, as he pointed out, be connected with the Indian trade). Jevons explored this new version of his theory in 1878 and 1879 and claimed to find strong evidence of the imported cycle in trade with India. One of Jevons' graphs (of which he was particularly proud), showing his evidence of 10–year variation in trade is given here (Figure 1). This moving average chart of the value of exports to India, on a logarithmic scale, is quite an advanced representation of data for the period. But the statistical arguments in this later work were less sophisticated than those used in his first paper, for he relied solely on the comparison of dates, the comparison of average periods and the visual evidence of his time-series graphs.

Jevons had little more to add either to his theory or to the evidence in succeeding notes and letters. Further evidence was in his own mind unnecessary, since he was by now thoroughly seduced by his 'treacherous', 'entrancing' and 'beautiful coincidence', as he referred to his theory.[5] He noted that the cycles in commercial crises were more regular than the sunspots! But he did not allow this interesting fact to cast any doubt on the causal relationship running from sunspots to commercial crises. Indeeed, he was so confident of this, that on several occasions he predicted the months of a future turning point in the commercial cycle and in his last paper on the subject in 1882, he even used the evidence of a cyclical peak in corn prices in Delhi to infer the presence of a preceding peak in the sunspot data (see Jevons (1981), VII, Paper XIV).

It is clear, from the accounts of his papers and from his own responses, that Jevons' sunspot theory was ridiculed, rather than criticised, by many of his scientific colleagues. They poked fun at the theory as a whole by suggesting unlikely relationships between sunspot cycles and other phenomena. Indeed, Jevons' articles and letters were part of a general literature of the time connecting sunspots with other recurring events. This literature involved a fair sprinkling of spoofs, and it is not always easy to tell which were meant seriously. Compare, for example, the titles 'Locusts and Sunspots' and 'Sunspots and the Nile' with one of Jevons' own short notes 'Sunspots and the Plague' (three articles from *Nature* in late 1878 and early 1879). Jevons felt that one anonymous contribution in the *Journal of the Royal Statistical Society* for 1879: 'University Boat Races and Sunspot Cycles' was particularly aimed at him.[6] Nevertheless, Jevons was not abashed; the more his theory was made fun of, the more serious Jevons became about it:

> I never was more in earnest ... It is no jest at all.
> (Jevons (1884), pp. 215 and 221)

Despite the ridicule of many of his colleagues, a few did take Jevons' work seriously. These tended to be those on the fringes of the profession, such as John Mills (a banker and frequent correspondent of Jevons on sunspots), whose prime area of influence was in commercial life. One exception was his successor at Manchester, Adamson, who

---

[5] Such language was sprinkled through Jevons' work on the sunspot cycle; these three come from letters 488 and 566 (1877 and 1878) in the *Papers* (1977, IV), and the 1878 *Nature* paper (1884, p. 207).

[6] See Jevons (1977, V, p. 51) for this particular episode and S. M. Stigler (1982).

wrote to Jevons towards the end of 1878 with some detailed criticism of the theory and its presentation.[7] Adamson criticised the validity of some of the 'crises' dates found by Jevons and he doubted that cycles would be exactly the same in length because he thought that there would be an increasing interval between crises as industrialisation took place. The lack of exact cycles in corn prices and output also worried him and he found Jevons' hypothesis of the link between these cycles unconvincing. On the other hand, Adamson was willing to believe that the sun would have an impact on the economic environment; but he complained that Jevons had provided no 'mode of connexion' between sunspots and agricultural output.

Adamson's criticisms were unusual in that he attacked Jevons' work at the level of evidence and the causal mechanism of his theory. It might be thought surprising that more of his contemporaries did not take this line, since it is clear that the evidence was not convincing, even by the standards of Jevons' earlier statistical work on other topics. But this was not the main thrust of most contemporary criticism. Yet nearly 60 years later, in his 'Centenary Allocution' on Jevons in 1936, J. M. Keynes took precisely this line of attack, criticising Jevons directly for the flimsy evidence on which he based his inductive argument and for the lack of attention to the time relation between cause and effect (and only indirectly for not making an economic factor the main cause of the cycle).

How did Jevons attempt to justify his views in the face of the derision of his colleagues and defend the fact that, despite the lack of convincing evidence, he gave credence to an imported periodic economic cycle? The answer lies in Jevons' use of an inductive methodology which formed an important element of his philosophy of science writings. In the context of defending his sunspot theory, Jevons explained his inductive logic as follows:

> We must proceed upon the great principle of inductive method, as laid down by Laplace and the several great mathematicians who created the theory of probability. This principle is to the effect that the most probable cause of an event which has happened is that cause which if it existed would most probably lead to that effect ... if we perceive a distinctly periodic effect, and can discover any cause which recurs at exactly equal intervals, and is the only discoverable cause recurring in that period, this is probably the cause of which we are in search. Such is the *prima facie* result, drawn simply on the ground that such a cause if existing would have effects with the required period, and there is no

---

[7] Letter 564, Adamson to Jevons, in *Papers* (1977, IV). Adamson took over Jevons' chair at Owens College, Manchester in 1875 when Jevons moved back to University College, London, as Professor of Political Economy (1875–81).

other cause which could be supposed with any probability to give that result. But this *prima facie* probability is immensely strengthened if we can give other reasons for believing that a cause of the nature supposed, apart from the question of its period, is likely to have effects of the kind we are attributing to it. In short, mere equality of period is a perfectly valid ground of inductive reasoning; but our results gain much in probability if we can analyse and explain the precise relation of cause and effect.[8]

(Jevons (1981), VII, pp. 93–4)

From this passage, it is clear that for Jevons, the similarity between the lengths of the sunspot cycle and the intervals between commercial crises was the primary evidence. (It has to be confessed that Jevons' imagination also played an important initial part in the induction. Once he had spotted his 'beautiful coincidence' he became hooked, alighting upon every new scrap of evidence on the timing of a crisis in a particular year to back up his coincidence.[9]) This coincidence, through the use of *probability inference*, became for Jevons a causal relationship. Evidence of the explanatory links in the causal chain between sunspots and economic cycles would, he argued, increase the probability of the theory being correct but it was not essential to his argument. The evidence of causal connection, then, was not an important consideration either for Jevons or for those contemporaries who ridiculed his work.

The unsympathetic attitude of Jevons' contemporaries is equally understandable, for both Jevons' methodology and the domain of his theory were beyond the pale of late nineteenth-century economics. The method of theorising in classical economics involved deductions from premises which were 'known to be true' partly, at least, on the basis of internal personal knowledge, while Jevons' method of theory building was an inductive process dependent on external statistical evidence. His vision of periodic economic cycles was also alien to the nineteenth-century concern with 'crises', a term which was applied to many different circumstances and involved many different causes. Even those few economists in the nineteenth century who believed in the idea of cycles in economic activity, such as Marx and Juglar, did not see them as exact cycles. Jevons' idea that spots on the sun, an entity outside the economic system, should directly cause exact cycles in the economy was considered quite bizarre.

---

[8] This was the methodological and intellectual side of his elaborate defence in an unfinished piece intended for the *Princeton Review*. In this paper, reproduced in Jevons (1981) *Papers*, Jevons perceived the arguments against him to be twofold: the second argument was concerned with the possible influence of the sun on economic life and was at a commonsense level.

[9] Jevons even passed on his obsession to his son, H. Stanley Jevons who continued to proselytise the sunspot cause; in 1910 he published a paper linking the sun's activity with a 42-month cycle, the so-called short business cycle.

So, while Jevons was proposing a general explanation of a general cyclical phenomenon, others were busy explaining individual 'crises' by a large number of different causes. Juglar was proposing a general cycle theory built on statistical data but, as we shall see in the next chapter, he analysed and used the evidence on each individual cycle separately. Jevons' induction was of a different and an unusual kind: the evidence on individual cycles was not important, it was the standard or average characteristics of the data which were paramount. His theory was about an underlying exact cycle not about the observed cycles of different lengths. This is why Jevons' work, despite its paucity of statistical evidence and serious analysis, marks an important step in the development of econometrics: he relied on evidence of uniformity in statistical data, from which a general theory was derived using inductive reasoning.

1.2   Moore's Venus theory

If Jevons' sunspot theory appeared to be cranky, it was nothing to the theory eventually proposed by Henry Ludwell Moore to account for economic cycles.[10] Moore seemed to have suffered from the same fatal fascination that afflicted Jevons; once persuaded of the idea of some outside periodic cause of economic cycles Moore could not give it up but strove to take the explanation back to its first cause. He developed his theory in two books. The first in 1914 found weather cycles to be the cause of business cycles. The second book in 1923 extended the causal chain back to movements to the planet Venus. Yet Moore's work represented a considerable advance over Jevons'. The main difference, which will quickly become apparent, was that for Moore, the causal chain of explanation between the weather and business cycles was the main object of study. He arrived at his explanatory theory from a mixture of prior economic theory and a serious statistical investigation into the regularities and relationships in the evidence.

It was Moore's belief that explaining the cyclical fluctuations of the economy and finding laws to fit them constituted the

fundamental problems of economic dynamics.   (Moore (1914), p. 1)

In solving this problem, he proposed to abandon the standard methodological approach (which he variously described as the deductive *a priori* method, the comparative static or the *ceteris paribus*

[10] Henry Ludwell Moore (1869–1958) led a very sheltered academic life with few professional responsibilities until his retirement in 1929 (unlike Mitchell, his contemporary and fellow American who features in Chapter 2). His mathematical and statistical knowledge were

method) on the grounds that it could never tell economists anything about the real dynamic economy which was constantly shifting and changing like the sea. The mainstream theory and method were of course interconnected: comparative statics was concerned with comparing two positions (not with explaining the path of change between them), and was perhaps appropriate for understanding endogenously caused irregular cycles. Moore believed that an exogenously determined periodic cycle theory demanded different methods of study. Method and theory had to be appropriately matched and he was very conscious that in adopting a periodic cycle theory and statistical analysis he was flouting conventional methods of analysis as well as conventional theory.[11]

Moore began his first book, *Economic Cycles – Their Law and Cause* (1914), by fixing on weather cycles as the exogenous cause of economic fluctuations and set about 'proving' this hypothesis by providing the evidence for the explanatory links in the theory. He started his statistical investigation with the harmonic analysis of rainfall from 1839 to 1910 in the Ohio Valley (for which meteorological records were the longest available). He decided that the periodogram showed two significant cycles, one with a period of 8 years and one of 33 years. The best fit to the data was obtained with these two periods plus their semi-harmonics. After this initial frequency analysis, he moved on to find the correlation between the Ohio Valley rainfall series and rainfall in Illinois (the most important state for corn production, and, luckily, one which had long kept weather records) for the period 1870–1910. He then worked out the critical growth periods for grain crops by correlating rainfall in each month with yields. By assuming that the same periodic cycles he found in the initial Ohio Valley rainfall data followed through to the months of critical growth in Illinois grain crops and thence to the crop yields in the USA as a whole, he felt able to conclude

largely self-taught, although he did attend courses on correlation from Karl Pearson. His five books – all utilising the econometric approach – spanned the years 1911 to 1929. G.J. Stigler's (1962) illuminating study of Moore gives further biographical details; Christ (1985) surveys his econometric work.

[11] Surveys of business cycle theories in the 1920s and 1930s (e.g. Haberler (1937)) show that amongst professional economists, only Jevons and Moore believed in an exogenously caused cycle based on weather cycles. It should also be clear that Moore's is a broader argument about the theory, the way it was constructed, and the way data were used. For example, a contemporary mainstream study of the cycle by Robertson (1915) used comparative static arguments with statistical data series, but without any statistical analysis or explanation of the dynamic path of the economy. It is, of course, arguable whether Moore succeeded in his aims; Schumpeter (1954) believed that Moore never got beyond a 'statistically operative comparative statics'; true dynamics coming with Frisch and others in the 1930s (see Chapters 3 and 4).

that the rhythmical movement in rain and in crop yields were causally related.

In the next section of this book, Moore examined the relationship between crop yields and crop prices. He found that yield/price schedules moved up and down with the general level of prices. Moore then tried to relate crop yields to production. Using the production of pig-iron as the proxy for output, he discovered that the best correlation between output and crop yields was for a two-year lag (yields preceding pig-iron) and concluded that this was evidence of a

> positive, intimate connection and very probably a direct causal relation.
>
> (Moore (1914), p. 110)

The next link in his theory was between output and prices of pig-iron. His empirical work produced a relationship which he interpreted as a positive demand curve for pig-iron. This of course contradicted the negative relationship between the price and quantity stipulated by standard economic theory, and he used this opportunity to launch a strident attack on conventional economic method and demand theory. (In fact, contemporary reviewers claimed that Moore had found a supply curve; the whole episode is discussed in Chapters 5 and 6.)

Moore, like Jevons, was not deterred by an unusual result. He fitted the positive demand curve into his general picture of the cycle and his explanation ran as follows: crop yields rise (due to the stage of the rain cycle), so the volume of trade increases (with a lag), the demand for producers' goods rises, employment rises, demand for crops rises and so general prices rise. The process was reversed when the rain cycle caused yields to decline. This model was finally confirmed for Moore when he found that the correlation of crop yields and general prices was highest with a lag of four years. The chart, Figure 2, shows the degree of concurrence between the two series in this final relationship (note that trends and the lag have both been eliminated). He used this correlation to justify his inference that the rhythmical features of crop yields are duplicated in prices; thus completing the cycle explanation, from weather through to general prices.

Moore concluded:

> The principle contribution of this Essay is the discovery of the law and cause of Economic Cycles. The rhythm in the activity of economic life, the alternation of buoyant, purposeful expansion with aimless depression, is caused by the rhythm in the yield per acre of the crops; while the rhythm in the production of the crops is, in turn, caused by the rhythm of changing weather which is represented by the cyclical changes in the amount of rainfall. The law of cycles of rainfall is the law of the cycles of the crops and the law of Economic Cycles. (Moore (1914), p. 135)

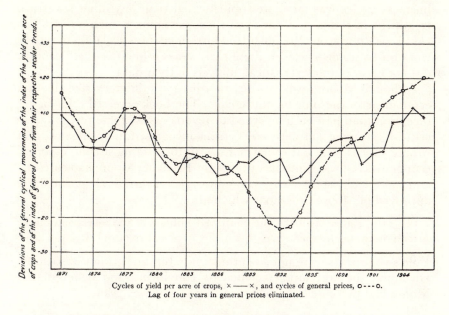

Cycles of yield per acre of crops, × —— ×, and cycles of general prices, o - - - o.
Lag of four years in general prices eliminated.

Figure 2   Moore's business cycle graph
Source: Moore (1914), p. 123, Figure 27

Moore's conviction that rainfall cycles caused economic fluctuations rivalled Jevons' belief in his sunspot theory. But, whereas for Jevons the evidence for his theory was only of secondary importance, for Moore it was primary. He worked industriously to discover and statistically verify the causal connections in the chain of evidence in order to provide a convincing explanation of the economic cycle.

Moore's handling of the evidence can be characterised as highly technological compared to those of both his predecessors and his contemporaries. His range of statistical methods included harmonic analysis, correlation, multiple regression with three variables (mainly in fitting cubic trend lines) and time-series decomposition (into three components: trend, cycle and temporary fluctuations). He worried about the goodness of fit of the lines and curves he used, particularly the sine curves, and worked out the standard error to measure the goodness of fit. Like Jevons, Moore imputed causality to certain empirical results, such as to correlations of a certain level. Unfortunately, Moore used his rather high-powered methods somewhat carelessly and uncritically. His work contrasts with Jevons who, with less concern for evidence and far less data at hand, had carried out his modest data manipulations with some care. Despite his faults, Moore's analysis of business cycles was far more sophisticated than any other statistical treatment of the period, for even those economists such as Mitchell (1913) or Robertson (1915) who did introduce statistical data into their work on economic cycles in these early years of the twentieth century did not carry out any statistical analysis of their data.

Although Moore's work was extraordinary, it did not strike all other economists of the time as outrageous. The book received a far better reception than had been awarded to Jevons' work; some reviews were critical, but none was derisory. Persons recognised, in his review, that Moore's ideas were out of harmony with those of most contemporary economists but was himself enthusiastic, believing Moore had carefully and successfully shown why economic cycles occurred. He particularly approved of Moore's methods which allowed

> the data, rather than the pre-conceived notions of the investigator to mould the conclusion.   (Persons (1915), p. 645)

Yule's comments were not so enthusiastic, but he was not unfriendly. He found the correlation coefficients convincing and believed that Moore had presented a strong case that weather cycles were

> at least a very important contributory cause of economic cycles.
>   (Yule (1915), p. 303)

But Yule criticised Moore for not using harmonic analysis directly on the economic data to reveal and analyse the economic cycles.

Lehfeldt's review, on the other hand, was one of those that made enjoyable reading for everyone except the author of the book. Lehfeldt decided that the best way to defend the application of statistical methods to the discovery of economic laws (i.e. econometrics) was to attack Moore's practice of the subject:

> In economics, hitherto, the sources of light available have been two: abstract reasoning of what should happen under certain simplified assumptions, and undigested statistics as to what does happen in the real world. Each of these is important, indeed indispensable ... But though abstract economic reasoning can be put into algebraic symbols, it leads to nothing quantitative, and, in the opinion of the reviewer, the greatest step forward in the science, possible at the present time, is to apply the modern methods of statistics to yield quantitative generalisations, under the guidance of abstract analysis, and so slowly and cautiously to build up flesh on the skeleton of theory.
>
> There are very few workers in this field as yet, which makes it all the more of a pity that one of them should lay himself open to accusations of unsoundness. Research along these lines is not easy, for it requires a thorough grasp of the mathematical theory of statistics, patience to do the

lengthy arithmetic involved, and ceaseless and acute criticism of the mathematical processes in the light of common sense and everything that is known about the subject-matter. Prof. Moore is weak in this last arm; he has, let us say, the artillery of mathematics and the plodding infantry of numbers, but not the aerial corps to save him from making attacks in the wrong directions. (Lehfeldt (1915), p. 410)

P. G. Wright's review (1915) was in rather similar vein but kindlier in manner and with some compliments to Moore's pioneering efforts. Wright was not convinced by Moore's theory and evidence and he reported some results from his own calculations with Moore's data. Moore had not analysed effective rainfall (rainfall in the critical growing months), just assumed that the 8-year cycle he found in annual rainfall was applicable. Wright carried out an harmonic analysis of effective rainfall to reveal a 4-year cycle instead of Moore's 8-year cycle. Wright believed that evidence from correlations would be consistent with the harmonic analysis but easier to understand and interpret, so he also worked out the correlogram of various data series to see if these gave evidence of cycles and of what length. To his surprise, the correlogram evidence was not consistent with Moore's, for he found a 3- to 4-year and a 7-year cycle in rainfall; a 7-year cycle in crop yields; and a 9-year cycle in general prices. No wonder Wright found Moore's 8-year cycle theory not proven! This is one of the earliest examples in econometrics where a criticism was made more pointed by reworking the author's data with a different hypothesis or method of attack.[12]

The fundamental difference in attitude in these reviews of Moore's work, compared to the contemporary response to Jevons, was that the evidence and the way it was analysed was being taken seriously, seriously enough indeed to prompt one reviewer to undertake his own data analysis. The econometric approach, though still relatively crude and untried, was treated with sympathy and accepted as having something to offer. But Moore's reviewers were part of the small group of economists involved in statistical economics and econometrics and they applauded Moore's pioneering spirit while criticising his performance. It would be wrong therefore to take their sympathy as evidence that econometrics had become in any sense a mainstream activity by 1914, for it certainly had not.

Moore's second book on the business cycles, *Generating Economic Cycles*, was published in 1923. In response to the criticisms of his earlier book, Moore carried out his statistical work on the economic cycle with

---

[12] These data experiments made very effective arguments and were a feature of the more theoretical investigations into time-series methods undertaken by Yule and others in the late 1920s, discussed in Chapter 3.

more diligence. For example, he used harmonic analysis directly on the economic data as suggested in Yule's review. Moore also widened the applicability of his economic theory by extending the time period he used and the coverage to three countries, namely Britain, France and the USA. The persistence of the 8-year cycles he was interested in and the fact that they occurred, according to his evidence, not only in all three countries but in synchronisation in those countries, made his case more convincing.

In terms of the content of his business cycle theory, Moore was still, like Jevons, searching

> for a single explanation of the entire rhythm and its constituent parts.
> (Moore (1923), p. 15)

The new version of Moore's theory involved a relaxation of his earlier view that there was one single generating cycle (the exogenous or propagating cycle). He now believed that the economic cycle was the result of economic and social influences combined with the main exogenous cause. But although Moore was no longer prepared to claim that 'the law of cycles of rainfall is . . . the law of Economic Cycles', his claims as to the nature of the generating cycle (the main cause) were far more extravagant. In an imaginative search for the mechanism generating the weather cycles, he fixed on Venus as the first cause, and in particular the fact that, at 8-year intervals, Venus came between the earth and the sun. The last chapter of the book went into various recent discoveries in physics which Moore believed shed light on exactly how Venus, in conjunction with the earth and the sun, might be supposed to cause rainfall cycles on earth. Sunspots were just one part of this explanatory chain which involved Venus causing interference in solar radiation to the earth, negative ionisation, weather disturbances and finally rainfall cycles.[13] He must have guessed that his Venus theory would not be well received because he opened his book with a report of Galileo's rejection of Kepler's idea that the moon caused the tides. Moore pleaded by analogy that readers should not dismiss his own ideas as ridiculous out of hand.

Moore's ideas on the cause of economic cycles had already appeared as separate articles between 1919 and 1921, so by the time of his 1923

---

[13] It is interesting to note that Davis (1941) suggested that if there was a connection between ionisation and health then Jevons' sunspot theory might be rehabilitated in conjunction with the psychological cycle theories. Those who have become addicted to the sunspot theory from reading this chapter might like to know that Garcia-Mata and Shaffner (1934) attempted to connect sunspots with a psychological explanation and that an ionisation/ health connection has recently been made by some environmental health specialists! For those more interested in the econometric tests of the theory, see the recent debate on Granger-type causality testing of Jevons' hypotheses in the *Southern Economic Journal* (1982 and 1983).

book, the Venus theory was no longer new. Perhaps this was why his theory met with polite scepticism from the serious commentators rather than with the outrage accorded to Jevons' sunspot theory.[14] For example, Hotelling commented on Moore's Venus theory as follows:

> The trouble with all such theories is the tenuousness, in the light of physics, of the long chain of causation which they are forced to postulate. Even if a statistical test should yield a very high correlation, the odds thus established in favour of such an hypothesis would have to be heavily discounted on account of its strong *a priori* improbability. (Hotelling (1927), p. 289)

The basic theory of periodic economic cycles caused by an outside body appeared to be no more acceptable to Moore's audience than it had been in Jevons' day. It comes as no surprise then to learn that as a theory of the cycle, his work had no direct influence on other economists.[15] Moore's reviewers essentially urged the same sort of criticisms of his second work as they had of the first, in challenging his periodogram method and his evidence of 8-year cycles in the economy, rather than in seriously arguing with the Venus theory. Indeed, Moore's assumption of periodic cycles and use of frequency analysis methods on economic data were rarely copied in econometrics during the remainder of the period covered by this study.[16] The reasons for this are discussed in the next section.

Of importance for the history of econometrics is that Moore, in both his cycle books, had concentrated his energies on the statistical evidence of the economic interactions involved in the business cycle and the statistical analysis of these relationships rather than on the relation between the economic cycle and the exogenous causal factor. Moore's concern with evidence and statistical explanation compared to that of Jevons, and the matching change in contemporaries' responses, are both indicative of the development of the econometric approach by the early years of the twentieth century. Yet, it was some years before

---

[14] The theory gained him a certain notoriety in the popular press. Academic reviewers may have been kind to Moore because it was known that he was particularly sensitive to criticism (see G. J. Stigler (1962) for discussion of this point).

[15] For this reason G. J. Stigler (1962) judged it to be a failure. However, Moore's cycle work did prove an influential example in econometrics, particularly, as Stigler himself argued, in the field of statistical demand curves. Moore developed dynamic econometric models of the demand and supply for agricultural commodities in the 1920s and, as we shall see in later chapters, these cobweb models fed back into mainstream economic dynamics and thence into Tinbergen's econometric work on business cycles in the 1930s (see also Morgan (1988)). Thus, the correct judgement seems to be that Moore's cycle work did influence economics, but only indirectly.

[16] The time-series approach has of course been revived more recently, beginning with the Princeton Time Series Project directed by Morgenstern (see Chapter 3 n. 10, and Chapter 8.1) and Tukey in the early 1960s (see Granger (1961)).

Moore's broad econometric approach to the explanation of economic cycles, involving a large number of relationships linking different parts of the economy, was taken up by Tinbergen who produced the first macroeconometric models in the late 1930s.

1.3   The decline of periodic cycle analysis

Few economists between 1920 and 1950 followed up Moore's promising start in using periodogram analysis in economics. Those few who did use the idea of periodic cycles and its associated methods were much less ambitious in their theorising and in the scope of their studies than Moore had been, as the following two examples by William Beveridge and by E. B. Wilson show.[17]

Beveridge's studies of wheat prices, weather and export cycles were published in 1920–2, but his data and main results have been used since as a textbook example. He gathered annual data on wheat prices which covered 4 centuries and 48 different places in Western and Central Europe. These observations were then reduced to one single index of wheat prices. He noticed that the shape of the graph of this index (once it had been detrended) changed quite dramatically with the onset of industrialisation, becoming less jagged and irregular after 1800. He believed that this was because

> another disturbing influence – the credit cycle – begins to show itself, and cannot be eliminated by any simple method. The character of the curve is visibly altered in these later years; beyond 1869 it could not without correction be trusted as an indication of harvest conditions.
>
> (Beveridge (1921), p. 432)

Beveridge then applied frequency analysis to his data, calculating over 300 different periods, and made a detailed examination of the results. He selected 19 dominant cycles (noting especially that Moore's 8-year cycle was not one of these). Beveridge sought corroborating evidence for these 19 cycles in the behaviour of the weather and of heavenly bodies, but caution prevented him making the sort of leap from slight evidence to total belief in a periodic connection between variables that Jevons had made. Instead, he suggested reasons why the exact periodicity might not hold in economic cycles, arguing that, because weather

---

[17] W. H. Beveridge (1879–1963) was an economist and statistician who specialised in applied social questions. He was director of the London School of Economics (1919–37) but is more famous as the architect of the British welfare state of the post-war era. E. B. Wilson (1879–1964) was a Harvard mathematician associated with econometrics and on the editorial board of *Econometrica* from 1933 until the late 1940s. The other early work besides Moore's to use harmonic analysis has been reviewed by Cargill (1974).

cycles are temporary phenomena, or span more than the unit of one year, they would affect crops differently in different periods.

While Beveridge had the residues of a causal model behind his analysis of the relationship between wheat prices and weather cycles, there was no explanatory model behind Wilson's 1934 analysis of monthly data on business activity covering 140 years. His work was really a test of the hypothesis that business cycle data show definite periods: the results rather suggested that they do not. In particular, he found neither Jevons' sunspot-related cycle nor Moore's Venus-related cycle of significance. Both Wilson and Beveridge tested the cycles they found in the data. Beveridge concentrated on whether his results were compatible with other evidence. Wilson used statistical tests to see whether the cyclical patterns of business cycle data were similar to those found in chance series. (He found that his dominant periods were rejected as not significant by the test recommended by Schuster and by the tests of others who rejected Schuster's test.) Wilson and Beveridge both tested subperiods of the data to see whether the results were the same for both periods, and Wilson also tried forecasting from subperiod to subperiod with little success.

Beveridge and Wilson showed a decline in confidence in the idea of periodic economic cycles compared to Moore and a preference for using the periodogram method to describe data and analyse its characteristics, rather than letting it play a central role in theory-building, as Moore had done. There were a number of sound reasons for this decline in confidence and for the relatively sparse usage of the periodogram method in economics in the period. By virtue of his leading example in this field, Moore's work naturally provided the focus for contemporary discussion of these issues.

One obvious reason for the decline in the periodic cycle programme was that economists did not believe that the business cycle was anything more than roughly regular. Critics of Moore's work were suspicious of the periodicity claimed for the economic cycle, a double claim since it was central to his hypothesis and it was implied by his usage of the periodogram method. Ingraham, for example, believed that *a priori* it was more probable that business cycles had an average length of 8 years, rather than Moore's hypothesis of an exact periodicity of 8 years. Ingraham showed that Moore's evidence was not inconsistent with this alternative hypothesis of an average cycle length, and was thus able to conclude his review of Moore's second book:

> All [Moore's] data could be explained as well by a theory of cycles which merely assumed that in general the length of cycles is close to that of their average length, showing no true periodicity. This is to the average

economist much the more likely hypothesis on an a priori judgement, and so it should stand until we have much more complete statistical data.

(Ingraham (1923), p. 765)

The assumption of periodicity also implied a symmetric shape to the cycle, whereas Crum (1923) pointed out that observed economic cycles tended to be asymmetric in form (i.e. the upturn is different from the downturn).

Even if economists were willing to suspend their disbelief in periodicity, the difficulties of interpreting the periodogram results remained. On the one hand, the method seemed to produce too many cycles to allow sensible economic interpretation: for example, Beveridge's (1922) tally of 19 significant cycles was followed by a lengthy and confused discussion of the meaning of his results. Mitchell (1927) and Schumpeter (1939) refer to similar difficulties of interpretation. On the other hand, Moore's exclusive concentration on the 8-year cycle seemed to be too simplistic a characterisation of economic cycle data. P. G. Wright (1924) considered, after experimenting with the data, that it was more likely Moore had two superimposed periodicities, or different periodicities for different subsections of the data, than a single 8-year cycle. Wright believed his interpretation was compatible with an internal origin to the business cycle from psychological or economic factors, which might be expected to vary their time periods. Others also suggested that over the long term, periodicities in economic series were likely to change rather than remain constant and Frisch (1927) concluded the method was too rigid for this reason.

But apart from these rather nebulous problems of interpretation, there were a number of technical difficulties in using the periodogram method which were recognised at the time. Moore's early discussion of what he required from the method indicates some of these difficulties. In the first place, Moore said of the method:

> It must exhaust the data in the search for possible cycles; that is to say, the data must be made to yield all the truth they contain relating to the particular problem in hand. Frequently in the past, spurious periodicities have been presented as real periodicities, chiefly because the investigator started with a bias in favor of a particular period and did not pursue his researches sufficiently far to determine whether his result was not one among many spurious, chance periodicities contained in his material. In the search for real periodicities the data must be exhaustively analyzed.

(Moore (1914), p. 137)

Despite his wise words, Moore's own work did not live up to the standards of unbiased behaviour that he had set himself. His 1914 theory had involved an 8-year cycle and his affection for this result led him astray when in 1923 he found that an harmonic analysis of British prices indicated significant cycles of 8.7 years and 7.4 years but not 8.0 years. Moore had tried to retrieve his theory by averaging the results from the two significant periods to gain a significant result for the 8-year cycle, a procedure which Ingraham (1923) pointed out was invalid in harmonic analysis.

Exhaustive and unbiased analysis was not sufficient to counteract the manifold dangers of spurious periodicities for as Moore reminded his readers there was a second technical difficulty:

> The method must render possible the discrimination between a true periodicity, having its origin in a natural cause and persisting with a change in the samples of statistics, and a spurious periodicity which is purely formal, having its origin in accidental characteristics of the statistical sample and disappearing, or radically altering its character, when different samples of statistics are made the basis of the computation.
>
> (Moore (1914), pp. 137–8)

Once again Moore failed to follow his own good advice, although others did so. Beveridge and Wilson were both aware of the problem and tried to eliminate spurious periodicities due to sampling by testing different subperiods of the data and Wilson applied statistical tests to try and determine real from chance periodicities.[18] Crum (1923) perceived this problem differently. He believed that non-homogeneity of the sample due to long-term trend changes, as well as irregular disturbances and even seasonal variations in the data, lead to a 'blurring' in the measurement of the maxima of the periodogram, making it difficult to determine the true periodicities. Yule (1927) went further with this argument and claimed that, if the effect of the disturbances were to carry through into later periods, the true periodicities could not be recovered by harmonic analysis.

Another way of avoiding 'chance' or 'spurious' periodicities, and thus one of the requirements for successful use of the method, was to use a long data period. Yet, economic time-series data, as Mitchell (1927) pointed out, usually covered only rather short periods and were therefore inadequate. For example, Moore's data set was only 40 years in length which, Ingraham argued, was

> insufficient to establish the existence of any period of length as great as eight years. (Ingraham (1923), p. 765)

P. G. Wright (1922) confirmed that this was so by carrying out a die throwing experiment to demonstrate that using harmonic analysis on

---

[18] Kendall (1945) afterwards claimed that most of Beveridge's 19 significant periods were accounted for by sampling error.

his chance series of numbers gave results similar to those Moore had obtained on his rainfall data. Data series were rarely, like Beveridge's series of wheat prices, long enough to make accurate results possible. Yet the periodogram method and the calculation it required gave a specious accuracy to results, of which economists – for example, Crum (1923) – were justly suspicious. On the other hand, use of a long data series brought a severe computing problem: periodogram analysis was very laborious to carry out by hand because it required such a large amount of computation. Contemporary evidence of the time taken to carry out periodogram analysis by hand calculator is difficult to gain, but Beveridge's work in particular must have taken many hours.[19]

Last, but by no means least, of the technical issues was that periodogram analysis could be of only very limited use to econometricians. Economists, even the most empirically minded, were primarily interested in *the relationships between variables* rather than *the behaviour of one variable*, while the harmonic analysis available at the time was applicable to one variable at a time and could not be used to investigate relationships between variables. This was certainly one of the drawbacks which struck Frisch when he started a theoretical study of time-series methods in the mid-1920s.[20]

With all the drawbacks of assumption, interpretation and technique mentioned here, it is no wonder that Crum (1923) concluded the synopsis of his critical study of the method with these words:

> The average form of the cycle is at best not very precisely determined, and its breaking up into a group of harmonic components of differing periods and amplitudes is certainly bewildering and probably furnishes no true insight into the nature of economic fluctuation.   (Crum (1923), p. 17)

Yet there was one very good reason why econometricians might have persevered with harmonic analysis: the method was specifically applicable to time-related data. The alternative correlation methods, to the degree that inference from them was dependent on data observations being independent through time, were therefore unsatisfactory for prediction purposes. Indeed, it was the general view of economists analysing business cycle data in the 1920s and 1930s that methods which involved the theory of probability could not be used because the observations of business cycle data were related through time. This

---

[19] Some idea is given by the report that the time taken for an harmonic analysis on an early IBM computer in 1961 using 400 observations (about the size of Beveridge's data set) was three hours.

[20] Frisch (1927), p. 2. This point was entirely missed by both Cargill (1974) and Morgenstern (1961) in discussing the way frequency analysis was discarded in econometrics during the 1930s.

view was not considered inconsistent with the wide use of a whole range of statistical techniques on time series (this apparent paradox will be further discussed in Chapter 8). The fact was that for contemporaries, most other statistical techniques were preferable to periodogram analysis. The methods of correlation and decomposition of time series into component parts were more widely understood than harmonic analysis which demanded a relatively high level of mathematical comprehension. P. G. Wright (1922) also argued that the method of correlation was better than harmonic analysis because it was more sensitive to changes in cyclical features and trends, and allowed more thoughtful interpretation and critical judgement. In addition, the correlation method could be used directly to measure the association between variables.

Despite the fact that Jevons and Moore are recognised as pioneers in econometric business cycle research, the reasons for their lack of continuing influence on cycle analysis are now clearer. First, their assumption of a periodic cycle generated from outside the economy was unattractive to most economists and the frequency methods which accompanied their assumption were found to be ill-suited for econometric work. In the second place, there was a positive burgeoning of statistical work on the business cycle in the 1920s which involved alternative ideas and methods and which were more easily accessible to business cycle students of the period. Thirdly, a preference for description over explanation was a common trait of the development of statistical work on business cycles in the 1920s and 1930s regardless of the actual tools used. In the face of this strong alternative empirical statistical programme, the econometric approach advanced by Jevons and Moore, which tried to build theories of the cycle out of the statistical regularities and relationships in the data, lay dormant until revitalised by Tinbergen in the late 1930s. Meanwhile, the alternative programme deserves our attention.

CHAPTER 2

Measuring and representing business cycles

Clément Juglar, Wesley Clair Mitchell and Warren M. Persons used statistics in a different fashion from Jevons and Moore. These three economists believed that numerical evidence should be used on a large scale because it was better than qualitative evidence, but their use of data was empirical in the sense that they did not use statistical features of the data as a basis for building cycle theories. Further generalisations are difficult, because their aims differed: Juglar wanted to provide a convincing explanation for the cycle, Mitchell sought an empirical definition of the cyclical phenomenon, whilst Persons aimed to provide a representation of the cycle. The chapter begins with a brief discussion of Juglar's work in the late nineteenth century, and then deals at greater length with the work of Mitchell and Persons, whose empirical programmes dominated statistical business cycle research in the 1920s and 1930s.

The applied work discussed here grew in parallel to that described in Chapter 1, for Juglar was a contemporary of Jevons, and Mitchell and Persons overlapped with Moore. The developments that the three economists, Juglar, Mitchell and Persons, pioneered came to be labelled 'statistical' or 'quantitative' economics but never bore the tag of 'econometrics' as Moore's work has done. These statistical approaches are important to the history of econometrics, not only because they provide a comparison with the work of Chapter 1, but also because it was by no means so clear to those who worked in the early twentieth century that econometrics was a distinctly separate programme from statistical economics. The distinction was clear enough by the 1940s for the two rival parties to indulge in a methodological debate over the correct use of statistics in economic research. Comparisons between the statistical and econometric programmes are drawn at various points during the discussion and an assessment of the two approaches comes at the end of the chapter.

2.1 Juglar's credit cycle

Clément Juglar's[1] interest in business cycles was stimulated in the 1850s by his study of a table of financial statistics for France. Like his contemporary Jevons, he was immediately struck by the recurrence of 'crises' evident in such data. Unlike Jevons, Juglar set out to find all the causes of these crises and eliminate the secondary causes one by one to leave only the necessary determining cause which was constant for every cycle. The theory that Juglar proposed was more acceptable to economists of the late nineteenth century than Jevons' sunspot theory, both because it was developed from current ideas on credit crises and because his way of reasoning from statistical data was less alien to them.

In the first edition of his book on crises in 1862, *Des crises commerciales et de leur retour périodique*, Juglar studied the histories of all the crises in the nineteenth century in three different countries, France, England and the USA. He discussed each crisis in turn and argued that events such as wars, revolutions and famines were causes of the moment, which might determine the exact crisis date or the particular character-istics of the cycle but they did not determine the fact of the crisis or cycle. Such causes were only the 'last drop which caused the basin to overflow' (Juglar (1862), p. v), not determining causes in the true sense. He concluded that the one constant common cause of all these cycles was changes in the conditions of credit. Juglar's 'proof' of the constant or determining cause rested on two planks: one was an appeal to the regularity of certain sequences or patterns in the tables of data, and the other was the novel reason that a discussion of the monetary history of each crisis was repetitious and liable to cause ennui in the reader, a proof by boredom!

The second edition of Juglar's book (1889) was very much enlarged and enriched with further evidence although the method of approach was essentially the same. He presented much of the evidence in distinctive exhibits. These were in the form of tables, to be read downwards (containing only the maxima and minima figures of each cycle) with a graphic indication (not drawn to scale) of the cycle by the side of the figures. An example is presented here (Figure 3). He concluded that over the nineteenth century the credit cycle was common to, and more or less simultaneous in, three countries with

---

[1] Clément Juglar (1819–1905) trained as a physician but became interested in demography and statistics and thence economics in the 1840s (see entry in the *International Encyclopedia of the Social Sciences*).

**Différence en plus ou moins des principaux articles des bilans
de la Banque de France.**

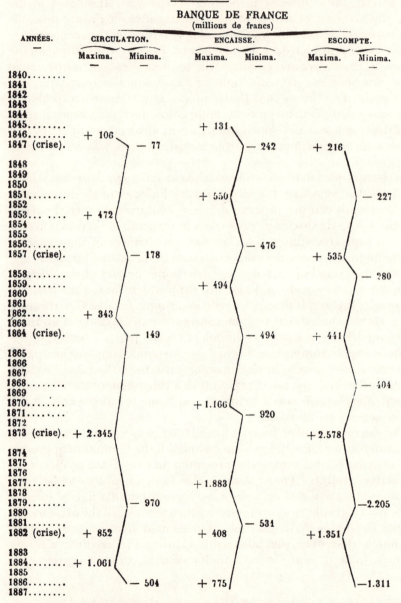

	BANQUE DE FRANCE (millions de francs)					
ANNÉES. —	CIRCULATION.		ENCAISSE.		ESCOMPTE.	
	Maxima. —	Minima. —	Maxima. —	Minima. —	Maxima. —	Minima. —
1840.......						
1841						
1842						
1843						
1844						
1845.......			+ 131			
1846.......	+ 106					
1847 (crise).		— 77		— 242	+ 216	
1848						
1849						
1850						
1851.......			+ 550			— 227
1852						
1853...	+ 472					
1854						
1855						
1856.......				— 476		
1857 (crise).		— 178			+ 535	
1858.......						— ?80
1859.......			+ 494			
1860						
1861						
1862.......	+ 343					
1863						
1864 (crise).		— 149		— 494	+ 441	
1865						
1866						
1867						
1868.......						— 404
1869						
1870.......			+ 1.166			
1871.......				— 920		
1872						
1873 (crise).	+ 2.345				+ 2.578	
1874						
1875						
1876						
1877.......			+ 1.883			
1878						
1879.......		— 970				—2.205
1880						
1881.......				— 531		
1882 (crise).	+ 852		+ 408		+ 1.351	
1883						
1884.......	+ 1.061					
1885						
1886.......		— 504	+ 775			—1.311
1887.......						

Figure 3   Juglar's table-graph of credit cycles
Source: Juglar (2nd edn, 1889), p. 154

different institutional regimes (that is, complete freedom of the banking system in the USA, freedom and monopoly in England and monopoly in France).

It was clear to Juglar, from the evidence of the first edition of his book, that cycles were variable in length and in amplitude, but that the sequence of activity was regular. He described this sequence as 'periodic', by which he meant that the sequence repeated itself, not that there was an exact periodic cycle. The terms 'constancy' and 'regularity' in Juglar's discussion referred to the necessary cause of cycles and the sequence of events not to the timing or appearance of cycles. This view was unchanged by his further research, although by the second edition he had developed a definite phase categorisation of his credit cycle sequence: prosperity (5–7 years), panic or crises (a few months to a few years) and liquidation or depression (a few years). Since his own evidence 'did not allow one to do more than observe that a crisis returned in a period of between 5 to 10 years' (Juglar (1889), p. 164), Juglar strongly rejected Jevons' theory of regular periodic cycles.[2] Juglar also found Jevons' sunspot theory untenable on other grounds. First, he believed that the changing environment of commerce and industry would cause changes in the cyclical pattern. Secondly, he believed that exogenous factors like the weather (or sunspots) could only be disturbing influences, not true causes. Lastly, he challenged those who believed in such meteorological causes to find a good economic barometer!

The novelty of both Juglar's and Jevons' work to contemporaries was that they used lots of data instead of a few odd numbers, that they were concerned with cycles not crises, and that they used statistical data to recognise regularity in the behaviour and causes of economic cycles. These general similarities hid important differences, for Juglar differed from Jevons about the nature of the regularity involved, the causes of economic cycles and, most important, they used their data in different ways. Juglar justified the usage of unusually long runs of statistics on the grounds that it added scientific rigour to his work. He argued that statistical evidence was better than verbal evidence because it uncovered the regularity in events and enabled him to see causes and links which might otherwise be hidden in the historical description. Despite his belief that statistical evidence was somehow more scientific

---

[2] Despite Juglar's insistent rejection of statistical regularity, cycles of 9–10 years in length are called 'Juglars'. This was due to Schumpeter (1939) who classified the various cycles by average length and named them after their main exponents (thus Kitchin, Juglar, Kuznets and Kondratieff cycles). His two-volume study of the business cycle contained no statistical analysis to speak of, but developed a complex theory of the interactions of these different cycles.

than qualitative evidence, Juglar used his statistical data in much the same way as qualitative evidence. He discussed the data on each individual cycle and then, as it were, piled up the cases to provide support for his theory by repetition. Each cycle was treated as an individual event with certain features in common; but these features were not connected to statistically measurable regularities of the data. Indeed, he made a point of their statistical variability. So Juglar's explanation and evidence for his theory was based on the aggregate of the individual occurrences, although it could have been built up on the basis of one cycle only. Jevons, on the other hand, expected the constancy of economic behaviour to be reflected in statistical regularities in the mass of the data. Not only was the pattern of economic activity to be revealed in statistically regular cycles, but these statistical regularities also played an important part in the development and design of Jevons' sunspot theory of their causation.

Historical judgement suggests that because of the way each used statistical data, Jevons' work more nearly qualifies as the first econometric theory and treatment of the business cycle, while Juglar is more appropriately seen as a pioneer in the important and parallel programme in 'quantitative economics'. Their contemporaries made no such distinction, rather they were impressed by Juglar's sensible economic reasoning about the cyclical nature of economic activity and deplored the eccentricity of Jevons' sunspot theory.[3]

2.2   The statistical approach of W. C. Mitchell

2.2.1   *Mitchell's first statistical study of business cycles*

Wesley Clair Mitchell, like Jevons, had a history of statistical studies to his credit when his first book on business cycles appeared in 1913, one year before that of Moore.[4] The aim and overall method of *Business Cycles and their Causes* were described in only two pages (out of over 600) and are best presented by direct quotation:

[3] For example, Schumpeter (1954) suggested that the cycle ousted the crisis in the period 1870 to 1914 and credited Juglar's work as the decisive factor in this change of perception. He conceived Mitchell's (1913) work to be in the same spirit as Juglar's and to mark the start of the next generation of business cycle study.

[4] Wesley Clair Mitchell (1878–1948) was a member of the loosely knit group of American economists known as the institutionalist school. The main influences on his work were Veblen and Dewey. Mitchell helped to found the National Bureau of Economic Research in 1920 and was its director 1920–45. He also helped found the New School for Social Research in New York. There are many sources of information about Mitchell, a contemporary starting point is Burns (1952).

One seeking to understand the recurrent ebb and flow of economic activity characteristic of the present day finds these numerous explanations [of business cycles] both suggestive and perplexing. All are plausible, but which is valid? None necessarily excludes all the others, but which is the most important? Each may account for certain phenomena; does any one account for all the phenomena? Or can these rival explanations be combined in such a fashion as to make a consistent theory which is wholly adequate?

There is slight hope of getting answers to these questions by a logical process of proving and criticizing the theories. For whatever merits of ingenuity and consistency they may possess, these theories have slight value except as they give keener insight into the phenomena of business cycles. It is by study of the facts which they purport to interpret that the theories must be tested.

But the perspective of the invesigation [*sic*] would be distorted if we set out to test each theory in turn by collecting evidence to confirm or to refute it. For the point of interest is not the validity of any writer's views, but clear comprehension of the facts. To observe, analyze, and systematize the phenomena of prosperity, crisis, and depression is the chief task. And there is better prospect of rendering service if we attack this task directly, than if we take the round about way of considering the phenomena with reference to the theories.

This plan of attacking the facts directly by no means precludes free use of the results achieved by others. On the contrary, their conclusions suggest certain facts to be looked for, certain analyses to be made, certain arrangements to be tried. Indeed, the whole investigation would be crude and superficial if we did not seek help from all quarters. But the help wanted is help in making a fresh examination into the facts.

(Mitchell (1913), pp. 19–20)

It would be a mistake to think that Mitchell rejected any role for business cycle theories, for he recognised here quite clearly that theories determined which 'facts' should be examined. But although theories dictated which data to look at, Mitchell was not sure whether he ought to test each theory of the cycle individually (and notice that his idea of testing included both verification and refutation) or attempt to investigate all the theories together. He decided that the principal need was for more detailed information on business cycle behaviour.

Mitchell's empirical programme was to start with the facts and determine the relative importance of different causal factors in the cycle, using both quantitative and qualitative research. Quantitative evidence predominated because, as Mitchell said,

in his efforts to make accurate measurements [of the causal factors] the economic investigator cannot devise experiments, he must do the best he can with the cruder gauges of statistics. (Mitchell (1913), p. 20)

He decided to study only a short period, 1890–1911, making up a 'sufficient number of cases' from which to generalise by looking at the evidence of four countries. His study of the facts consisted of an exhaustive 350-page presentation of the statistics of business cycles for the four countries, accompanied by a commentary and arranged by topic. These topics included the usual ones of prices and profits, but also the less usual aspects of cycles such as the behaviour of migration. His analysis of the data was severely limited, consisting of taking averages for each of the two decades and comparing the behaviour of different countries using graphs.

Following his statistical enquiry Mitchell attempted to redefine what an adequate business cycle theory should look like. His study suggested that

> A theory of business cycles must therefore be a descriptive analysis of the cumulative changes by which one set of business conditions transforms itself into another set.
>
> The deepest-seated difficulty in the way of framing such a theory arises from the fact that while business cycles recur decade after decade each new cycle presents points of novelty. Business history repeats itself, but always with a difference. This is precisely what is implied by saying that the process of economic activity within which business cycles occur is a process of *cumulative* change.   (Mitchell (1913), p. 449)

In this definition, no general theory is completely adequate because each cycle is unique and demands a unique explanation. Since each cycle grows out of, and is dependent on, the previous events, it is impossible completely to explain any cycle because the analysis can never be carried back far enough. Mitchell realised these difficulties and proposed that instead of seeking a general theory, attention should be focussed on the recurring phases of the cycle, from revival to depression.

Having presented the data, Mitchell set himself to study the interactions of the elements of the cycle as the cycle passed through its various phases. There was no natural starting place for the process and arbitrarily he chose the point following on from a depression. This investigation did not involve quantitative analysis, but the knowledge of the statistical evidence was used to evaluate the various cycle theories. He suggested that

> none of the theories of business cycles ... seems to be demonstrably wrong, but neither does any one seem to be wholly adequate.
>   (Mitchell (1913), p. 579)

He concluded that cycles are not uniform but irregular; that they do not always follow the same pattern of phases and their intensities and

elements differ. He claimed these differences were often due to 'extraneous factors' such as weather, war, government policy changes, etc. In
addition, Mitchell thought that, with improved business barometers
(already widely used in the US and commercially successful), future
cycles could be predicted and might be controlled to some extent.

Lastly, Mitchell believed that longer term changes in economic
organisation (being cumulative) had an evolutionary effect on cycles.
To illustrate this point he discussed the changes that had occurred in the
nature of cycles from agricultural crises (in the pre-industrial period) to
credit crises and thence to business cycles (as industrialisation had taken
place). These long-term developments he claimed were gradual and
continuous (unlike the earlier stage theories of development held by
some nineteenth-century German economists), and were associated
with institutional or organisational change in the economy.

Mitchell's book was very well received and was regarded by contemporaries as an important contribution to statistical economics.
Pigou was particularly convinced by Mitchell's description of the
complexity of the cycle:

> For the great value of this lies in its realism and concreteness – in the fact
> that the skeleton does not appear as a skeleton, but as a being of flesh who
> lives and moves.   (Pigou (1914), p. 81)

Persons, who was also very taken with the book, wrote:

> It is comprehensive; it contains the most complete and careful statistical
> study of the phenomena connected with business cycles; . . . it is a scientific
> study by an author who, obviously, is not seeking to establish a pet theory.
>   (Persons (1914), p. 795)

In a later judgement, Dorfman (1949) suggested that the theoretical
contributions in Mitchell's book were not appreciated by contemporary
readers because the language was commonplace and the method
descriptive.

There was some truth in this latter point for Mitchell had presented
the statistical evidence and other evidence before discussing theories;
he had then drawn his conclusions about the nature of the cycle from an
investigation in which theoretical ideas and statistical evidence were
discussed in conjunction. Despite admitting (though only in a footnote)
the difficulties of studying such a complex phenomenon in this way,

> the intellectual instruments of analysis are unequal to the complex problem
> of handling simultaneous variations among a large number of inter-related
> functions.   (Mitchell (1913), p. 450)

Mitchell's descriptive analysis remained wedded to conventional methods based on the unaided intellect; he spurned the aid of both mathematical and statistical tools.[5] It is not clear that these tools would have helped him, for his investigations into the evidence had convinced him that not only was each cycle a unique event, but that cycles did not even possess unifying characteristics such as the same pattern of phases or the same elements in their changes. These beliefs coupled with his empirical approach made it impossible for Mitchell to produce a simple but general model of the cycle as Juglar had done from his observation that the cycle had a standard sequence of events.

The fact that Mitchell believed each cycle was different also precluded him from adopting a data reduction approach involving either the summary statistics such as means and variances, like Jevons' reliance on average cycle length, or using regression and correlation as Moore was to do in 1914. Moore's book provides the obvious contemporary comparison. Their divergent views on the nature of the business cycle were naturally reflected in the way that each used statistical evidence. For Mitchell, the raw data gave evidence for the lack of uniformity, and this effectively excluded both statistical analysis and any general explanation or theory of the business cycle. For Moore, the raw data hid the uniformity and constancy of the cycles; he therefore depended on statistical analysis in his search for regularity and relationships in the data and a general theory of the cycle.

Despite their differences, both Mitchell and Moore were pioneers in their time. Few other economists had followed the pointers laid by Juglar and Jevons. Like these predecessors, both Mitchell and Moore were seeking a theory which would explain all the characteristics of the whole cycle (not just upturns or turning points as in early theories of the business cycle which derived from crises theories), and both relied on masses of statistical data in their search. Yet here the similarities between Mitchell and Moore end. Mitchell's cautious use of statistical data and empirical approach to analysing the business cycle are as clearly distinguishable from Moore's careless but imaginative econometric work as Juglar's work was from Jevons'.

2.2.2   *The problems in Mitchell's cycle analysis*

In 1921, the National Bureau of Economic Research, under Mitchell's direction, took up his statistical business cycle programme. Among many results of this programme was a second book by Mitchell *Business Cycles: The Problem and its Setting*, in 1927, which is best described as

---

[5] Mitchell was not trained as a statistician and apparently thought of himself as a theorist who used statistical evidence and later, only by necessity, statistical tools. Seckler (1975) discusses Mitchell's attitude towards evidence and Veblen's influence in this respect.

Mitchell's search for the definition and the correct analytical approach to the business cycle: a survey of the problems in the field rather than a new empirical study solving these problems. He again discussed the role of theory, of institutional descriptions, of statistics and of commercial history (records of business annals) in the analysis of business cycles. As in his 1913 book, all these elements seemed to have equal status in his investigation.

Throughout the book runs an attempt to define the concept of the business cycle. The more Mitchell tried to define the phenomenon, the more it seemed to slip away from his grasp:

> The more intensively we work, the more we realize that this term [business cycles] is a synthetic product of the imagination – a product whose history is characteristic of our ways of learning. Overtaken by a series of strange experiences our predecessors leaped to a broad conception, gave it a name, and began to invent explanations.   (Mitchell (1927), p. 2)

He sought help with the conceptual problem in an analysis of business cycle theories, but once again he found that there were too many theories and all were plausible:

> the theories figure less as rival explanations of a single phenomenon than as complementary explanations of closely related phenomena. The processes with which they severally deal are all characteristic features of the whole. These processes not only run side by side, but also influence and (except for the weather) are influenced by each other ... Complexity is no proof of multiplicity of causes. Perhaps some single factor is responsible for all the phenomena. An acceptable explanation of this simple type would constitute the ideal theory of business cycles from the practical, as well as from the scientific, viewpoint. But if there be one cause of business cycles, we cannot make sure of its adequacy as an explanation without knowing what are the phenomena to be explained, and how the single cause produces its complex effects, direct and indirect.
> (Mitchell (1927), p. 180)

Mitchell now had a clearer notion of the roles of data and theory. Data were useless without theory:

> the figures are of little use except as they are illuminated by theory,
> (Mitchell (1927), p. 54)

and, he argued, data in the form of economic statistics and commercial records could be used to

> suggest hypotheses, and to test our conclusions. (Mitchell (1927), p. 57)

But the issue of how to 'test the conclusions' remained problematic in Mitchell's eyes. On the one hand, he rejected the idea of testing theories individually against the evidence as being repetitious and indeed restrictive if the theories were complementary. On the other hand, he believed there was a danger of hopeless confusion of an empirical classification, such as the phases of the cycle (i.e. depression, revival and prosperity), were to provide the framework for investigation.

Of particular interest in this book is the long section in which Mitchell discussed the merits and disadvantages of the statistical techniques which were then in popular use on business cycle data. He thought that the two main statistical techniques, data decomposition (discussed later in this chapter) and periodogram analysis (discussed in Chapter 1) were both inadequate because neither measured the business cycle directly. The data decomposition technique involved, in Mitchell's view, the dubious separation of an economic time series into cyclical, trend, seasonal and accidental elements. (The cycle element was what was left when the others had been removed.) Of the alternative periodogram analysis, Mitchell noted that this had technical difficulties and, like most economists, he clearly doubted the periodicity of business cycles. Indices of the cycle (made up of several variables) were treated more leniently by Mitchell because he believed they measured the business cycle directly, although he felt that none of the indices available at the time was entirely satisfactory. Correlation of one time series with another (with or without lagging) was another popular tool of data analysis in the 1920s. Correlation techniques were not rejected outright, but Mitchell distrusted the technique because he believed correlations could easily be manipulated. In addition, contemporaries tended to take high correlations as evidence of causal connections, an inference Mitchell believed to be invalid.

This book, with its exhaustive discussion of current statistical methods, fully established Mitchell's reputation as the preeminent figure in statistical business cycle research of the interwar period. The book was an impressive survey of the field of business cycle research in the 1920s and was justly praised by his contemporaries, both for his insights into the phenomenon and for the rich discussion of business cycle research methods, particularly the statistical approaches.[6] Yet Mitchell's book contained almost nothing of direct importance to the development of econometric work on the business cycle in the 1920s and 1930s, and was, if anything, negative towards further statistical research on cycles.

The circumspection evident in the book might easily strike the modern reader as Mitchell's inability to make up his mind. He had rejected the idea of using any one theory (but conceded the necessity of theories in general); had rejected currently available methods of

[6] See, for example, H. Working (1928).

analysing statistical data (but depended on statistical data as evidence); and he also expressed doubts about the role of business records (though once again he wanted to use their evidence). One reason for this equivocation was that the difficulties of any particular approach or method loomed large in Mitchell's mind.[7] Another reason was that Mitchell could not, or would not, deal in abstract notions. Much of the statistical analysis by this time, assumed that there was some 'normal' cycle: a hypothetical cycle which would exist if there were no short-term disturbances or long-term influences. Mitchell, on the other hand, was interested in the 'typical' cycle: the cycle which was characteristic of business cycles in the real world. Mitchell's priorities in business cycle research were description and measurement of real cycles.

2.2.3   Mitchell and Burns' cycle measurements

The third of the major volumes in Mitchell's research programme on cycles was *Measuring Business Cycles*, written jointly with A. F. Burns and published by the NBER in 1946.[8] Their aims were to study the fluctuations in the individual sectors of the economy and to use the individual data series available to provide good measurements of the cycle. This was the programme which had been laid down at the end of Mitchell's 1927 book, but the problem of measuring business cycles turned out to be far more difficult than Mitchell had envisaged and took a long time to solve.

Measurement was seen by Mitchell and Burns as a prior requirement for testing the theories of other economists, of which they wrote:

> Their work is often highly suggestive; yet it rests so much upon simplifying assumptions and is so imperfectly tested for conformity to experience that, for our purposes, the conclusions must serve mainly as hypotheses. Nor can we readily use the existing measures of statisticians to determine which among existing hypotheses accounts best for what happens. Satisfactory tests cannot be made unless hypotheses have been framed with an eye to testing, and unless observations upon many economic activities have been made in a uniform manner.   (Burns and Mitchell (1946), p. 4)

---

[7] Dorfman's judgement on the influence of Veblen on his pupils seems particularly apt in describing Mitchell's approach to business cycles: 'Several of Veblen's students chose a concrete field of economics for detailed inquiry and found themselves moving gradually into ever-widening realms. Veblen had had the effect of stripping them so thoroughly, though unconsciously, of their complete confidence in the old way, that they tended to base their inquiries closely upon the existing facts' (Dorfman (1949), p. 450).

[8] The initial collaborator at the NBER was Simon Kuznets; Arthur Burns took over as researcher when Kuznets left the project to work on national income accounts.

In order to test theories, the statistical data had to be reformulated into measurements of the business cycle itself. Measurement in turn required a prior definition of the phenomenon to be measured. Mitchell's definition of business cycles had by this stage become a description of observable characteristics, and since 'equilibrium', 'normal' and 'natural' were theoretical notions, not observable characteristics, they did not form part of this definition.

In his 1927 book, Mitchell had criticised statistical workers for their failure to provide direct measurements of the cycle. In this new book, Mitchell and Burns evolved a new set of statistical measures of the business cycle called specific cycles and reference cycles. Specific cycles were cycles specific to an individual variable, dated on the turning points of that variable and divided into the nine phases of that variable's cycle. As a benchmark for comparison of the different variables and to trace their interrelationships and timing, each variable also had its own reference cycle based on the timing of the business cycle as a whole (measured on the basis of business annals and the conjunction of important variables of the cycle). They wrote of the reference cycle idea:

> This step is the crux of the investigation; it involves passing from the specific cycles of individual time series, which readers not embarrassed by experience are likely to think of as objective 'facts', to business cycles, which can be seen through a cloud of witnesses only by the eye of the mind.
> (Burns and Mitchell (1946), p. 12)

Both reference cycles and specific cycles were averages of the individual cycle data in which seasonal variations had been excluded and the data were deviations from the average for each cycle (to avoid interference from trends). In practice, these cycle measurements were arrived at by a mixture of mechanically applied rules and ad hoc judgements.

The specific and reference cycles were presented in numerous tables and in graphs. An example of these graphs (the one used by Burns and Mitchell as an illustration, with their explanations) is reproduced in Figure 4. The Burns–Mitchell measurements of specific and reference cycles were quite difficult to understand. Although Burns and Mitchell gave hints on how to read them, the very newness of the graphs made it difficult to gain a clear picture of each variable's characteristics. (For the importance of graphs in general in statistical economics see Addendum to this chapter.) The position was made more difficult for the reader because the graphs were not only used to present measurements of each element in the business cycle but the relationships between the variables had to be understood largely from comparison of the graphs.

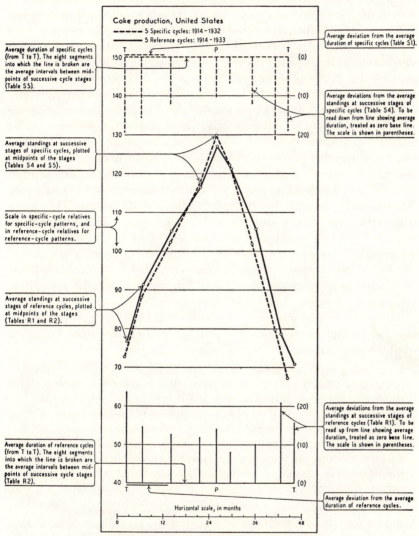

Figure 4   Mitchell's specific and reference cycle chart
Source: Burns and Mitchell (1946), p. 35, Chart 2

Mitchell and Burns did not test any theories that purported to explain cycles, but did test a number of hypotheses about the long-term behaviour of economic cycles using their measurements. For example, they tested Schumpeter's hypothesis about the relationship between different cycles, which suggested that there were three 40-month cycles (Kitchins) to each cycle of 9–10 years (Juglars) and six of these to each long wave (or Kondratieff cycle). They found it very difficult to fit their own specific cycles into the pattern proposed by Schumpeter for there was no consistent agreement of timing and dates and they therefore refused to accept Schumpeter's hypothesis. They also investigated one of Mitchell's own hypotheses, that there was a long-term secular change in cyclical behaviour. This test was more interesting for they examined whether their specific cycle measurements exhibited stability, first by fitting trend lines to their cycle durations and amplitudes, and secondly by dividing their cycles into three groups and testing for differences in the variance in amplitudes and durations. They used correlation tests and F-tests of significance, which failed to provide support for their hypothesis. They concluded that such changes as were observed were irregular or random, rather than consistent and due to secular change. Similar tests on their reference cycle measurements also failed to support the hypothesis, but these results did give them further confidence in their measurements.

Their own explanations of what happens during business cycles and how the various parts of the economy fit together were to be held over until the next volume:

> Later monographs will demonstrate in detail that the processes involved in business cycles behave far less regularly than theorists have been prone to assume; but they will demonstrate also that business-cycle phenomena are far more regular than many historically-minded students believe...
>
> Our theoretical work leans heavily on cyclical averages, such as are described in this book, and we hope that others will find them helpful. Instead of setting out from the dreamland of equilibrium, or from a few simple assumptions that common sense suggests ... our 'assumptions' are derived from concrete, systematic observations of economic life.
>
> (Burns and Mitchell (1946), p. 491)

Mitchell and Burns had codified their 'concrete observations' into representations of the cycle. This necessarily imposed some uniformity or regularity on the cycles. By thus retreating from Mitchell's earlier (1913) position that there was no uniformity in the patterns or elements in the business cycle, they left the way open for theoretical explanations of the cycle. Unfortunately, Mitchell died before the important final volume discussing their theoretical conclusions was complete. Burns carried on the work at the NBER, but the impetus of the programme was lost.

Mitchell's business cycle programme had begun in 1913 when he had prophesied that

> it is probable that the economists of each generation will see reason to recast the theory of business cycles which they learned in their youth.
>
> (Mitchell (1913), p. 583).

He had himself pointed out the change from crises to cycles. Yet he had been unable to foresee the future. The cycle was no longer, by Mitchell's death in 1948, the defining unit of analysis. During the course of Mitchell's working life, cycle theories had been recast twice: the theory of crises had given way to the theory of business cycles and this in turn had given way to macroeconomic theory. At the same time, the fashions in methodology also changed. Mitchell was an empirical economist primarily concerned with describing, classifying and measuring the 'typical' economic cycle.[9] His use of statistical evidence had made him a pioneer in 1913, but his lack of analysis made his statistical economics look increasingly dated as the econometric programme grew more sophisticated.[10] While Mitchell was still struggling with raw business cycle data in the 1930s, Tinbergen was busy formulating macroeconometrics. By the time of the Burns and Mitchell volume, the yawning gap between statistical economics and the more technically advanced and theoretically minded econometrics programme was evident in a highly critical review of their book by Koopmans, one of the leading econometricians of the day.

Tjalling Koopmans was a member of the Cowles Commission, which had been set up in 1932 to undertake econometric research and was *the* centre of econometric research in the 1940s.[11] Koopmans' 1947 review initiated the famous 'Measurement Without Theory' debate in which

[9] His rejection of mechanical analogies in favour of evolutionary and organic ones combined with his descriptive and classificatory approach suggests that whereas many economists looked to nineteenth-century physics for their model science, a more apt comparison for Mitchell is with the descriptive and categorising activities of nineteenth-century naturalists.

[10] It is not clear exactly when these programmes became distinct to contemporaries. The econometric programme must have been fairly clear by 1929 when the Econometric Society was formed, but because of the lack of econometric work on business cycle models in the late 1920s and early 1930s, this did not necessarily help to distinguish the business cycle programmes.

[11] The Cowles Commission for Research in Economics was set up in 1932 and funded by Alfred Cowles specifically to undertake econometric research. The journal *Econometrica* was run from the Commission, and there were close links with the Econometric Society. (Details of the history of the institution and its activities are described in Christ (1952), Hildreth (1986), Epstein (1987) and in the annual reports of the Commission for 1943–8.) Koopmans' review sparked a reply by Vining and a further response from Koopmans published in 1949, see Vining and Koopmans (1949). On Koopmans, see Chapter 8 n. 6.

he accused Burns and Mitchell of trying to measure economic cycles without having any *economic* theory about how the cycle worked. Koopmans' group had advanced a Walrasian model based on the aggregation of individual economic agents as units and in which the cycle was seen as a deviation from an underlying equilibrium level. In reply to Koopmans, Vining (1949) (a visiting research associate at the NBER) charged the Cowles group of being guilty of the same sin of measurement without economic theory in their own work. Vining took the position that the theory of how agents behaved had not been sufficiently worked out, and that the Cowles model was therefore a 'pretty skinny fellow' upon which to base so much high-powered statistical estimation: in essence, measurement without economic theory. Further, Vining argued in defence that Mitchell took a holistic view of the economy in which behaviour of the whole economy was more than a simple aggregate of individuals' behaviour and in which cycles and trends could not be unravelled because both were subject to the impact of institutional and evolutionary factors.

There was a second serious charge made by the econometricians: that the NBER group were trying to undertake measurement without *statistical* theory. Following Haavelmo's work in the early 1940s, econometricians believed that economic theories should be explicitly formulated as statistical hypotheses, so that methods of inference based on probability theory could be used to measure and test the relationships. Klein was in the process of testing a cycle (or macroeconomic) model for the Cowles group, using their newly developed methods of estimation and inference. It is true that Mitchell and Burns had not tested theories which explained the cycle, because they believed such theories had not yet been properly formulated for statistical testing; but they had (as noted above) used probability inference in their tests of theories about long-term behaviour.

This debate of the late 1940s showed the clearly irreconcilable differences both in theoretical conceptions of the cycle and in methodological approaches between Mitchell's statistical programme and that of the econometricians. The 'measurement without statistical theory' aspect of the debate is particularly important, but we need to know more about the development of the econometric programme before we can deal with it in detail in Chapter 8.

2.3   Persons and business barometers

In 1919, soon after Mitchell had produced his first statistical study of business cycles, another empirical economist, Warren M. Persons published his first main results using an alternative analytical approach to cycles based exclusively on statistical evidence.[12] This second main strand of statistical business cycle research was largely descriptive in aim and was associated with the production of time-series representations of cyclical activity called business barometers. Persons is much less well known than Mitchell, but his work was more important for econometrics because he was primarily responsible for developing data preparation and data adjustment methods which quickly became and remained standard in applied econometrics.

The methods Persons used to decompose economic time series into components and expose the business cycle were not entirely new, but had been used piecemeal in economic statistics from the late nineteenth century. Commercially produced indicators of economic activity, based on statistical series and used to forecast future business conditions, were of a similar age.[13] However, Persons developed the methods to a much higher state of sophistication and was particularly responsible for initiating serious academic study of these methods. His initiative temporarily gave academic respectability to business cycle barometers. This academic respectability led in turn to the setting up of a number of university business cycle research institutes in the 1920s which constructed their own national barometers. The barometers suffered a subsequent decline from respectability, but their descendants live on in the field of commerce and of government statistical services which publish leading and lagging series of economic statistics called indicators.

Persons was already well known in the field of economic data analysis when he was asked in 1917, by the newly established Harvard Committee for Economic Research, to undertake a study of the 'existing methods of collecting and interpreting economic statistics'. Two years later, the Committee established the *Review of Economic Statistics*,[14] with the aim of providing

> a more accurate record of economic phenomena than is now available, and [it] will also supply a method of interpreting current economic statistics which will make them more useful and significant than they are today

---

[12] Warren M. Persons (1878–1937), statistician and economist, was educated at the University of Wisconsin. He joined the Harvard faculty in 1919 and resigned in 1928 to become a consultant economist. Persons had produced an earlier barometer, but it was a limited affair based on little data or analysis (see Persons (1916)).

[13] This was a profitable business in 1913 (according to Mitchell), but Persons' work stimulated further commercial activity and by 1925 (see I. Fisher (1925)) there were 40 successful commercial forecasting agencies in the USA.

[14] The Harvard Committee was set up in 1917 and started the *Review* in 1919. (In 1949 the journal's name was changed to the *Review of Economics and Statistics*.) These three quotations on aims and methods come from the 'Prefatory Statement' in the first issue of the *Review* by C. J. Bullock.

and the method of interpreting economic statistics was to be developed by the application of

> modern methods of statistical analysis which have hitherto been utilized more extensively in other sciences than in economics.
>
> (Bullock (1919), Preface)

Persons' contributions to the first year's issues of the *Review* in 1919 included two major articles, one on the method of analysis of economic time series and the second on the development of business indicators. The first of these is more interesting from the point of view of the development of econometric thought. Persons' stated aim in these papers was to find a method to determine the significance of statistical data in indicating current and future business conditions. Persons believed that the first priority (addressed in his first paper (1919)) was to obtain long data series of reliable (accurate) and homogeneous data in order to make comparisons. His approach to the problem of which methods to use in the investigation of data was experimental in the sense that every procedure that he suggested was tried out on a number of data series. He strived for methods which would be objective and leave no room for subjective judgement for, as he said,

> No method is thought worth while testing that cannot be made entirely objective, that cannot be reproduced exactly by an individual working according to the directions laid down. The primary requirement in the argument is that each step be tested; the primary requirement in the method evolved is that the operations should be fully explained and reproducible.   (Persons (1919), p. 7)

The basic conceptual framework, from which Persons proceeded, was that fluctuations in economic series occur as a result of various forces: secular (or long-term) forces, seasonal forces, cyclical (or wavelike) forces and accidental (or irregular) forces. These all occur simultaneously:

> Those fluctuations are thus a confused conglomerate growing out of numerous causes which overlie and obscure one another.
>
> In view of this complexity the simple comparison of items within time series, in what may be termed their crude state, is of but little significance.
>
> (Persons (1919), p. 8)

The aim of the method was to eliminate the unwanted fluctuations and reveal the business cycle:

> the problem is to devise a method of unravelling, in so far as may be, the tangle of elements which constitute the fluctuations in fundamental series; that is, of distinguishing and measuring types of changes; of eliminating

certain types; and thus of revealing in the corrected data the quantitative effect of those forces which underlie the business and industrial situation.

(Persons (1919), p. 8)

Persons attacked the problem of measuring the secular trend first, since he needed a benchmark from which to measure the cyclical changes. Ideally, he thought, the secular trend should be determined by the data, rather than *a priori*, because he had no foreknowledge of which periods were homogeneous. He tried two empirical means of determining the trend, one by the method of moving averages and one by curve fitting. For the former, rather than take a centred moving average, each observation was taken relative to the preceding average period. He tried this with different numbers of terms in the moving average period (e.g. 5 years, 10 years, etc.) to provide different trend-adjusted series. But this proved unsatisfactory, because when he fitted a straight line to each of the new (detrended) data series he found that these lines had different slopes including, in some cases, slopes of opposite signs, whereas he felt that they should have produced the horizontal lines of detrended data.

After further experimentation Persons decided that the direct trend-fitting method, in which simple curves or straight lines were fitted to the raw data, would be less cumbersome and more reliable than the moving average method. However, this direct method was far from mechanical. It required a number of judgements about the period to be used, with little guidance from Persons. Was it homogeneous? Did it cover a full cycle or was it a peak to trough measure? Was the function to be fitted linear? Persons advocated that there was no mathematical substitute for the 'direct analysis of homogeneity'. By this, he meant fitting trends to a number of different periods and looking for radical changes in the slope of the fitted line, which he took to indicate non-homogeneous periods. For example, he found evidence of a change in the trend component in various business cycle data between the two periods 1879–96 and 1896–1913 and therefore fitted two different trends to the subperiods.

It was inevitable that Persons should fail to find adequate mechanical rules for this problem of trend fitting. The lack of natural base periods (the open-endedness of the time unit) meant that once the time period had been chosen, the technical criteria of success in trend fitting (that is, the appearance of horizontal trend lines in trend-adjusted data) could always be fulfilled. But the question of how to choose a homogeneous time period remained to a certain extent arbitrary and depended on individual judgement in each case.

These problems were not evident in the second component of time series, seasonal variations, which did have a natural time unit. Persons' work in this area was correspondingly more successful. His procedure was: first to establish that such fluctuations existed, then to measure them and finally to eliminate them from the data series. Again after a number of experiments on different data series he settled on link relatives, month to month changes, to give the basis for measurement of the seasonal variations. He looked at the frequency distribution of these percentage monthly changes for each month of the year and chose the median value as the best measure of the seasonal pattern. Following an adjustment for trend effects over the year, these medians were then formed into an index which began at 100 and returned to the same value for each January. This index could then be used to correct the original data series.

Lastly, Persons went on to study the other two elements in the time series, the irregular and the cyclical fluctuations. He did not regard cyclical fluctuations as being exactly periodic or regular. Irregular fluctuations might be large or small and isolated or occurring in succession like the cyclical fluctuations. The cyclical and the accidental components might therefore have similar data characteristics. Persons took this to imply that the forces behind the two elements were interconnected and that it would be impossible to distinguish the two elements:

> No distinction, therefore, between 'cyclical' and 'irregular' fluctuations may be obtained simply by study of the statistical data.
>
> (Persons (1919), p. 33)

Later he used a short period moving average to smooth away the irregular fluctuations. By a process of subtracting the seasonal and trend elements, he was then left with the remaining cyclical fluctuations.[15] He tried out these measurement methods on 15 economic series of monthly data covering 15 years. Persons concluded that his study of economic time-series data revealed considerable support for the 'realistic character of the concepts' of the four components.

In his second major article for the *Review* (1919a) Persons' aim was to construct an index of general business conditions with particular emphasis on the cyclical aspects:

> It is the cyclical fluctuations which have received especial attention. Further, in dealing with the cyclical fluctuations the aim has been to measure them, rather than to utilize the results in constructing a theory of business cycles.   (Persons (1919a), p. 115)

[15] In order to make the cyclical fluctuations comparable within and between data series, he calculated 'normal' (or standardised) fluctuations by dividing the percentage deviations from the secular trends by their standard deviations.

Constructing an index of the cycle raised the important question of how variables were related to each other. For Persons this was a question of fact not theory, to be answered by empirical research. He began by studying 50 data series and chose 20 of these which had similar periods but differently timed turning points. Persons relied on the methods he had already established in his previous paper to decompose the data and derive the individual cyclical series, but the problems of determining the sequence of the variables and combining them to make indices remained open.

His first step was to compare the variables and classify them according to the timing of their fluctuations to find the 'typical or average sequence' of the variables in the business cycle. With 20 data series, he needed to make 190 comparisons to cover all possible cases. These 190 comparisons were each carried out by three 'observers' with the use of an illuminated screen or light box on which were laid graphs of the two data series being compared. One graph was then moved back and forth on top of the other to try and match the movements in the two series. (Each series was expressed in terms of its standard deviations to make such comparison possible.) Each 'observer' was supposed to record the observed level of correlation (no arithemetical calculations: high, medium or low correlations were judged by eye), the sign of correlation (positive or negative) and whether the relationship was lagged forwards or backwards and by how many months. There was considerable disagreement, as might be expected, between the 'observers' as to whether a lag was positive or negative, and a correlation high or low.

Persons worked out the correlation coefficients for the lag periods suggested by his 'observers' and fixed the lag length according to the highest value of the correlation coefficient. This gave him the time sequence of the variables, and the timing of changes in the cycle. The variables were then grouped together to reflect this sequence and synthesised into three indices which would 'epitomize the business situation' and act 'as a guide to the relations that exist among economic phenomena' (Persons (1919a), p. 117).[16] Persons' indices of the business cycle were called the Harvard A-B-C curves, representing

---

[16] On this final aspect, of combining those series which the correlations showed to have similar timing and turning points into indices, there was no discussion and the data series in each group appear to have been averaged with no weighting involved. This omission is surprising in view of the known and much discussed statistical problems of weighting components in, for example, price indices. There was no discussion either, in this article, of the problem of forecasting from these indices, also strange given the purposes of barometers to forecast the turning points of the cycle. Both these points were discussed briefly in Person's earlier paper (1916).

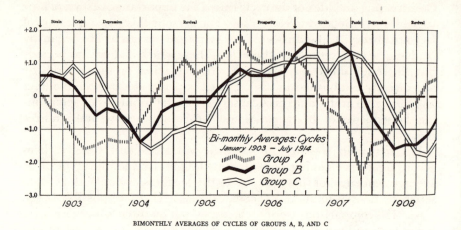

BIMONTHLY AVERAGES OF CYCLES OF GROUPS A, B, AND C

Figure 5   Persons' business barometer
Source: Persons (1919), p. 112

respectively: speculation; physical productivity combined with commodity prices; and the financial markets. (Index B seemed to be rather
a strange collection, made up of pig-iron production, bank clearings
outside New York, indices of commodity and retail prices and the
reserves of New York banks.) The A-B-C curves laid out Persons' view
of how groups of variables were empirically related in cycles. An
example of the A-B-C graph is given in Figure 5.

Persons had set out in his first article in 1919 to measure various
components of the data so that the interpretation of economic time-
series data would be more enlightening. Though, like Mitchell, he
wanted to avoid the use of *a priori* theory in making his measurements,
preconceived ideas were bound to enter any measurement process.
First, as Schumpeter pointed out, the concept of data series being made
up of four components associated with particular groups of causes or
influences: cyclical, seasonal, long-term and accidental, implied underlying ideas about economic behaviour which constituted:

a theory that was all the more dangerous because it was subconscious:
they [the Harvard approach] used what may be termed the Marshallian
theory of evolution ... they assumed that the structure of the economy
evolves in a steady or smooth fashion that may be represented (except for
occasional changes in gradient, 'breaks') by the linear trends and that

cycles are upward or downward deviations from such trends and constitute a separate and separable phenomenon . . . this view constitutes a theory, or the backbone of one. (Schumpeter (1954), p. 1165)

Secondly, once involved in the measurement process, Persons could not avoid making some theory-based decisions, for example about what constituted a homogeneous period in economic terms and where the breaks between these periods occurred.

In his second paper of 1919, Persons had set out to show the typical empirical relationships of the cycle in the form of indices of business activity. Business cycle theory was, as already noted, fashionably new at this time, but concern about the economic theory relationships between variables was largely absent from Persons' discussion. He was concerned only with methods of representing the cycles in business activity. His process of deriving the indices which represented the cycle was based on highly subjective visual judgements about how series were related in time and which series should be grouped together. The actual measurements of the relationships were only made at the last point in his procedure when these decisions had been more or less taken by the three 'observers'. This was particularly unsatisfactory in those cases where his 'observers' disagreed as to which series were connected with others and (more problematically) what the lag length should be.

Persons was left with a number of questions as a result of his empirical approach. If one series preceded another did that mean that it caused the other? If so, Persons wondered, how similar must the cycles be? Or are both to be considered the joint effects of joint causes? These questions arose, and were unanswerable, because Persons had neither a theoretical economic answer as to how variables were related in a complex world, nor did he use any consistent statistical measurement or inference procedures which might have helped him. He used only two-variable correlation techniques which could not reveal, for example, joint connection with a third variable. This dependence on simple, rather than multiple, correlation techniques was exceedingly limiting. But despite these problems Persons' methods for the removal of trends, seasonal and irregular components quickly became commonplace in statistical business cycle research and pervaded econometrics generally. His methods (or closely related ones) for detrending data, for removing seasonal variations and for smoothing out erratic fluctuations are now such a standard part of data preparation for econometric work that they are barely given a thought.

2.4   The business cycle research institutes

The decade of the 1920s witnessed an explosion in statistical business cycle research. Institutes entirely devoted to statistical analysis and research on the business cycle were established in Germany, France, the Netherlands, Italy, Sweden, Britain, indeed throughout Europe generally, and even in post-revolutionary Russia. Though the detail of the methods adopted and the overall concept used differed from institute to institute and country to country, all relied on an empirical methodology using statistical data in which the work of both Mitchell and Persons were highly influential. Evidence suggests that Mitchell's name was invoked as the foremost exponent of statistical research of the period, although his methods were not always followed. The examples presented in the *Review of Economics and Statistics* by Persons were less acknowledged, but were at least as influential judging from the publications of the new institutes.[17] An analysis of the work of the Berlin Institute (as represented by the main work of its director, Ernst Wagemann) illustrates the way this joint influence worked. An examination of the work of the Konjuncture Institute of Moscow shows that the influence was two-way.

Wagemann's 1928 book of business cycles was translated into English as *Economic Rhythm* (1930) at the instigation of business cycle scholars in the USA and prefaced by Mitchell. Wagemann in turn much admired Mitchell's work on business cycles which seemed to him to be the ideal synthesis of the theoretical, statistical and historical schools of economics. Unfortunately, the nineteenth-century *methoden-streit* between the theoretical deductive and the empirical inductive approaches was still sufficiently alive in Germany to stifle synthetic work (particularly quantitative and econometric developments) in the 1920s.[18] These factors made Wagemann self-conscious about his own attempts to combine the theoretical and empirical methods and whilst

[17] Mitchell (1927) himself credited Persons with setting the trend for statistical analysis, both in the US and in Europe. As an example of their influence, Snyder (1927) dedicated his book jointly to Mitchell and Persons with the descriptive tag: 'pioneers in the quantitative study of business cycles'. See Schumpeter (1954) for his contemporary observations on these influences.

[18] Economists descended from the historical school believed that there were no constant laws in economics and, like Mitchell, that business cycles were individual historical occurrences, therefore it was not possible to analyse the business cycle as a uniform event. German theoretical economists scorned any empirical work and maintained a detached indifference to any actual economic event. This was true, as Wagemann (1930) pointed out, even to the extent of ignoring the infamous German inflation of 1923 and the 'miracle' of the subsequent currency stabilisation.

he acknowledged the influence of American thought, he tried to strike out afresh. For example, he claimed not to follow the Harvard (Persons') decomposition method, in the first place because he saw their classifications as statistical rather than economic. Instead, he classified movements as changes in structure (isolated changes which were continuous or discontinuous) and periodic fluctuations (changes with either a fixed or free rhythm). But despite his claims, the description of these reveal just how close his categorisation was to Persons'; continuous changes were more or less equivalent to secular trends, discontinuous changes were large irregular changes (closer in conception to changes in structure than to small random events), fixed rhythm changes were, for example, seasonal fluctuations and free rhythm changes were business cycles.

The second problem of the Harvard method, according to Wagemann, was that having eliminated the unwanted series components, this provided only a negative definition of the business cycle, that is, as the residual element in the data. In addition, Wagemann judged both the single and multiple cycle indices, such as the Harvard A-B-C curves, inadequate. The Berlin Institute developed a more sophisticated system of indices (as far as economic content was concerned) consisting of eight sectoral barometers covering production, employment, storage, foreign trade, transactions, credit, comparative prices (in security, money and commodity markets) and commodity prices. Wagemann's aim was to forecast three months ahead with these barometers once they had established a model of how they fitted together. Successful forecasting depended, however, on correct diagnosis of the events which in turn depended on there being some typical movements (or 'symptoms') in the data.

Wagemann's book is full of interesting speculations. For example, he thought that forecasting might be improved by examining the plans of individual firms (by questioning the firms) and by using statistics of orders or of raw material inputs. On the one hand, he argued, firms' plans meet obstacles, which would reduce the accuracy of forecasts based on barometric diagnosis. But on the other hand, the reactions to obstacles may be reflected in the barometers themselves, which would help forecasting. In any case, he thought, completely successful forecasts would never be possible because movements are never identical (variables are subject to structural changes), and because a static system of classification underlies the whole.

While his applied work and its definitions reflected the influence of Persons' work, Wagemann's methodological statements and conceptual definitions were extraordinarily reminiscent of Mitchell's empirical (but non-operational) ideas. Two examples make this point neatly. One is the positive definition of business cycles as

> the total complex of economic reaction phenomena
> (Wagemann (1930), p. 68)

that Wagemann adopted in preference to the negative, but practical, definition of the cycle as the residual series. The second is his call for a study of the facts before fitting business cycles into a deductive theory; to theorise without detailed study would be, he said,

> as though a doctor were to try to find a pathogenic agent before he had formed a proper notion of the disease itself by a study of the symptoms. To look for the causes of a phenomenon before acquiring a fairly adequate knowledge of its external manifestations is an absurdity; how can one search for causes before one has a grasp of the subject itself?
> (Wagemann (1930), p. 217)

Wagemann made the interesting suggestion that approaches to statistical business cycle study could be characterised nationally: German economists viewed the economy from the point of view of a doctor dealing with a human patient while the Americans saw the economy as 'a powerful piece of machinery' (Wagemann (1930), p. 9).[19] Wagemann claimed that the Russians viewed the economic system rather like the planetary system and adopted the statistical approach used in astronomy. As a result, some of their statistical work had a different flavour, and involved stochastic theory to help analyse the movements of economic variables.

The Konjuncture Institute of Moscow was founded in 1920 under the direction of Kondratieff. The institute fed information directly into the state planning organisation to help produce the 'Gosplan' (the national plan) and an important part of their analysis was concerned with more general developments of the economy. The Moscow Institute produced a number of statistical publications which contained statistical data and analysis of the sort standard from other cycle institutes. From 1925, it also published a theoretical journal to which workers at the Institute, such as Oparin, Ignatieff, Slutsky, Konüs and Kondratieff, contributed.[20] Judging by the English summaries of the

---

[19] There may be some truth in this latter observation in relation to economic theory but the three American economists discussed here, Persons and Mitchell, and more interestingly Moore, showed marked preferences for sea metaphors such as 'ebb and flow', 'drifting' and 'buoyant', rather than mechanical ones, in describing the cycle.

[20] The journal, called *Problems of Economic Conditions* (in its English translation), was published from 1925 to 1928 in Russian with English-language summaries.

articles and the works referenced by the Russian authors, they were keenly aware of, and much of their work was closely related to, the work done elsewhere. For example, the journal published some of Mitchell's work on the use of business records in cycle research.

Workers at the Moscow Institute used their theoretical journal to publish experiments on cycle data which sometimes involved novel hypotheses and unusual techniques. These works became available to the other business cycle institutes and some proved very influential. One important work, which quickly became widely known, was by Slutsky, in which he examined the ways in which stochastic processes could form cyclical patterns in the data. (This article is sufficiently important to be discussed in its own right in Chapter 3.) Another important article contained Kondratieff's first applied results on his long wave thesis. (This 1925 paper was not his original paper on the subject, but it was the first to be translated and published in the West.) Kondratieff's long wave theory was highly controversial, even within the business cycle Institute, and he was removed from his position as director. In 1928 the Moscow Institute was closed down and Kondratiev was sent to Siberia, his long wave theory dismissed as 'wrong and reactionary'.[21]

The Harvard business cycle work suffered the far less dramatic fate which comes to those in the West whose forecasts have failed, namely loss of credibility. The Great Depression was commonly believed to have seen the decline from academic respectability (and perhaps a temporary wane from commercial use) of business barometers.[22] There were other reasons why these empirical approaches, so strong in the 1920s, lost their dominant role in academia in the 1930s. One was the work by Yule and others critical of the methods of statistical analysis used in cycle research. The second reason was the development of the alternative quantitative programme in econometrics. After a temporary lull following Moore's work, the econometric approach to business cycle analysis had moved on in the early 1930s to the development of small macrodynamic models of the business cycle and these by the late

---

[21] Röpke (1936) claimed that the Institute was closed because it was 'reactionary' and 'the staff was sent to Siberia or shot'. This report seems to have been overstated since Slutsky continued to hold an official university mathematics post until his death in 1948, while another member of the group, Konüs, was recently made a Fellow of the Econometric Society. The story is told in Garvy (1943).

[22] Schumpeter claimed that in fact the Harvard barometer successfully predicted both the 1929 crisis and subsequent fall into the Great Depression, but 'the trouble was that the interpreters of the curves either would not believe their own methods or else would not take what they believed to be a serious responsibility in predicting depression' (Schumpeter (1954), p. 1165). Schumpeter indeed argued for a kinder reassessment of the whole barometer episode than that which had been offered by other contemporaries.

1930s grew into full-scale macroeconometric models of the business cycle.

Despite the loss of academic credibility, statistical business cycle study continued to be an important government and professional activity in the 1930s. The Dutch Statistical Office, for example, began their own statistical business cycle journal in 1929, under Tinbergen's editorship. Further, cycle indices (as leading and lagging indicators) have continued their useful role in commercial and public sector economic analysis and forecasting services. The statistical study of business cycles has continued because, as Mitchell, and more particularly, Persons and the work of the Institutes have shown, a great deal of understanding about the economy can be gained from the rich statistical descriptions of business cycles which they presented.

2.5   Statistical economics and econometrics

The parallel approaches of statistical economics and econometrics shared two traits: both recognised economic cycles in the statistical data and rejected the notion of crises as independent events caused by local circumstances. But economists involved in the two programmes differed in their aims, their beliefs about the cycle and their use of statistical methods. The statistical research programme of Mitchell and Persons can be summarised as follows. They both started from the position of wanting to describe and measure business cycles as a way of finding out all about them. Their desire to find the facts required that they first defined what the business cycle was, so that they knew what data to look at and how to set about isolating or measuring the cycles. Having no theory of the cycle, and thus no theoretical definition of what it was, both were inclined to interpret the phenomenon rather broadly. Persons was untroubled by difficulties of definition for he avoided them by turning them into questions of statistical method: the business cycle was defined by the methods he used to isolate and represent its fluctuations in barometer form. Defining and describing the phenomenon and producing measurements of it proved more difficult for Mitchell since theoretical ideas were a part of his process. As an aid in definition and a way of providing measurements, Mitchell and Persons developed different visual representations of the cycles: Mitchell's (and Burns') reference cycle charts and Persons' A-B-C indices. For Mitchell and Persons, then, statistical work was concerned with constructing representations of the business cycle itself, although for Mitchell this was but a prelude to later understanding. A comparison may make this point clearer. Jevons and Moore (and as far as aims go, we should include Juglar here) did not worry about defining the cycle as a phenomenon and describing it because their theories told them what facts or data to study and their aim was to explain what caused the cycle.

Beliefs about the nature of economic cycles determined the extent to which each economist used statistical analysis. For Jevons and Moore (the econometricians), the cyclical regularity was hidden in the statistical features of the data set, whereas for Juglar and Mitchell (the statistical economists) the regularities were visible in the pattern of events of the cycle, not in statistical features of the cycle itself such as average cycle lengths or periodicities. Thus Mitchell and Juglar treated the cycles as individual, irregular events and sought typicality of behaviour within the cycles. Both were precluded from using more sophisticated statistical methods by their belief in non-uniformity in the statistical data. Persons did not believe in regular cycles either, but he did believe that certain other regularities or constants of behaviour would be reflected in statistical data (for example, seasonal variations and correlations between variables), so he made use of analytical techniques on these aspects. By contrast to the work of these statistical economists, Jevons, and more especially Moore, used statistical analysis not only to determine the nature of the underlying cycle, but to try and establish and verify the causal relationships which made up their theories as well. That is why I have labelled their work 'econometrics'.

The question of what 'theory testing' meant is more complex and can not be answered simply by knowing whether an economist was working in the econometrics or in the statistical economics tradition. Persons was at one extreme: a pure empiricist within the statistical programme, interested only in presenting facts and not at all in theory testing. At the other extreme in the econometrics programme, Moore and Jevons held strongly to their own pet theory of the cause and course of the cycle. These two believed that theory verification, not theory testing, was required; but this meant different things to each. For Jevons, evidence was not particularly important; verification was achieved primarily through an induction resting on probability inference. For Moore, statistical evidence which verified the theory was important, but he only sought confirming evidence in favour of the relationships of his theory not negative evidence which might refute it.

There was considerable muddy ground between these two positions, suggesting a complex partition of beliefs on theory testing. Juglar has been defined in this chapter as Mitchell's forerunner in the statistical tradition of analysis because of his use of statistical evidence, yet he fits most neatly with Moore in his attitudes to theory validation. Mitchell was also in the middle, an empiricist but not anti-theory. He had thought hard about the difficulties of finding out which were useful theories and had concluded that of the large number of possible cycle theories, some were complements and some were rivals. His attitude towards testing theories was rather natural in the circumstances: if many theories were possible, they could not all be verified, some would necessarily have to be rejected. (Mitchell, remember, did examine – and reject – some theories concerned with the appearance of cycles (the changing shape or time period of cycles) over the long term, but did not test theories about the cause and process of the economic cycle itself.) Further, as Chapter 4 will show, Tinbergen, though clearly in the econometric tradition, was in this respect like Mitchell, for he also saw that theory testing in the face of a multiplicity of theories involved both refutation and verification. Before we move on to Tinbergen's macro-econometrics, Chapter 3 explores how the idea of random shocks came to infiltrate formal business cycle analysis. But first, a brief aside on graphic methods.

Addendum: graphs and graphic methods

Graphs have played an important part in both statistical economics and econometrics. In the first place, they formed one of the main ways of presenting evidence. The aim and effect of graphing time-series data was to reduce a mass of figures to a single picture showing character-istics such as cycles more clearly than in tables. (Juglar's table-graphs (see Figure 3) were a halfway house, which give vivid demonstration to this point.) Discussions of the best ways to achieve these aims can be found in the economic and statistical journals of the late nineteenth century (documented by Funkhouser (1938) and Spengler (1961)).[23] Early statistics textbooks used by economists typically included a chapter on methods of graphing data (for example, Mills (1924)) and the interwar period saw a rash of books entirely concerned with advising economists on how to present data in graph form. Secondly, graphs often formed an important element in statistical analysis in the early twentieth-century work (for example, in Bowley (1901)). Graphs were used to help explain statistical methods, and graphic methods were even used as alternatives to aglebraic methods of manipulating variables and arithmetic methods of calculation. For example, graphs were used to explain and to calculate correlation and regression coefficients (see Ezekiel (1930) and Davis and Nelson (1935)). Thirdly,

---

[23] See also J. L. Klein (1987a) for an interesting analysis of the early use of graphs in economics.

graphs were used to report the results of statistical work, and various forms of graph were devised especially for this purpose.

In the work of business cycles reported in the last two chapters, graphs were used extensively. In the Jevons/Moore tradition they were used primarily to show regularity in the data on individual variables (as in Figure 1), to provide evidence of relationships between variables and to report the results of analysis (see Figure 2). The Mitchell/Persons tradition relied on graphs and graphic methods to a greater degree. Persons used every opportunity to use graphs to illustrate his methods of data decomposition and the experiments he carried out in arriving at those methods. Graphs were more fundamentally important to his work on indices; the relationships between the individual variables, and thus the content of the indices, were determined from studying graphs of the data series. Graphs were used in a standard way to represent data in Mitchell's 1913 book, but played a more central role in his 1946 volume with Burns, where their new measurements of cycles were dependent on pictorial representations of the data and presented in graph form. Though these Burns–Mitchell graphs (see Figure 4) did reduce the mass of figures to one diagram, the novelty of the measurements and their presentation made them difficult to understand. In comparison with the standard representations of the cycle, of the sort given by Persons (see Figure 5) which showed the cycles as a time series, the meaning of Mitchell and Burns' standardised reference and specific cycles was opaque. Comparison of these graphs underlines the point made earlier, that Mitchell and Burns gave representations of the typical cycle, while Persons gave representation to the cycles over time.

In the next two chapters there are further examples of the use of graphs. In Chapter 3, there are examples of how graphs were used to express the results of data experiments (Figures 6 and 7) and of methods of data analysis (Figures 8 and 9). In Chapter 4, there is an example of Tinbergen's use of graphs (Figure 10), used both to analyse the relationships (and thereby reduce the amount of arithmetic) and to report the results of his analysis. These sorts of graph were distinctive to Tinbergen's work, and were copied by relatively few other economists of the period,[24] even though they contained more information than the conventional algebraic reports.

Graphs were a particularly important element in the analysis of time-series data and business cycles; but it was commonplace throughout the econometric work of the period to give the data used

---

[24] Two notable exceptions who did use Tinbergen-type graphs were Stone (1954) in his work on consumers' expenditure and the US macroeconometric model by L. R. Klein and Goldberger (1955).

either in graph or table form (or both) and to use graphs to help explain methods and to report results in conjunction with algebraic methods and representations. Although graphs have continued as an important element in the *statistical* programme, algebraic representation of both methods and results had come to dominate the *econometrics* programme by the 1950s.

CHAPTER 3

Random shocks enter the business cycle scene

The introduction to this book suggested that econometrics developed as a substitute for the experimental method in economics, and that the problems which arose were connected with the fact that most economic data had been generated in circumstances which were neither controlled nor repeatable. By using statistical methods, econometricians also obtained access to an experimental tradition in statistics. This tradition consisted of generating data artificially, under theoretically known and controlled conditions, to provide a standard for comparison with empirical data or to investigate the behaviour of data processes under certain conditions. Such experiments now form a significant part of the work in econometric theory (under the title Monte Carlo experiments) and are sometimes used in applied work (model simulations), but their use dates from the early years of econometrics. Experiments played a particularly important role in the work of the 1920s which is discussed here.

This chapter deals with technical issues of data analysis and associated explanations of the generation of economic cycle data as investigated by Yule, Slutsky and Frisch. The account begins with the work of Eugen Slutsky and George Udny Yule in the 1920s both of whom made considerable use of statistical experiments.[1] Yule criticised the methods of analysing time-series data described in the previous two chapters. Slutsky explored the role of random shocks in generating cyclical patterns of data. At the same time (the late 1920s) Ragnar Frisch was experimenting with his own method for analysing economic time-series data. Although his method turned out to be a dead end as an analytical tool, Frisch used his understanding of economic time-series data, together with the suggestions of Yule and Slutsky, in his 1933 design for macrodynamic models. So it appears that the Yule and Slutsky

---

[1] Their work was also important in the development of theoretical work on time series. Davis (1941) has traced these developments through to Wold's (1938) analysis of stationary time series.

critique, which at first had seemed entirely negative towards the analysis of economic data, was transformed into an important element of econometric work on the business cycle.

At the same time as the statistical genesis of business cycle data was being investigated in the late 1920s and early 1930s, there were parallel developments in the mathematical formulations of dynamic theories of the business cycle. Frisch's 1933 model is the most important of these mathematical models from the point of view of the history of econometrics because he was the only economist to combine the insights of the statistical analysis with a mathematically formulated dynamics in his cycle model.

3.1   The experiments of Yule and Slutsky

3.1.1   *Yule, measurement error and the pendulum and peas model*

Since Hooker's paper of 1901 on the relationship between the marriage rate and trade, it had been recognised by contemporary researchers that correlations of time-series variables had to be carried out with some care. Hooker found different correlations between the oscillations of the variables and between their trends: over the short term, the marriage rate was positively correlated with the trade cycle, but over the long term the trend relationship was negative. Various methods were suggested to get at the 'true' correlation, including the variate difference method: taking differences between successive observations. George Udny Yule's 1921 survey of the problem of 'time-correlations' found that the field was full of confusions; time-series correlations were not well understood and there was disagreement about exactly what problem the variate difference method was supposed to solve.[2]

In his 1926 paper, 'Why Do we Sometimes Get Nonsense Correlations between Time-Series?', Yule set about his own analysis of the problem and discovered that correlations between two sets of data in which the observations were time related were likely to be very misleading, in fact, they would generally be biased upwards. The high correlations often found in time-series work were, according to Yule, not 'spurious' but 'nonsense' correlations. His critique naturally threw suspicion on the findings of business cycle analysts whose observations were related through time and who relied on the evidence of high

[2] George Udny Yule (1871–1951) trained as an engineer and then learnt statistics from Karl Pearson. Yule's contributions to the field of mathemataical statistics were many and varied and his statistics textbooks (1911) (later editions by G. U. Yule and M. G. Kendall, then by M. G. Kendall and A. Stuart) has been used by many econometricians. (See S. M. Stigler (1986) for a recent account of his place in the history of statistics.)

correlation coefficients to establish relationships between variables. For contemporaries, Yule's article was yet another nail in the coffin of the business barometers and time-series methods discussed in Chapter 2.

Yule defined the problem as follows:

> It is fairly familiar knowledge that we sometimes obtain between quantities varying with the time (time-variables) quite high correlations to which we cannot attach any physical significance whatever, although under the ordinary test correlation would be held to be certainly 'significant'. As the occurrence of such 'nonsense correlations' makes one mistrust the serious arguments that are sometimes put forward on the basis of correlations between times series . . . it is important to clear up the problem how they arise and in what special cases.
>   (Yule (1926), reprinted in (1971), p. 326)

(Yule rejected the usual 'spurious correlation' argument: that an unexpectedly high correlation found between two variables was due to the influence of the 'time factor', taken as a proxy for some other variable or variables, which indirectly caused the two variables to move together. He had been the originator of this 'spurious correlation' notion in 1895, but here he favoured a more technical explanation of the problem:

> But what one feels about such a correlation is, not that it must be interpreted in terms of some very indirect catena of causation, but that it has no meaning at all; that in non-technical terms it is simply a fluke, and if we had or could have experience of the two variables over a very much longer period of time we would not find any appreciable correlation between them. But to argue like this is, in technical terms, to imply that the observed correlation is only a fluctuation of sampling, whatever the ordinary formula for the standard error may seem to imply: we are arguing that the result given by the ordinary formula is not merely wrong, but very badly wrong.   (Yule (1926), reprinted in (1971), p. 328)

On considering the assumptions underlying the calculation of the standard error formula for the correlation coefficient, Yule decided that there were two of these which did not hold good in economic and social time-series data. The two conditions breached were, first, that each observation of the sample was equally likely to be drawn from any part of the aggregate population (when in fact successive observations were drawn from successive parts of the aggregate), and, second, that each observation in the sample was independent of the observation drawn either before or after it.[3] Since social and economic time-series data did

---

[3] Persons had also by this stage realised that the standard error formula did not apply, but he did not go on, as Yule did, to analyse how far wrong the normal correlation coefficients would be. Instead, as we shall see in Chapter 8, he believed that since the data did not behave according to the assumptions of probability laws, then probability methods could not be applied to business cycle data.

not constitute independent series of observations but series in which successive terms were related, Yule argued that

> the usual conceptions to which we are accustomed fail totally and entirely to apply.   (Yule (1926), reprinted in (1971), p. 330)

Yule investigated how such time-related series of observations gave spuriously high correlations by considering two sine waves, differing by a quarter period. These two series have a correlation of zero over their whole length; however, over any short period of time, the correlation between the two series will be either $+1$ or -1. In fact as the centre of a short observation period moves along the curves, the correlation coefficient between the two series switches between $+1$ and -1. This gives a U-shaped frequency distribution of the correlation coefficients obtained from simultaneous observations on the two curves, always giving values furthest away from the true value (zero) as the most frequent. One of Yule's frequency distributions is reproduced here (Figure 6).

Yule analysed what sorts of series would produce the nonsense correlations found in his experiments on harmonic curves. His results were partly based on experimental work on artificial series (a random number series, and series derived from that), and partly on existing data series. He found that he could predict which series would give nonsense correlations on the basis of their serial correlation characteristics. Samples of observations from two positively serially correlated series (a 'conjunct' series), which had random differences, would produce a higher standard error for the correlation coefficient than that obtained for a random series. The distribution of correlation coefficients, though not definitely misleading, was far from bell-shaped and might possibly be bi-modal. On the other hand, two positively serially correlated series with positively serially correlated differences (a conjunct series with conjunct differences) would produce a U-shaped distribution or correlation coefficients like those of the harmonic curves and would therefore lead to nonsense results.

Yule found it more difficult to reach any conclusions about the case of oscillatory series: series where the serial correlation changes sign often but which are not well-behaved sine waves. (He used Beveridge's series of wheat prices as an example of this common type of series). Given these difficulties, Yule carefully cautioned against the comparison of artificial series (possessing known or engineered characteristics) with real series of unknown characteristics:

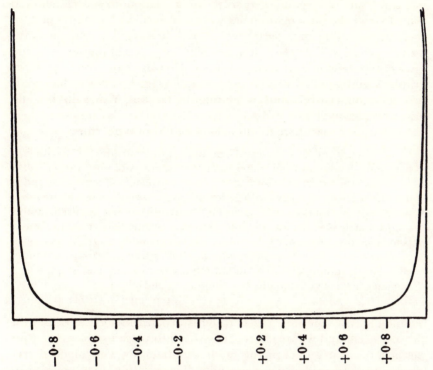

-0.8   -0.6   -0.4   -0.2   0   +0.2   +0.4   +0.6   +0.8

Frequency-distribution of correlations between simultaneous elements of the harmonic curves.

Figure 6   Yule's graph of the distribution of correlation coefficients for time series
Source: Yule (1926), reprinted in (1971), p. 334

it is quite possible that what looked a good match to the eye would not seem at all a good match when subjected to strict analysis.

(Yule (1926), reprinted in (1971), p. 350)

In 1927, the year following his analysis of the problem of nonsense correlations, Yule published an investigation of the frequency analysis of sunspot data, 'On a Method of Investigating Periodicities in Disturbed Series'. By the obvious association of sunspots with business cycles (following Jevons' work), this paper also dealt indirectly with the use of frequency analysis to decompose economic time series. The focus of the paper was on the role played by errors when combined in different ways with an harmonic process. Yule believed that frequency analysis of cyclical data usually began with the hypothesis that the periodic function was masked solely by added-on errors. He showed that if small measurement errors were added to an harmonic process then the resulting data series would look less regular, but the wave pattern would still be clear and frequency analysis of the series would always recover the underlying process. If such errors were large the graph would appear very irregular and jagged and the harmonic process might not be clearly visible to the eye but, Yule said, it could always be recovered.

Yule argued that there might also be other sorts of errors:

> If we observe at short intervals of time the departures of a simple harmonic pendulum from its position of rest, errors of observation will cause superposed fluctuations ... But by improvement of apparatus and automatic methods of recording, let us say, errors of observation are practically eliminated. The recording apparatus is left to itself, and unfortunately boys get into the room and start pelting the pendulum with peas, sometimes from one side and sometimes from the other. The motion is now affected, not by *superposed fluctuations* but by true *disturbances*, and the effect on the graph will be of an entirely different kind. The graph will remain surprisingly smooth, but amplitude and phase will vary continually.   (Yule (1927), reprinted in (1971), p. 390)

Yule found by experiment that true disturbances which feed into the process itself, and whose effects are carried through to successive time periods, result in a data picture with smooth cycles which looked very similar to that produced by sunspots. These results may seem to be counterintuitive since superimposed (measurement) errors gave Yule a jagged data picture which looked less like an harmonic function than the smooth picture produced by disturbances.[4]

The obvious question was whether the underlying harmonic function could be revealed in the case of true disturbances? Using ordinary harmonic analysis led to results which were liable to error and to be misleading. Yule found that the best way to replicate such data, that is the best model to use to describe the data, was the regression of a linear difference equation:

$$X_t = B_1 X_{t-1} - B_2 X_{t-2}$$

He fitted this regression equation to his experimentally obtained disturbed harmonic process, and the sunspot data, and found that both difference equations had as their solution a heavily damped harmonic

---

[4] A physical experiment with a galvonometer was carried out in the 1930s by Davis at the Cowles Commission to replicate Yule's pendulum being hit by peas (see Davis (1941)). The oscillations were set to match the periodicities observed in the Dow Jones Industrial Average index and then subjected to shocks. This produced very irregular data, closer in appearance to economic cycle data than the smooth picture of Yule's demonstration.

movement. Yule claimed that the role of the disturbances 'deduced' from the fitted sunspot regression equation (the residuals) was to maintain the amplitude of the harmonic period in the observed data:

> The distribution of the disturbances seems to me to have some bearing on the question whether we may perhaps, tentatively regard the damped harmonic formula at which we have empirically arrived as being some-thing more than merely empirical, and representing some physical reality. As it seems to me, the disturbances do occur just in the kind of way that would be necessary to maintain a damped vibration, and this suggests that broadly the conception fits the facts.
>
> (Yule (1927), reprinted in (1971), p. 408)

Yule's conclusions suggested that any variable subject to external circumstances would be affected by disturbances:

> many series which have been or might be subjected to periodogram analysis may be subject to 'disturbance' in the sense in which the term is here used, and that this may possibly be the source of some rather odd results which have been reached. Disturbance will always arise if the value of the variable is affected by external circumstance and the oscillatory variation with time is wholly or partly self-determined, owing to the value of the variable at any one time being a function of the immediately preceding values. (Yule (1927), reprinted in (1971), p. 417)

Since economic variables were undoubtedly subject to external circum-stances and were probably self-determined in Yule's sense, economic time-series data probably contained disturbances of the sort Yule had in mind. We have already noted Yule's paper in connection with the decline in periodic business cycle analysis which followed Moore's work: if disturbances were present, the use of harmonic analysis would be an inappropriate way of finding the underlying economic cycles. The implication was that harmonic analysis, like correlation analysis, seemed a dangerous tool for econometricians to use. But, although Yule had alerted economists to another danger, he had also proposed a solution to the problem in the sense that he had found a model (the linear difference regression model) to describe the vagaries exhibited by such disturbed data.

3.1.2 Slutsky's random waves

In the same year (1927), the Russian economist Eugen Slutsky suggested a more deeply worrying possibility than the presence of measurement errors or disturbances in economic data.[5] His idea was

[5] E. E. Slutsky (1880–1948), a Russian economist of considerable reputation in the field of economic theory, but whose publication record was more heavily weighted towards

that cycles could be caused entirely by the cumulation of random events. The article, 'The Summation of Random Causes as a Source of Cyclic Processes', was published in the theoretical journal of the Moscow Institute for Business Cycle Research in 1927 (with a summary in English). Though it appeared in an unusual source, Slutsky's paper was immediately widely reported in the West via academic books and journals.[6]

Slutsky was responsible in this paper for one of those crucial experiments much beloved by historians and philosophers of science. Crucial experiments are usually taken to mean decisive experiments but I prefer to follow Hacking's (1983) suggestion and use this term in the sense of a signposting experiment which points out the ways. Slutsky did not indulge in repetition of his experiment. There was no need, for he had made his point and he preferred to use his resources to carry out several different experiments. As already noted, these sorts of experiments in statistical theory rely on artificially generated data; the outcome of such an experiment is an insight into what might be the process generating some real data series. I will return to this point following a discussion of Slutsky's work and his results.

Slutsky wanted to know whether the combination of random causes would be sufficient to generate regular cycles. He posed the question as follows:

> is it possible that a definite structure of a connection between random fluctuations could form them into a system of more or less regular waves? Many laws of physics and biology are based on chance, among them such laws as the second law of thermodynamics and Mendel's laws. But heretofore we have known how regularities could be derived from a chaos of disconnected elements because of the very disconnectedness. In our case we wish to consider the rise of regularity from series of chaotically-random elements because of certain connections imposed upon them.
>
> (Slutsky (1937), p. 106 (quoting from the 1937 English version))

His method was to be experimental:

> Generally speaking the theory of chance waves is almost entirely a matter of the future. For the sake of this future theory one cannot be too lavish with experiments: it is experiment that shows us totally unexpected facts,

statistical work of an experimental and theoretical kind on stochastic processes and correlation. He worked on time-series problems at the Moscow business cycle institute in the 1920s and later used sunspot data as the raw material for some of his work (see the entry in the *International Encyclopedia of the Social Sciences* and Allen (1950)).

[6] Slutsky's 1927 article was fully reprinted in English in 1937 at the instigation of Schultz and Frisch. The first five sections of the 1937 article were similar (but with some revisions) to the original 1927 article; the latter part of the 1937 paper draws on results he published in

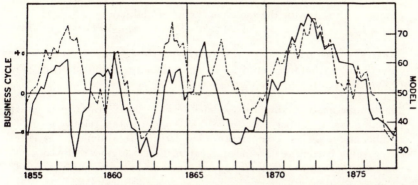

——————An index of English business cycles from 1855 to 1877; scale on the left side. ------Terms 20 to 145 of Model I; scale on the right side.

Figure 7   Slutsky's random series juxtaposed with business cycles
Source: Slutsky (1927), p. 38, Chart 3; reprinted in (1937), as Figure 3, p. 110

> thus pointing out problems which otherwise would hardly fall within the
> field of the investigator.   (Slutsky (1937), p. 107)

and his raw material consisted of a data series of numbers drawn in the People's Commissariat of Finance lottery, which he took to be a random series (that is, a series with no serial correlation).

Slutsky then generated different models of empirical data processes using the basic data series, and defining a model in the following words:

> Any concrete instance of an experimentally obtained chance series we
> shall regard as a model of empirical processes which are structurally
> similar to it.   (Slutsky (1937), p. 108)

The first model was based on a cumulative process – each new observation (X_t') was based on a simple 10–item moving summation of the basic random number series (X_t):

$$X_t' = \sum_{i=1}^{10} X_{t-i}$$

He plotted a section of the data of this first model next to a chosen section of an index of business cycles in England, reproduced in Figure 7. A close similarity between the two graphs was readily apparent. Further experiments, using models with different weighting patterns in the summation, reinforced Slutsky's first results and he claimed

Russian, French and Italian journals in the intervening period. This activity suggests that he avoided the miserable fate of some of his colleagues at the Moscow Institute (see Chapter 2.4).

an inductive proof of our first thesis, namely that the summation of random causes may be the source of cyclic, or undulatory processes.

(Slutsky (1937), p. 114)

The rest of his article was concerned with the regularity of the cycles involved and with a frequency analysis of the experimental series. This led him to make the following generalisation:

> The summation of random causes generates a cyclical series which tends to imitate for a number of cycles a harmonic series of a relatively small number of sine curves. After a more or less considerable number of periods every regime becomes disarranged, the transition to another regime occurring sometimes rather gradually, sometimes more or less abruptly, around certain critical points.   (Slutsky (1937), p. 123)

That is, random terms can generate data series which appear to consist of a number of sine waves and are thus amenable to frequency analysis; whereas in fact the periodic components are not well behaved but irregular.

Slutsky's juxaposition of the random cumulated series with the business cycle data was not supposed to be a proof that random events had caused the business cycle index shown. Nor was any such claim made by Slutsky. He neither established that business cycle data were generated by random events, nor that they were not generated in some alternative way. The experiment was an artificial 'as if' experiment, rather than real experiment. The inference was therefore more limited: the graph merely suggested that such a data generation process could give very similar data to that produced by economic activity.

Slutsky was not responsible for the idea that random events have a role in business cycles, for it was a long-held view that accidental or outside disturbances formed the immediate impetus behind economic crises or turning points. No statistical model of how this occurred had been advanced prior to the work of Yule and Slutsky. Yule's model (the pendulum being pelted with peas) suggested a cyclical mechanism, whose oscillations were maintained by random shocks. Slutsky's hypothesis went further by giving random causes sole responsibility for the complete cyclical movements in economic activity, rather than for just the turning points or the maintenance of oscillations.

It seems that Slutsky's insight into how random events might cause business cycles captured the imagination more than the partial role for disturbances suggested by Yule. Slutsky's idea was rapidly reported and discussed in business cycle circles. It was discussed briefly by Mitchell in his influential 1927 book. Then Holbrook Working (1928), in reviewing Mitchell's book, seized on this brief report of Slutsky's work and suggested that, although he was not prepared to accept it as a complete explanation, there might be considerable elements of truth in the idea. In 1929 Kuznets discussed Slutsky's work at length and reproduced the crucial graph (Figure 7) in the context of carrying out some of his own experiments on time-series data. He wrote of Slutsky's theory:

> If cycles arise from random events, assuming the summation of the latter, then we obviously do not need the hypothesis of an independent regularly recurring cause which is deemed necessary by some theorists of business cycles. Indeed, if one can explain how in certain processes of economic life, the response to stimuli is cumulative, then the whole discussion of the cause of business cycles becomes supererogation.   (Kuznets (1929), p. 274)

As Kuznets pointed out, Slutsky's work not only removed the necessity for periodic cause of economic cycles (an idea which had been persistently followed by Jevons and Moore, but which had made most economists feel distinctly uneasy), but might also, if the cumulative mechanism were understood, make any further discussion of the cause of business cycles superfluous.

Later in 1939, with the benefit of some hindsight, Schumpeter gave a different interpretation of the signposts which pointed from Slutsky's experiment:

> that proof did two things for us: first, it removed the argument that, since our series display obvious regularities, therefore their behaviour cannot result from the impact of random causes; second, it opened an avenue to an important part of the economic mechanism, which has since been explored by R. Frisch in a powerful piece of work.
>
>   (Schumpeter (1939), p. 181)

This interpretation recognised both the possibility of random causes (by rejecting the notion of their impossibility) and the possibility of a new sort of business cycle mechanism. Schumpeter referred here to Frisch's 1933 business cycle model (discussed later in this chapter), but the avenue of thought which Frisch was actually exploring in the late 1920s was the composition of economic time-series data.

3.2   Frisch's time-series analysis

Ragnar Frisch was one of the leading practioners of econometrics in the 1920s and 1930s.[7] His leadership of the econometric movement was exercised through his personal style whilst Editor of *Econometrica* (from

[7] Ragnar Frisch (1895–1973), one of the founders of the Econometric Society and a very influential figure in the development of econometrics (see, for example, Tinbergen's (1974) sketch of his role). His first degree was in economics and his doctorate was in mathematical

1933 to 1954), at meetings of the Econometric Society and through his writing and teaching. He was a prolific writer: a number of his articles quickly became classics; but some of his econometric papers, particularly those on econometric methods and ideas, are as hard to comprehend today as they were to his contemporaries. Despite his dominant role, Frisch's work on time-series analysis has been largely forgotten. It is important to understand something of this work bacause his analysis helped him to understand economic time-series data and thus to produce an innovative model of the business cycle.

In the middle 1920s Frisch, dissatisfied with the available methods, decided to invent his own method of time-series analysis.[8] He wanted to develop a totally objective method of analysing time-series data which was more flexible yet more rigorous than the methods in current usage. Despite a lengthy and massive research effort, his results were reported in just three papers in 1927 (unpublished), 1928 and 1931.[9] This description of his method is based on all three.

According to Frisch, the problem of existing time-series decomposition methods (of the sort used by Persons, for example) was that different methods were used to isolate each component, and there was

> no logical relation between the various methods ... no general principle from which these various methods may be derived.[10]
>
> (Frisch (1927), p. 4)

Frisch thought that if all the usual components (trends, cycles, seasonal and erratic variations) were regarded as cycles, then trends were merely part of a long cycle and erratic elements were short cycles which

---

statistics. He spent his career at the University of Oslo (though he travelled widely) and his intereests ranged over the whole field of economics. J. C. Andvig (1985) gives a comprehensive account of Frisch's work in building macroeconomic models which parallels his work described here in econometrics. (See also Andvig (1978) and (1981).)

[8] It is not clear exactly when Frisch started to work on time-series problems for he gave no hint of the impetus behind it. But this was not unusual with Frisch; he often did not deign to fit his own work into the literature or to say specifically who he was arguing against. Davis, who worked with Frisch on these problems in the 1930s at the Cowles Commission, stated that it was Yule's (1927) ideas on disturbed harmonic processes and his analogy of the pendulum and peas which first stimulated Frisch into working on the decomposition problem. Andvig maintains from his study of Frisch's papers that the work started earlier in 1925.

[9] Frisch produced a mimeographed paper (circulated privately with the help of Mitchell) on his time-series methods in 1927. The two published articles are (1928) and (1931). Andvig (1985) also reports a mimeographed paper in Norwegian.

[10] Wald (1936) agreed with this criticism in an interesting critique of the decomposition method, undertaken at the request of Morgenstern, head of the Vienna business cycle research institute (see Chapter 8 n. 5). Wald suggested that since there were no generally consistent and complete ways of defining the components of economic data series according to the outside groups of causal forces, a more fruitful approach was to do a complete frequency analysis of the components of a series and then identify those internal components found with groups of external causes. Wald's work on the subject was and is

appear jagged because the data were not available in short enough time units. Time series could then be regarded as a suite of cycles in which only the middle waves can be traced. Frisch called each component a 'trend' denoting a changing, probably cyclical, form. (This is a good example of Frisch's confusing habit of changing the meaning of existing terminology.) A low order 'trend' (such as seasonal variation) involved a short period length and a high order 'trend' was one of long length (for example, a Kondratieff long wave). This, he claimed, enabled a unified approach to all the components of a time series, instead of the mixed approach adopted by Persons.

Frisch also proposed to abandon the standard periodogram analysis which involved the assumption of constant and fixed periodicities because he believed economic cycles were variable (both in length and shape) rather than constant phenomena. He proposed instead a 'moving method' which would show how component cycles ('trends') evolved and trace these changing cycles in the historical data series. His analysis was concerned with local properties rather than the total properties of the whole series. That is, Frisch wanted each component of the time series at any given point of time to be determined from the data in the vicinity of that point rather than by the course of the time series in all years. He described his method as a 'principle of moving fit' or 'curvefitting without parameters' (Frisch (1928), p. 230).

In his first paper on the subject in 1927, Frisch began by assuming that a time series W is a complicated function made up of many different 'trends', Y_i, each of which are assumed to be changing sine waves (i.e., waves of changing period length):

$$W = Y_0 + Y_1 + Y_2 + \ldots + Y_n$$

He claimed that these component Ys could be unravelled relatively easily if the order of each 'trend' were very different from the others. That is, provided the period of one 'trend' component was, say, 7 to 10 times greater than that of the next 'trend', both components could be found. Frisch's method of unravelling the different 'trends' he called the 'method of normal points'. It was based on the observation that if the 'trends' were of different orders, the curvature of Y_0 would be very much greater than that of Y_1, which would be that much greater again than the curve of Y_2 and so on.[11] Figure 8 illustrates Frisch's idea (but it

little known (an extract is printed in the forthcoming volume of classic readings by Hendry and Morgan) but is cited in connection with the 1960s revival of frequency analysis in econometrics (see Morgenstern (1961)).

[11] Frisch also suggested a second method, called the 'method of moving differences'. to be applied when there were several component 'trends' of the same order of magnitude in each series. The general approach was the same but it involved the higher derivatives of W,

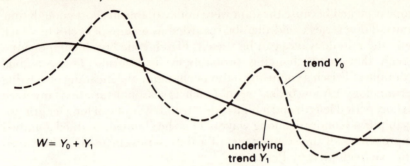

Figure 8   Frisch's time-series method – graph 1

is not an illustration from Frisch, for he used none): a time series W, consisting of two components, in which the slope of the shorter period component, Y_0, is steeper in general than that of the longer period component, Y_1.

Frisch argued that if you took the second derivatives of the data series that is, W''', the dominant element in it would be Y_0'' except at the 'normal point' defined as the point where Y_0'' vanishes. At a slight displacement from its normal point, however, Y_0'' would continue to dominate, since at the normal point, the first derivative Y_0' is at its maximum (or minimum). In practice, if the period of Y_1 is several times greater than that of Y_0, then the dominance of Y_0 is such that the normal points of the lowest order (smallest period) 'trend' Y_0 would be found where W''' is zero. These normal points could then be used as observations in a new time series W_1 where the trend of lowest order, Y_0, had been eliminated. This is shown in Figure 9 (which is adapted from an illustration of Frisch's method given in Schumpeter (1939), p. 469), where the original series W_0 consists of three 'trends', Y_0, Y_1 and Y_2 and the new series W_1 consists of only the two longer period trends Y_1 and Y_2.

Following the elimination of Y_0 from W_0, the 'trend' Y_1 could be eliminated from the new composite series W_1 to give the remaining $W_2 = Y_2$ series. The deviations between the old series W_0 and the first new series W_1 would give the 'trend' Y_0, and successive Y_1 components ('trends' of higher order) could be found in the same way.

In practice, the second derivatives could not be found because the data were discrete, so Frisch used the second differences of the data series, denoted V, as an estimate of the second derivatives W'''. That is, he calculated the individual data points from:

required more reliable and regular material than the first method and was considerably more complicated.

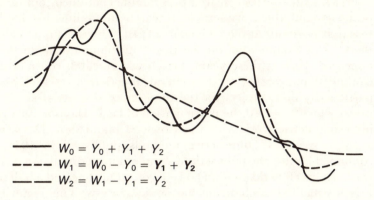

$$W_0 = Y_0 + Y_1 + Y_2$$
$$W_1 = W_0 - Y_0 = Y_1 + Y_2$$
$$W_2 = W_1 - Y_1 = Y_2$$

Figure 9   Frisch's time-series method – graph 2

$$\hat{W}_t'' = V_t = W_{t+1} - 2W_t + W_{t-1}$$

Plotting this second difference series revealed the estimated 'normal points' (where V_t equalled zero) providing, Frisch argued, that two conditions hold. First, the distance between the three data points used in calculating the second difference of W must be small in relation to the distance between the normal points of the lowest 'trend'; secondly, accidental errors must not dominate in the data and lead to false zeros. So, if the graph of V_t changed signs frequently within short intervals, Frisch suggested that the 'trend' was of too low an order (relative to the data frequency) to be investigated. Such a 'trend' should be treated instead as accidental components, eliminated by taking a moving average of the original series W. These problems might arise, for example, in the attempt to isolate a seasonal component using monthly data.

In his 1928 article, Frisch presented a generalised and condensed version of his method which he described as the use of linear operators to measure changing harmonics in time series. These linear operators could be derivatives, but were more likely to be difference operators or weighted moving averages of various kinds. In a further short paper in 1931, Frisch turned his attention to the Slutsky effect and experimented with different linear operators acting on random terms. He regarded Slutsky's cycles as spurious and was interested in finding a way of telling whether cycles in data were spurious (caused by the Slutsky effect: the cumulation of random terms) or not. He found, as Slutsky had done, that certain linear operators acting on random shocks would produce changing harmonic waves.

Frisch's time-series research programme continued, but despite his promises and the considerable research input into his method by research assistants at the University of Oslo, by students at Yale and at the Cowles Commission during the 1930s, none of this further work appeared. During these years, Frisch was research consultant to the Commission, advising on the general direction of research and more particularly on a project on the time-series analysis of stock market prices which involved the participation of H. T. Davis.[12] As a result of his econometric work with the Cowles Commission, Davis wrote a massive survey of time-series methods published in 1941, which contained almost the only serious contemporary discussion of Frisch's work. In his 600-odd pages, Davis devoted only one and a half pages to Frisch's method of changing harmonic analysis. This is not because Davis disagreed with Frisch's view of the nature of economic time series. On the contrary, he rejected periodogram analysis on exactly the same grounds that Frisch had done. Davis himself worked out a more straightforward way of treating moving components involving a small modification of the standard periodogram method. He carried out empirical work to demonstrate that his own method obtained results similar to those obtained by Frisch, and that both were more successful in reducing the residual variance of a series than standard harmonic methods using a small number of harmonic terms. After all Frisch's hard work on the topic, it is ironic that Davis arrived at his quicker method because of a hint from Frisch.[13]

Given his prestige, it is perhaps surprising that Frisch's theoretical work on time series has received so little attention (Davis apart) from those assessing his work.[14] Yet, as a practical method of time-series analysis, Frisch's work was a failure. Moreover, this was evident at the time, for in marked contrast to other innovations that Frisch proposed, contemporaries did not adopt his time-series methods. With hindsight, there are a number of convincing reasons why this was so. One reason was the communication difficulties generally evident in Frisch's writing

---

[12] Harold T. Davis (1892–1974), a mathematician, became associated with econometrics through his connection with Alfred Cowles. Davis worked with the Cowles Commission research staff particularly on mathematical problems and on the analysis of time-series data. He wrote one of the first econometrics textbooks (1941a), mainly on mathematical economics. He also published widely on pure and applied mathematical problems.

[13] Davis' hint from Frisch was acknowledged. Cargill's (1974) survey paper claims that the contribution of Davis' book on time series was the treatment of changing cyclical components, but he ignores Frisch's work.

[14] Schumpeter (1939) is the other contemporary exception to this rule. Recent assessments by, for example, Arrow (1960) and Edvardsen (1970) also ignore this work. Andvig (1985) is, of course, comprehensive in this respect.

on statistical methods. Frisch usually presented his work in this field as if it were a brand new approach to a problem and invented his own new terminology. In this case for example, he confused the reader by using the term 'trend' for all the components of the data. He was particularly interested in the problems of computation and sometimes invented new algorithms for calculating terms, but, as here, he failed to give proper examples illustrating his new methods. He rarely rewrote his results in order to make them comprehensible, preferring instead to move on to a new problem. He often failed to relate his analytical techniques to economic problems so their relevance was not always obvious. Because of these characteristics, much of Frisch's written work in this area is therefore very difficult to understand and his analysis of economic time series illustrates these communication problems vividly.[15]

A more potent reason for the failure of Frisch's time-series method to make much impact on econometrics was that his methods were not particularly original, although Frisch's written style obscured this fact. Frisch's work appeared novel because his analysis was based on a continually changing series of components. But the techniques he used, linear operators of various sorts, were also used in different guises by Persons and in the variate difference approach and, most important, they suffered from the same problems as other business cycle methods of the 1920s. Specifically, despite all his mathematics, Frisch had failed in his desire to invent a totally objective method; in practice, some judgement was needed. Frisch's method therefore possessed no real advantages over Persons' decomposition approach.

Further, as Davis pointed out, any method of treating changing harmonics, either his own moving periodogram method or Frisch's method of linear operators, raised questions about degrees of freedom and significance of the results. The ideal representation of data should account for as much variation in the data with as few parameters or functions as possible. Any method which fitted each segment of data (or each observation) individually, as in Frisch's method or in fitting a polynomial of order nearly equal to the number of data points, is not a very efficient representation of the data. Frisch's method accounted for more variation than the standard method, but just how many degrees of

---

[15] They are also evident in another research project of Frisch of the late 1920s and early 1930s. This was on confluent relationships: several relationships holding between a set of economic variables at the same time. He viewed both as problems of unravelling components from the data; in one case these were cycles and in the other relationships. His method of attacking these problems and some of the techniques he used were similar. (See Chapter 7 Letter 11 for a discussion of confluence analysis.)

freedom were left, and thus how significant were his results, would be difficult to determine.

A further comparison with another contemporary approach is pertinent here. In Frisch's method, each cycle of each component 'trend' was treated as an individual event. His method therefore suffered from the same difficulties as beset Mitchell's analysis, namely the inability to support general explanations of economic data or explanations based on constant relationships. These problems were the inevitable result of theory-free data analysis applied at the level of the cycle. It is the cycle unit which is the real problem here, not the theory-free analysis. Remember, Yule had analysed the problem of changing components in terms of a stochastic process which generated the data: this enabled theory-free analysis, but allowed for a generalised model of the process. But, unlike Yule's analysis or Slutsky's work, Frisch's unravelling of time-series data produced no general model of how time-series data were generated.

In his 1931 paper, Frisch had defined the general problems in the analysis of economic time-series data. The first was the question of the composition of economic time series. Frisch's programme to solve this problem and

> find out on more or less empirical grounds what is actually present in the series at hand, that is to say, what sort of components the series contains
>
> (Frisch (1931), p. 74)

has been described in this section. He believed he had succeeded in this task and although he failed in his attempts to revolutionise the field of economic time-series analysis, he had learnt a considerable amount about the behaviour of economic time-series data from his investigations. The crucial issue which remained unexplained was how the time-series components, which Frisch had spent so much energy trying to unravel, came to be combined together in the first place. His solution to this puzzle is discussed next.

3.3   Frisch's rocking horse model of the business cycle

In marked contrast to his work on time series, Frisch's 1933 paper on business cycle models presented few communication problems. It was an ambitious paper but was highly successful and quickly became a classic in its field, for it both told economists how to do macrodynamics and showed what an econometric model of the complete cycle should look like. As we shall see later, Frisch's small theoretical model provided the design for Tinbergen's full-scale applied macroeconometrics in the later 1930s.

The advent of mathematically formulated, dynamic models of the business cycle was, as I said earlier, a parallel story to the development of statistical work on business cycle data. The focus of endeavour was to produce an economic theory to explain business cycles and, particularly by the early 1930s, to explain the Great Depression. This required a dynamic model of the whole economy, a task in which econometricians (as mathematical economists) played a very important role. During the 1920s econometricians had explored the cycles that occurred in prices and outputs of agricultural goods and modelled these as systems of lagged relationships. Frisch developed these ideas further in the business cycle field to form a model of the cycle in its entirety. But he was not the only economist to do so in the late 1920s and early 1930s. As Tinbergen's 1935 survey of the field showed, apart from the cycle models of other econometricians such as Vinci, Roos and Tinbergen himself, there was also the work of Kalecki.

The development of small mathematical dynamic macromodels was very important for the history of econometrics. But the unique importance of Frisch's paper lies in another aspect of his model, namely the integration of random shocks into the cycle model as an essential part of that model. In this chaper, I shall concentrate on those aspects of Frisch's model design which are of particular interest from the econometric point of view. An analysis of the macroeconomics of the model are contained in the definitive study of Frisch's work during the interwar period by Andvig (1985) (see also Andvig (1978)).

Frisch's paper, entitled 'Propagation Problems and Impulse Problems in Dynamic Economics', was concerned with the following problem: what should a model look like which accounts not only for cycles in economic variables but also does so in a way that can be reconciled with observed economic data? As we have seen from the reactions to Moore's cycle work, business cycle theories which specified regular forced oscillations (exogenous theories such as the sunspot theory) were thought by reviewers to be unsatisfactory since observed cycles were clearly not of exactly regular length and appearance. At the same time, although economists liked theories which suggested that a cycle was generated from inside the economic system (endogenous theories such as changes in credit availablity) and which involved a tendency to return to equilibrium, such theories failed to explain why it was that in observed data, the cycles in economic activity were maintained.

By the time Frisch wrote his paper in 1933, there had been two statistical demonstrations of how outside disturbing forces could generate the type of time-series data seen in economic variables. Yule had shown, in his 1927 investigation of sunspots, how the presence of shocks hitting an harmonic process would give rise to an irregular harmonic series. Slutsky's experiment of 1927 had shown how in the extreme case, the summation of a random series on its own would result in data series of the business cycle type. Frisch took note of these examples in his own attempts to postulate a mechanism that would generate the sort of economic time-series data which were observed.[16] Since Frisch himself believed that observed business cycle data consisted of a suite of changing cyclical components, in effect he sought an explanation of how these components were combined to form the economic time series.

Frisch suggested that the original idea of his model was due not to Slutsky or Yule but to Wicksell:

> Knut Wicksell seems to be the first who has been definitely aware of the two types of problems in economic cycle analysis - the propagation problem and impulse problem - and also the first who has formulated explicitly the theory that the source of energy which maintains the economic cycles are erratic shocks. He conceived more or less definitely of the economic system as being pushed along irregularly, jerkingly ... these irregular jerks may cause more or less regular cyclical movements. He illustrates it by one of those perfectly simple and yet profound illustrations: 'If you hit a wooden rocking-horse with a club, the movement of the horse will be very different to that of the club.'
>
> (Frisch (1933), p. 198)

This idea, termed here the 'rocking horse theory' of the business cycle (but usually known more prosaically as the Cassel paper, after the volume in which it appeared), provided a general explanation of the generation of economic time-series data. It had appeared in other guises in cycle analysis, for example, in Jevons' description of the economy as a vibrating ship being hit by waves and in Yule's analogy of boys pelting a pendulum with peas, but the rocking horse analogy, through Frisch's work, proved the most influential.

The particular attraction of Frisch's rocking horse model was that it allowed for the free and damped oscillations desired by economic theoreticians (the normal movement of the rocking horse which would gradually return the horse to a position of rest if left to itself) and yet was compatible with observed business cycle data which were irregular and undamped (the rocking horse movement disturbed by the random blows). As Frisch observed at the start of his paper:

[16] The influence of Yule and Slutsky on Frisch is clear in this case for he took unusual care to reference their work in his (1933) paper and later (1939) stated explicitly that one of the aims of his (1933) paper was to explain how Slutsky's 'shocks' came to be summed by the economic system.

The most important feature of the free oscillations is that the length of the cycles and the tendency towards dampening are determined by the intrinsic structure of the swinging system, while the intensity (the amplitude) of the fluctuations is determined primarily by the exterior impulse. An important consequence of this is that a more or less regular fluctuation may be produced by a cause which operates irregularly. There need not be any synchronism between the initiating force or forces and the movement of the swinging system. This fact has frequently been overlooked in economic cycle analysis.

If a cyclical variation is analysed from the point of view of a free oscillation, we have to distinguish between two fundamental problems: first, the *propagation* problem; second, the *impulse* problem.

(Frisch (1933), p. 171)

Frisch first of all turned his attention to the propagation problem and the question of dynamic economic models of the economic system:

The propagation problem is the problem of explaining by the structural properties of the swinging system, what the character of the swings would be in case the system was started in some initial situation. This must be done by an essentially dynamic theory, that is to say, by a theory that explains how one situation grows out of the foregoing. In this type of analysis we consider not only a set of magnitudes in a given point of time and study the interrelations between them, but we consider the magnitudes of certain variables in different points of time, and we introduce certain equations which embrace at the same time several of these magnitudes belonging to different instants. This is the essential characteristic of a dynamic theory. (Frisch (1933), pp. 171–2)

Frisch distinguished between the microdynamic models which had been developed of particular markets and his own macrodynamic analysis. Yet it is clear that his macromodelling was based on contemporary micro-models such as the cobweb model: a two-equation demand and lagged supply model first used by Moore in 1925 (and discussed in Part II). Although his model was to be of the whole economy, Frisch stressed that it had to be a simplified model otherwise it would not be possible to study

the *exact time shape* of the solutions, the question of whether one group of phenomena is lagging behind or leading before another group, the question of whether one part of the system will oscillate with higher amplitudes than another part and so on. But these latter problems are just the essential problems in business cycle analysis. (Frisch (1933), p. 173)

So he set up a small macroeconomic model, formulated as a determinate system of mixed differential and difference equations, and showed how it could give rise to oscillations.

Because of his earlier research on the nature of economic time series Frisch naturally wanted to investigate

> whether the system is satisfied if each of the variables is assumed to be made up of a number of *components*, each component being either an exponential or a damped oscillation.   (Frisch (1933), p. 183)

To do this, he first assumed that each of his three main economic variables ('consumption', 'capital starting' and 'carry-on-activity') were composed of a number of component cycles or waves. The period and form of these component cycles were dependent in turn on the structural parameters of the system that he had set up. In order to study the nature of the time-series solutions to these equations (between the structural parameters and the harmonic terms) he inserted his own guessed values for the structural parameters. These guesses he described as:

> numerical values that may in a rough way express the magnitudes which we would expect to find in actual economic life. At present I am only guessing very roughly at these parameters, but I believe that it will be possible by appropriate statistical methods to obtain more exact information about them. I think, indeed, that the statistical determination of such structural parameters will be one of the main objectives of the economic cycle analysis of the future. If we ask for a real *explanation* of the movements, this type of work seems to be the indispensable complement needed in order to co-ordinate and give a significant interpretation to the huge mass of empirical descriptive facts that have been accumulated in cycle analysis for the past ten or twenty years.   (Frisch (1933), p. 185)

The mathematical solution of the equation system with the inserted guesses was not easy.[17] Frisch used a system of 'numerical and graphical approximation' which resulted in a solution for each variable, consisting of a trend plus three component cycles. These cycles were a primary cycle of 8.57 years (the business cycle), a secondary cycle of 3.5 years (the short 42–month business cycle) and a tertiary cycle of 2.2 years. All of these were heavily damped. The first two cycle lengths were close to those found in actual business cycle data for the late nineteenth and early twentieth centuries. Further, these cycle lengths were fairly insensitive to changes in all of the chosen structural parameter values, except that representing the length of time required for the production of capital goods (the technical coefficient of 'carry-on-activity'). In order to show more clearly how the structural parameters determined the time shape of the solutions, Frisch also provided a step-by-step computation of the variables, assuming that certain

---

[17] The solution method was ad hoc but the problem prompted further research and a paper by Frisch and Holme (1935) gave a formal method of solving mixed differential-difference equations.

initial values of the system were given.

Frisch was clearly very pleased with his results and their closeness to observed average cycle lengths:

> Of course, the results here obtained with regard to the length of the periods and the intensity of the damping must not be interpreted as giving a final explanation of business cycles; in particular it must be investigated if the same types of cycles can be explained also by other sets of assumptions, for instance, by assumptions about the saving–investment discrepancy, or by the indebtedness effect etc. Anyhow, I believe that the results here obtained in particular those regarding the length of the primary cycle of 8½ years and secondary cycle of 3½ years, are not entirely due to coincidence but have a real significance. (Frisch (1933), p. 190)[18]

Remember that Frisch had simulated his economic system based on guessed values for the structural parameters rather than using real economic data in his work. He must have been very confident in his model, and in his experiment, to predict that a new cycle would be discovered in empirical data:

> I want to go one step further: I want to formulate the hypothesis that if the various statistical production or monetary series that are now usually studied in connection with business cycles are scrutinized more thoroughly, using a more powerful technique of time series analysis, *then we shall probably discover evidence also of the tertiary cycle, i.e. a cycle of a little more than two years.*
> (Frisch (1933), p. 190)

Having discussed the internal economic cycle mechanism (the propagation problem), Frisch turned his attention to the impulse problem and to the question of consistency between his theory and economic time-series data. How could the damped component cycles he found for his determinate dynamic system be reconciled with the absence of damping and smoothness in the data?

> there are several alternative ways in which one may approach the impulse problem and try to reconcile the results of the determinate dynamic analysis with the facts. One way which I believe is particularly fruitful and promising is to study what would become of the solution of a determinate dynamic system if it were exposed to a stream of erratic shocks that constantly upsets the continuous evolution, and by so doing introduces into the system the energy necessary to maintain the swings. If

---

[18] The dangers of making such inferences were discussed by Haavelmo (1940). Like Yule, Haavelmo discussed both the role of superimposed errors and disturbances in estimated economic relationships and pointed out the dangers of letting verification rest on periodicities equal or similar to those of observed cycles, for when shocks are added to the model, these periodicities may change or may not even exist. This point is discussed further in Chapter 4.4.

fully worked out, I believe that this idea will give an interesting synthesis between the stochastical point of view and the point of view of rigidly determined dynamical laws.   (Frisch (1933), pp. 197–8)

Frisch pointed out that both Yule and Slutsky had suggested how economic time series might be generated by irregular events. Yet Frisch felt that the central problem still remained. How are the time shapes of observed economic variables actually determined, that is, how do Slutsky's random terms come to be summed in economic activity or how are Yule's shocks absorbed into the system; and what economic interpretation can be given to the processes?

Frisch's explanation linked his two fields of enquiry: the time shape of the components and their generation. His earlier analysis of economic time-series data had made him characterise such data as a combination of *changing* component cycles and he had used linear operators to unravel the components in each variable. Later he had turned this method round to experiment with linear operators acting on shocks as Slutsky had done. Now he used this idea again to suggest that the observed time series of an economic variable was the result of

applying a linear operator to the shocks, and *the system of weights in the operator will simply be given by the shape of the time curve that would have been the solution of the determinate dynamic system in case the movement had been allowed to go on undisturbed.*   (Frisch (1933), p. 201)

That is, the economic system has its own time path (consisting in his model of the combination of three damped, but *fixed*, component cycles) which provides a set of weights. This acts as a linear operator on the random shocks in a cumulative fashion to produce a combination of *changing* component cycles like those he had observed in real economic variables. Frisch gave a 'proof' of this suggestion with another simulation which showed that a linear operator acting on erratic shocks produced a curve with a changing harmonic, a not quite regular cycle where

the length of the period and also the amplitude being to some extent variable, these variations taking place, however, within such limits that it is reasonable to speak of an *average* period and an *average* amplitude.
                    (Frisch (1933), p. 202)

These are precisely the sort of component cycles Frisch had analysed in his time-series work and which he believed were typical of economic time-series data. He felt that this provided further empirical support that his model design was on the right lines.

Thus the system and the shocks are both required to maintain economic oscillations and to produce data consisting of changing component cycles:

> thus by connecting the two ideas: (1) the continuous solution of a determinate dynamic system and (2) the discontinuous shocks intervening and supplying the energy that may maintain the swings - we get a theoretical set-up which seems to furnish a rational interpretation of those movements which we have been accustomed to see in our statistical time data. The solution of the determinate dynamic system only furnishes a part of the explanation: it determines the *weight system* to be used in the cumulation of the erratic shocks. The other and equally important part of the explanation lies in the elucidation of the general laws governing the effect produced by linear operations performed on erratic shocks.
>
> (Frisch (1933), pp. 202-3)

Frisch's finding was similar to Yule's result that the best way to model the process of a disturbed harmonic function was by a simple difference equation (a linear operator) with an added disturbance. It is interesting that, although Yule postulated the process for such a time series, estimated the process and then solved for the cycles, Frisch himself continued to shy away from estimating the process that generated the cycles. Thus, despite recommending that structural parameters of the equations in the system should be estimated, Frisch had preferred instead to guess these parameters. This might seem a puzzling decision, but there were several reasons for it. In the first place, despite Frisch's modern terminology of 'macrodynamics', the cycle still formed the central concept and unit of analysis in his work. This is reflected both in his practice of solving the system into the time-series domain to find the cycle lengths and in the novelty of his appeal to the resulting cycles as confirming evidence of the model. It was the shape and periodicity of the time-series solutions to the macroeconomic system, and not the structural parameters themselves, which interested Frisch.[19] His views in this respect were conventional since the intellectual context of economic thought in the early 1930s was still that of business cycles not macroeconomics.

But Frisch had other good reasons for avoiding the structural parameters. He was at this time involved in two separate investigations into econometric methods. One was his time-series work discussed earlier and the second was a study of parameter estimation methods in

[19] I am indebted to John Aldrich for this suggestion which is consistent with Frisch's apparent change of heart towards estimation of such cycle models by the time of the European Meeting of the Econometric Society in 1936. By that time he advocated estimating the final form equations (similar to Yule's difference equations) not the structural system of equations because of his worries about collinearity and this led naturally on to his 1938 paper on autonomy (see Chapter 4.4 and Aldrich (1989)).

the presence of confluent relationships: several relationships holding between the variables at the same time. He thought there would be a particular danger of confluent relationships in business cycle research because of the parallel movements in the data series, and that the usual least squares estimates of structural parameters would therefore be untrustworthy. He was heavily critical of the standard regression methods, but he had not yet (by 1933) worked out his own bunch map techniques to deal with this problem. On the other hand, his time-series research programme was well advanced and, in these circumstances, he perhaps felt more at home in seeking the solution to his system, in terms of component cycles than in working with the structural parameters.

Good intellectual reasons apart, Frisch, unlike Tinbergen, preferred to work on problems of the methods and methodology of econometrics rather than on applied econometrics using real data. Although he had not 'applied' his rocking horse model to real data, and had therefore made no direct recourse to evidence, Frisch had made two indirect appeals to evidence to convince himself that his design was on the right lines. The first was that his simulated system had certain numerical results on cycle lengths in common with those from standard business cycle analysis. This was highly satisfactory, but was insufficient for Frisch. It was the further fact, that by putting together his economic model and the shocks he could reproduce the features he believed characterised economic time-series data, which finally convinced him. Frisch's model design did provide an answer to his question of how the changing cycle components came together to form economic data series.

Frisch's 1933 paper was highly successful; it was referenced by all the main writers on business cycles working in econometrics and mathematical economics. As a dynamic macromodel, the rocking horse model of the business cycle was successful because it had all the 'correct' features. The models of Jevons and Moore had not been accepted by other economists, not primarily because the chain of causation was so tenuous, but because economists were unwilling to believe in an economy which was totally reliant on regular exogenous forces for its motion. Frisch's rocking horse theory rested on an essentially mechanical system, a system, with a natural tendency towards an equilibrium or position of rest; the motion of the underlying model was endogenous and had damped oscillations. Frisch's paper has been credited by Samuelson with causing a revolution in economics equivalent in effect to the revolution from classical to quantum mechanics in physics (Samuelson (1947), p. 284). The revolution in thought that Samuelson referred to, however, was not in econometrics but in economic theory, and the transition in question was from the method of comparative statics to what might be called comparative dynamics.[20] Frisch had shown economists how to manipulate dynamic macromodels.

Yet there was more involved than suggested by Samuelson's judgement. Non-mathematical models of the trade cycle could not usually be translated into macromodels, let alone into potential econometric models, because such theories were often indeterminate or incomplete and the time relations were rarely specified. Frisch's model was dynamic, determinate and complete, a model which theorists could explore and manipulate for insights into how the economy might work, but one which was also amenable to econometric analysis. Econometricians such as Frisch and Tinbergen played a crucial part in developing mathematical macroeconomic models that could be made operational.

The rocking horse model was also a landmark in econometrics. Statistical work on the business cycle, such as that by Persons and Mitchell, had mostly been concerned with attempts to measure or isolate the cycle rather than to provide explanatory models of the cycle or test the many theories of the cycle. Moore had worked out a viable explanation of the business cycle and estimated it by a process of defining successive relationships, but it was limited in its design to fit the dynamic pattern of a particular time and place. Frisch's model was not built to fit any particular data set; it is not even clear that it was intended as a serious economic theory of the cycle, but rather as an illustrative exercise in method in which Frisch showed the sort of model or explanation econometricians should be using.

The importance of Frisch's paper for econometrics lies therefore in his model design. The economic dynamics are one important element of this. His model could generate economic cycles through the interactions of the equations in its system. But of course, whether the model did generate cycles depended on the parameters of the model and it was possible that with other parameters, the model might not necessarily produce cycles, the solutions might be undamped or even explosive. The second important econometric design feature was the role of random shocks in conjuction with the deterministic system. Although business cycle theory was non-stochastic, it was generally accepted in an informal way that observed cycles were influenced by non-regular outside events. Frisch recognised that these shocks were real disturbances (in Yule's sense), rather than either a measurement error (as in Yule's superposed errors) or an unexplained residual left after the

---

[20] See, for example, Merlin's (1950) analysis of equilibrium notions and the econometric contribution to cycle theory.

elimination of trend, seasonal and cyclical features from the data (as in Persons' work). The economic system provided the summation mechanism for these random errors as suggested in Slutsky's hypothesis about cycle data. The role of random shocks was crucial, it transformed the model from a theoretical model which could produce the underlying cyclical components to one which could lay claims to the data by producing the rather jagged appearance of economic data and by maintaining the oscillations of the cycle. The shocks provided the final important element which changed the dynamic economic model into an econometric model, a formal stochastic model of how real economic data might be produced.

Frisch's econometric model was successful and influential and yet the first attempts, by Tinbergen, to build a full-scale model of the economy and follow Frisch's suggestion of estimating the structural parameters using real data, rather than by guesswork, proved to be far more controversial.

CHAPTER 4

Tinbergen and macrodynamic models

Jan Tinbergen built and estimated the first macrodynamic model of the business cycle in 1936.[1] Amongst all the econometricians of his day, Tinbergen was ideally suited for such a task. He had been experimenting with small-scale models of the trade cycle since the late 1920s and was well versed in the ways of dynamic models. He also had a wide knowledge of quantitative business cycle research from his experience as Editor of *De Nederlandsche Conjunctuur* (the Dutch statistical business cycle journal). Yet, even for one so well qualified, it was a formidable undertaking, for there was a considerable jump from putting together a small cycle model to constructing an econometric model of the business cycle covering the whole economy, and Tinbergen was well aware that the difficulties were not merely due to the difference in scale.

Tinbergen had already given considerable thought to the problems involved in a 1935 survey of econometric research on business cycles commissioned for *Econometrica*. He had taken as his starting point Frisch's (1933) idea that a business cycle model should consist of two elements, an economic mechanism (the macrosystem):

> 'This system of relations defines the structure of the economic community to be considered in our theory' (Tinbergen (1935), p. 242)

and the outside influences or shocks. But, as Tinbergen had pointed out, this was only a basic design for an econometric model; the scope of Frisch's new term 'macrodynamics' was unclear. Just what variables and relations should a complete model of the business cycle include? How should these relations be put together to form an adequate

---

[1] The Dutch economist Jan Tinbergen was born in 1903. He graduated from the University of Leiden in 1926 and received a doctorate for his thesis on physics and economics in 1929. From 1929 to 1945 he worked on business cycle research at the Central Bureau for Statistics (apart from 1936–8 spent working for the League of Nations). He was appointed the first director of the Netherlands Central Planning Bureau in 1945 where he remained until 1955. Besides being one of the great pioneers in econometrics, he has made valuable contributions to several other fields of economics.

econometric model of the business cycle? What properties should this system of relations have? None of these questions should be considered trivial or obvious, for in the 1930s even the most sophisticated theories of the business cycle tended to be incomplete and the essential characteristics of an econometric model remained undefined.[2]

A second set of problems concerned how to choose the relations to make up the system when many theories and dynamic characterisations of those theories were available. The multiplicity of theories necessitated some form of test or verification in order, as Tinbergen had stated:

> To find out whether these schemes can explain real business cycles and which of them most resembles reality.   (Tinbergen (1935), p. 281)

Last, but certainly not least as far as Tinbergen's interests were concerned, was the question of how to use the model to investigate policy problems.

These were the issues and problems in Tinbergen's mind when he started work on his large model of the Dutch economy. They seemed to pull two ways. He saw that a successful applied model needed to replicate reality as closely as possible, but that the model would only be amenable to policy analysis if it were relatively simple. He gained some comfort from recognising that this tension between realism and simplicity was a standard problem of applied scientific research.

4.1   The Dutch model

Tinbergen's first macrodynamic model was built in response to a request from the Dutch Economic Association to present a paper in October 1936 on policies to relieve the depression. He was pleased to respond to this opportunity for he had switched out of his initial field, physics, into economics because he believed it was a more socially useful science. His model is a remarkable piece of work, involving not only building and estimating a model of the whole economy but also using the model to simulate the likely impact of various policies. His memorandum on the model was written in Dutch for a non-quantitative audience, and consequently avoided discussion of technical and methodological problems. But by the following February, Tinbergen had produced a full treatment of the econometric aspects of his work in an English-language version which is discussed here.[3]

The experience of building and estimating the Dutch model forced

---

[2] Tinbergen has recently discussed this problem in an interview (see Magnus and Morgan (1987)).

[3] The original Dutch model was published in Dutch in 1936, and is available in English in Tinbergen (1959). The revised English version was published in a French series edited by Gibrat in 1937.

Tinbergen to find practical solutions for some of the problems he had foreseen. First of all he described how he proposed to set up the system of causal relationships to form the model.

> We may start from the proposition that every change in economic life has a number of proximate causes. These proximate causes themselves have their own proximate causes which in turn are indirect 'deeper' causes with respect to the first mentioned change, and so on. Thus a network of causal relationships can be laid out connecting up all the successive changes occurring in an economic community. Apart from causal relationships there will also exist relationships of definition ... And, finally, there will be technical or institutional connections. All these relationships together form a system of equations governing the movements of the various elements in the community. Each of these equations can be looked upon as a determining equation for one of the elements, explaining what factors influence that element and how large is the effect of a given change in each factor. (Tinbergen (1937), p. 8)

He worried less about realism, aware that a model is but a stylised version of the economic system:

> I must stress the necessity for simplification. Mathematical treatment is a powerful tool; it is, however, only applicable if the number of elements in the system is not too large ... the whole community has to be schematised to a 'model' before anything fruitful can be done. This process of schematisation is, of course, more or less arbitrary. It could, of course, be done in a way other than has here been attempted. In a sense this is the 'art' of economic research. (Tinbergen (1937), p. 8)

Tinbergen explained his model building as an iterative process involving both hypotheses and statistical estimation:

> The description of the simplified model of Dutch business life used for the consideration of business cycle causes and business cycle policy commences with an enumeration of the variables introduced. The equations assumed to exist between these variables will be considered in the second place. This order does not correspond exactly to the procedure followed in the construction of the model. One cannot know *a priori* what variables are necessary and what can be neglected in the explanation of the central phenomena that are under consideration. It is only during the actual work, and especially after the statistical verification of the hypotheses, that this can be discovered. As a matter of fact, the two stages mentioned are really taken up at the same time; it is for the sake of clearness that the exposition is given in two stages. A glance at the 'kitchen' will nevertheless be occasionally made in order to avoid an impression of magic. (Tinbergen (1937), p. 9)

These introductory remarks portray Tinbergen's ideas and general approach to the task ahead.

The Dutch model was very much a simple model as far as Tinbergen was concerned but was huge and complex by the standards of the time. It contained 22 relationships and 31 variables (divided into prices, physical quantities and money values). The relationships were divided into technical equations, definitional equations (such as those defining value) and direct causal relationships which provided explanations of price movements, sales, competition and the formation and disposal of incomes. He estimated the 16 non-definitional relationships covering three sectors (domestic production, income and consumption, and international trade) for the period 1923 to 1935. Most of these equations involved only one or two systematic or explanatory variables. In addition, Tinbergen included time trends in the equations rather than working with variables in the form of deviations from trend values (considered to represent the long-run or equilibrium values).[4] Each of the equations was estimated separately and, for the most part, independently of the others; though in some cases, information from already estimated equations was incorporated in a new equation. Accidental influences were assumed to be small and random, leading to residuals in the regression, but these random error terms were not written into the relationships.

In contrast to the current publication conventions of econometrics, Tinbergen was not afraid to let his reader see the 'craft' element in his work. A summary of his discussion of the investment equation will give, to use Tinbergen's own words, 'a glance at the "kitchen"'. The principal factor determining investment was thought to be profit expectations, but, Tinbergen argued, these are probably based on previous profits, which can therefore safely be taken as the main explanatory variable. The influence of interest rates on investment was investigated statistically and found unimportant (as indicated by the regression coefficient). Finally he argued:

> economists would perhaps prefer a more complicated function ... Their argument would probably be that the volume of investment should be large enough to make marginal profits equal to zero. I think this argument only applies to long-run tendencies but not to the rather short-run tendencies represented by our equations.   (Tinbergen (1937), pp. 25–6)

This left a simple equation in which investment depended only on profits lagged by one year and a trend term. Tinbergen reported the equation's results in graph form, showing the observed and fitted

---

[4] In this he was following Frisch and Waugh's (1933) result which had shown the equivalence of the methods (discussed in Chapter 5). Tinbergen also calculated unusual regression coefficients: he divided each standard least squares regression coefficient by the correlation coefficient.

values of the dependent variable and the explanatory variables on one chart. These charts (an example of which is reproduced as Figure 10) were distinctive to Tinbergen's work and their role and importance will become evident during the course of the chapter.

As is clear from this example, the formation of each individual equation and the particular choice of variables were found by iterating between theoretical ideas and empirical investigations. This iterative approach was extended to the 'verification' of hypotheses. This consisted of judging whether the estimated relationships were reasonable, both in terms of their economic sense (the first criterion) and in terms of closeness of fit, judging by eye the distance between the observed and fitted values of the dependent variable on the graph. It should be clear that Tinbergen was not claiming 'statistical testing' of his model here, but 'statistical verification'. His purpose was to show that the model was compatible with the statistical observations and provided a sensible explanation of the observed movements in the economy over the previous years.

Business cycle historians, according to Tinbergen, could gain many insights into past economic experience by comparing the variations in the explanatory variables with those of the dependent variable. These comparisons could easily be made using Tinbergen's graphs and could reveal a specific cause of a crisis or a revival. For example, he found that a particularly large residual in one equation, suggestive of some outside cause, could be interpreted as the result of the introduction of an import quota system. But Tinbergen provided a sting in the tail by reminding his readers that such an interpretation of large residuals was only possible

in so far as we believe in the theory behind our hypotheses.

(Tinbergen (1937), p. 46)

The next stage of the investigation was to see if the model had a cyclical pattern as its solution. Why and how this was done requires further explanation for it was difficult for some of Tinbergen's contemporaries too understand and may still be opaque to the modern reader. The question was, in the absence of shocks and disturbances, would the economic system have a cyclical path? If it did, then Tinbergen argued that the model provided a theory of the business cycle. This test of the model was in line with Frisch's 1933 paper which required that the economic system part of a macrodynamic model show a cyclical tendency. Frisch had studied the time path of each of the three variables in his model. Tinbergen's system of equations was more complicated and none of the elementary equations could represent the system of the whole economy.

In order to discover what the natural tendencies of Tinbergen's model were, his large system of 22 equations first had to be reduced to one equation in one variable. By taking arbitrary values for the international variables (such as import prices) and by a process of substitution and elimination of the domestic variables in the model, one 'final equation' was obtained. This final equation was a simple difference equation in the variable Z (which represented non-labour income):

$$Z_t = .15Z_{t-1} + .26Z_{t-2} - 34.7$$

In a later discussion of this part of his method Tinbergen admitted the difficulty of following the economic meaning of the model when the original economic relationships were converted into one final equation.[5] This had led the analysis to be called 'night train analysis', because economists had to move from the elementary equations or relationships, with which they were familiar, to 'deduced economic laws' for which it was not easy to give an account. In this case, the final equation represented the structure of the Dutch economy because the coefficients of the difference terms depended on the estimated coefficients of the system of 22 elementary equations which formed the model. So, the equation was not itself a regression equation, but it depended on all those that were.

Of course, the final equation was not derived for its own sake, but as a preliminary step in finding the time path of the system. Tinbergen proposed two methods for this. There was a mathematically simple, but tedious, method, and a mathematically advanced alternative. The simple way involved taking two initial values of the variable Z in the final equation (assuming no disturbances) and simply extrapolating further values of Z from the equation. From this, other variables' paths could also be calculated because of the interdependencies in the system of equations. Of course, with different starting values, and different values for the international variables, other time paths would be found for the system. The more advanced method of finding the time path of the system, which avoided the problems of choosing starting values, was to solve the final linear difference equation in terms of its harmonic terms. This is the route both Yule (1927) and Frisch (1933) had followed in order to find out what the system's path looked like. The final equation of the Dutch model was solved by Tinbergen to show that the economy had a nicely damped cyclical path which would tend to an equilibrium position provided there were no disturbances. This

[5] See Tinbergen (1940) and the background to this paper in n. 19 below.

solution was taken to show that the model did provide an adequate theory of the Dutch business cycle.

In practice, the process of determining the dynamic character of the model was complicated by the presence of disturbance terms. These might be represented in the initial conditions of the system or they might occur as additive terms coming into the elementary equations at specific points due to, for example, changes in government policy. As an example, Tinbergen examined how an imported international cycle could disturb the Dutch economy. This exercise confirmed his belief that for a small country like the Netherlands, the shocks from the internal economy (through new inventions or good harvests, for example) would not be very large; they would be dominated by disturbances imported from the movements of larger economies.

Extrapolation of the model to show its time path was a test of whether the model provided a theory of the business cycle, but it was also a prelude to an investigation of the optimum policy. In Tinbergen's analysis (based on analogies from physics on the movements of a pendulum) policy changes either affected the relations superficially through the additive disturbance terms or more deeply by changing the coefficients and causing a change in structure. Tinbergen investigated six policy options: public works schemes, a protectionist policy, a rationalisation policy, a lowering of monopoly prices, wage reductions and devaluation. He modelled these simply as terms added to the estimated elementary equations of the system; and for each policy option the system was again solved to find the new final form equation. Tinbergen then compared the movements in two variables, non-labour income (Z) and employment, which would result if he extrapolated the system for seven periods ahead for each of the six different policies. (He also, by putting $Z_t = Z_{t-1} = Z_{t-2}$, compared the long-run equilibrium values for all the main variables under the different policies.) Of course which policy was considered optimum depended on the criteria chosen. Tinbergen's criterion in 1936 was to obtain the lowest unemployment, and, for this purpose, devaluation proved to be the most promising policy.

Tinbergen also tried to work out the best possible policy for stabilising an imported business cycle, either through making compensatory movements in the exchange rate or in public investment. Here some of his examples involved changing the coefficients on the equations, a more complicated problem than dealing with policies as added disturbances.

To conclude his study of the Dutch economy, Tinbergen offered a résumé of the advantages of the econometric approach to business cycle problems:

> The establishment of a system of equations compels us to state clear-cut hypotheses about every sphere of economic life and, in addition, to test them statistically. Once stated, the system enables us to distinguish sharply between all kinds of different variation problems. And it yields clear-cut conclusions. Differences of opinion can, in principle, be localised, i.e. the elementary equation in which the difference occurs can be found. Deviations between theory and reality can be measured and a number of their consequences estimated. Finally, the results of our calculations show, apart from many well-known facts, that, as regards the types of movement that are conceivable, there exist a number of neglected problems and of unexpected possibilities.   (Tinbergen (1937), p. 73)

Given the multitude of business cycle theories then available and the serious policy problems posed by the Great Depression, the benefits outlined by Tinbergen were potentially valuable. His comments perhaps appear overoptimistic now, but comparisons of his work on the Dutch model with Frisch's 1933 paper or with Mitchell's 1927 book on business cycles suggest that Tinbergen was justified in boasting the benefits of econometrics. He was soon given an opportunity for a deeper exploration of the subject's potential.

4.2   The first League of Nations' report

In 1936, Tinbergen was commissioned by the League of Nations to undertake statistical tests of the business cycle theories examined for the League by Haberler in *Prosperity and Depression* (1937).[6] Tinbergen worked at this task for two years and reported his results in two volumes, *Statistical Testing of Business-Cycle Theories* published in 1939. The first contained an explanation of the method of econometric testing and a demonstration of what could be achieved in three case studies. The second volume contained an ambitious macroeconometric model of the USA.

In order to air the problems involved in testing business cycle theories, Tinbergen opened his first report with some general comments on the methodology of econometric research. It is again worth quoting these more or less in full, so that we can understand Tinbergen's own ideas on testing. He believed that the empirical study of business cycle data, involving correlation and decomposition analysis

---

[6] I am grateful to Earlene Craver for pointing out the explanation for the apparent confusion in these dates: Haberler's book was widely circulated in draft by the League prior to publication.

of economic time series (of the sort discussed in Chapter 2), was of limited use when it came to testing theories.

> Certainly all this work had its value, especially for the *negative* evidence it afforded on the validity of certain theories. For the purpose of applying more searching tests, however, it is necessary to dig deeper. An apparently simple relation, such as that between prices and production, is often not a direct causal relation at all, but a more or less complicated chain of many such relations. It is the object of analysis to identify and test these causal relations...
>
> The part which the statistician can play in this process of analysis must not be misunderstood. The theories which he submits to examination are handed over to him by the economist, and with the economist the responsibility for them must remain; for no statistical test can prove a theory to be correct. It can, indeed, prove that theory to be incorrect, or at least incomplete, by showing that it does not cover a particular set of facts: but, even if one theory appears to be in accordance with the facts, it is still possible that there is another theory, also in accordance with the facts, which is the 'true' one, as may be shown by new facts or further theoretical investigations. Thus the sense in which the statistician can provide 'verification' of a theory is a limited one.
>
> On the other hand, the role of the statistician is not confined to 'verification' ... the direct causal relations of which we are in search are generally relations not between two series only – one cause and one effect – but between one dependent series and several causes. And what we want to discover is, not merely what causes are operative, but also *with what strength each of them operates*: otherwise it is impossible to find out the nature of the combined effect of causes working in opposite directions.
>
> (Tinbergen (1939), I, p. 12)

Tinbergen's view, then, incidentally a long-held opinion, was that statistical testing could lead to either disproof or to limited verification.[7]

Tinbergen's separation of the two roles, the statistician and economist, is disconcerting in this context. But he went on to explain how econometrics united these approaches. Tinbergen argued that economic theory must be expressed in mathematical form but that quantitative economics had chiefly been concerned with the long-run equilibrium conditions, to the neglect of short-run dynamic problems of the cycle:

> To be useful, therefore, for business cycle research, economic theory needs to be made 'dynamic'. A 'dynamic' theory, in the sense which is here attached to that ambiguous word, is one which deals with the short-term reactions of one variate upon others, but without neglecting the lapse of

---

[7] Tinbergen had suggested that statistics could not prove theories but could be used to help disprove theories as early as his first article in economics in 1927, see Magnus and Morgan (1987).

time between cause and effect. The equations in which it is expressed thus relate to non-simultaneous events, and take a form which Swedish economists have described as 'sequence analysis'

(Tinbergen (1939), I, p. 13)

At the same time, the conversion of theory into relationships 'capable of statistical test' required: that the economic relations be given in terms of cause and effect; that the time lag between these be specified; and that all the major causes of variation be specified rather than leaving them 'concealed in a *ceteris paribus* clause' (Tinbergen (1939), I, p. 13). The development of dynamic theory had sometimes, according to Tinbergen's view, resulted directly from statistical research rather than from purely theoretical research. Thus,

> we find that the correlation analysis suggested by statistical technique and the sequence analysis dictated by 'dynamicised' economic theory converge and are synthesised in the method employed in this study.
>
> (Tinbergen (1939), I, p. 14)

This synthesis of mathematically expressed dynamic theory and statistical method formed the ideal of the econometric method and so, in a practical way, the activities and aims of the statistician and the economist were united, as indeed they were in Tinbergen's work.

The main and novel feature of this first League of Nations report, subtitled: *A Method and its Application to Investment Activity*, was its marked emphasis on testing, using a very wide range of procedures involving both economic and statistical criteria; the substantive material was provided by three case studies on general investment, investment in housebuilding and in railway rolling stock. Tinbergen felt constrained from the start by the amount of calculation needed to cover all the cases he wanted to investigate. But he made a virtue of his necessity and used his limited resources to create another opportunity to test the model as follows. In his first case study on general investment, he began by working with a large model which incorporated all the variables suggested by theorists as influencing investment. He applied this full model to only a limited number of countries and time periods. After studying the results from this exercise, he reduced the size of the model to include only the variables which appeared to be most important. He then applied the reduced model to a number of different countries and time periods to see whether it worked equally well, and at this second stage was able to apply a full range of statistical testing procedures.

Once again, theoretical discussions were interwoven with the applied work in a recursive treatment. Tinbergen happily showed the 'cook at work' creating his investment model from a mixture of verbally expressed theories, correlations between various variables and empirical results. Prior to estimation, Tinbergen discussed the following sorts of questions. What variables should be included? What was the exact form of a variable to be used, for example, should it be profit margins, total profits, profit rates or expected profits? What were the expected signs of the variables? Was there a danger of multicollinearity?[8] He also thought about, and tried to sort out from the correlations, the problem of two-way causality between profits and investments and dealt with the parallel problem of determination of both demand and supply functions (discussed further in Part II).

Tinbergen used his distinctive 'stacking' technique, which involved graphing the causal variables one on top of the other like plates in an attempt to 'explain' the variation in the dependent variable.[9] These graphs both helped him to choose the contents of the individual relations, and delayed the calculation of the regression equation until he was reasonably sure of its contents (thus reducing the burden of computation on his assistants to a minimum). He had used this graphing technique earlier for the Dutch model, he now produced more complex charts containing more information. One of them, showing the regression equation for the production of pig-iron, is reproduced here as Figure 10. From my earlier comments and this illustration, it should be obvious that a large amount of information can be gleaned from Tinbergen's charts. As well as helping him to choose the model, they were a useful way of reporting the results. They showed the final calculated relationship and revealed the patterns of both the individual explanatory variables and the residuals.

Tinbergen felt it was important to calculate both regression and correlation coefficients for he had suggested earlier in his study that regression coefficients measured the strength of the effect of the explanatory variables in a relationship whereas the correlation coefficient gave evidence for the verification of a relationship, that is, a high correlation coefficient verified a theory. So, in calculating the regression relations, Tinbergen followed a sort of simple to general modelling procedure looking at the sign, stability and size of the regression coefficients and total correlation coefficient as each new variable was added in. He used the evidence from his calculations as further help in deciding the correct model (and in some cases the regression

[8] Fear of multicollinearity had been engendered by Frisch's confluence analysis (1934). Tinbergen's rule of thumb was that if the correlation coefficient between any two explanatory variables was particularly high ($| r | > .80$) then one of the variables was omitted (see also n. 11).

[9] The term 'plate stacking' was used by Tinbergen himself to describe his practice in an interview with him on 30 April 1980. Despite their usefulness, few copied his graphic methods, though see Chapter 2 n. 24.

"Explanation" of Pig-iron Production.
United States, 1919-1937.

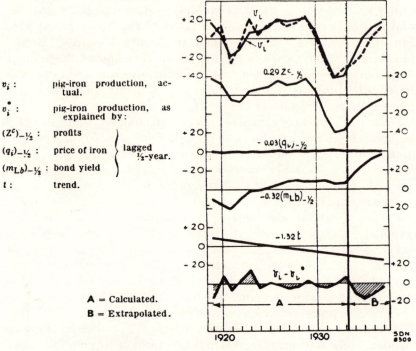

v_i :   pig-iron production, ac-
                tual.

$v_i^{\bullet}$:   pig-iron production, as
                explained by:

$(Z^c)_{-\frac{1}{2}}$:   profits

$(q_i)_{-\frac{1}{2}}$:   price of iron   lagged
                          ½-year.

$(m_{Lb})_{-\frac{1}{2}}$: bond yield

t :   trend.

A = Calculated.

B = Extrapolated.

Figure 10   Tinbergen's plate-stacking graph
Source: Tinbergen (1939), I, p. 73, Graph III.8

calculations were carried out ahead of the graphing study). He did not
always go along with its results; for example, he would sometimes
include variables which seemed ineffective in the relation but which
theorists argued should be present. In addition, Tinbergen tried a
number of different lags lengths to obtain the best time relation.[10]

Once estimated, the equations were subjected to several different
sorts of testing procedures. First, there was the already mentioned test
of the models on new countries and time periods. Second, Tinbergen
tried the models out on different subperiods to test for the possibility of
structural changes or non-constant coefficients and for different coefficients on the up-phases of the cycle compared to the down-phases.

[10] Tinbergen's initial assumption was that the explanatory variables entered the equations
with a half-year lag. He also experimented with no lag and a one-year lag. In addition, he
plotted out the frequency distribution of the coefficients on the lagged profit term in the
investment equation and found the average lag to be eight months.

Third, he carried out prediction tests by extrapolating the fitted equations for the next two years of the period (an example of this practice is evident on the graph reproduced above: 'B' is the forecast period) and he also checked the assumption of linear trends by looking at the partial scatter diagrams.

Last, but not least, Tinbergen followed a complete programme of statistical significance calculations. First, this involved testing the residuals. He had characterised the omitted and non-economic influences in the relationship as being many, small and of accidental character – traditionally the characterisation associated with the 'law of errors' or normal curve. Testing for first order serial correlation of the residuals, he wrote,

> serves to test the hypothesis ... that the residuals are to be considered as sample drawings from a 'normally distributed universe'. At the same time, it gives information as to whether the regression chosen satisfies the scheme of the shock theory. (Tinbergen (1939), I, p. 80)

In this he equated the shock scheme of Frisch's 1933 model with the assumption of a normal distribution of the residuals. The shock model was therefore in Tinbergen's treatment the same as the classical regression model. Tinbergen used the classical tests on ordinary least squares and Frisch's confluence analysis as complementary checks on the relations he had found. So his second statistical test was to look at the standard errors of the coefficients to check their significance, and thirdly, he looked at the bunch maps to check for collinearity and to get some idea of the error due to weighting. He even worked out limits for the errors of weighting in line with Koopmans' improvements to Frisch's confluence analysis scheme.[11]

Tinbergen's first example of macrodynamic modelling had been concerned with explaining the past behaviour of the Dutch economy and with judging the effects of various policies rather than with testing. In this first report for the League of Nations he concentrated whole-heartedly on the problem of testing at the level of the individual equations. He carried out an enormous range of different tests (16 in all) to demonstrate the extent to which a theory could be confirmed or refuted by using the econometric approach. Although it is probable that none of these tests was an innovation, the sheer range of tests that Tinbergen presented was entirely without precedent in econometrics in the 1930s. Other econometricians were beginning to get interested in testing models but few used many tests or understood what the

---

[11] Frisch's confluence analysis (1934) and Koopmans' 1937 critique and application of some of R. A. Fisher's ideas to Frisch's work are presented in Chapter 7 Letters 11 and 15.

problems were. Tinbergen clearly led econometrics in this field, but he still had to tackle the problem of the statistical testing of business cycle theories.

4.3   The second League of Nations' report

Tinbergen's commission, remember, was to test the theories of the business cycle which had been surveyed by Haberler. This did not mean that Tinbergen was faced with two or three well-prepared competing macroeconometric models. On the contrary, he was faced with a large number of verbally expressed economic theories in a form not immediately appropriate for statistical measurement or evaluation. In his second report for the League of Nations, Tinbergen therefore developed a three-stage procedure for evaluating theories of the business cycle. The first stage was to find out whether a verbal model could be translated into an econometric model. For stages two and three, Tinbergen returned to the approach adopted in his earlier Dutch model of 'statistically verifying' the relationships of the model first, and then deriving and testing whether the final equation had a cyclical solution. To provide material for his evaluation process he built the first large-scale macroeconometric model of the USA; and the report was consequently subtitled: *Business Cycles in the United States of America, 1919–1932*.

Tinbergen's first test of a verbal theory was whether it could be translated into a mathematically expressed econometric model. It was only while working on the US model that he began to understand and clarify what this meant in the business cycle context.[12] Tinbergen required that the theory should be able to form a model which was complete (as many relationships as variables to be explained) and determinate (the causal factors in each relation to be fully specified) and dynamic (the time lags fully specified). All three properties were needed to take sensible measurements of the model, but the first two properties were also required for the system of equations to be solved for the final equation while the shape of the time path of the system also depended on the dynamic aspects of the relationships. The qualities needed to make an economic model into an adequate econometric model were not widely appreciated at the time.

According to Tinbergen's view, most of the verbal theories of the business cycle failed at this important first hurdle because they were

---

[12] Tinbergen found this idea of a model very important and now sees it as one of the main contributions that econometrics has made to economic theory (see Magnus and Morgan (1987)).

incomplete or were indeterminate, while the dynamic aspects of a theory would almost certainly be couched in vague terms, if at all. It was certainly the case that most of the theories of the business cycle in Haberler's survey were likely to be incomplete since they dealt with only one or two relations of the economic system. Some of these theories could be considered complementary since they dealt with different parts of the economic system while others were directly competing theories. Like Mitchell, Tinbergen rejected the notion of testing each business cycle theory one by one as being too repetitious. The most efficient way to test these theories seemed to Tinbergen to combine the theories into one system of relations to form a model. Indeed, since most existing theories failed the first test, it was obviously *necessary* that some theories be combined in order to make a complete model. The theories, and the equations which represented them, became inter-related by their place in the whole model. Inevitably this process also involved making some choices between competing theories.

In the second stage of evaluating business cycle theories, the individual estimated equations were to be tested for their correspon-dence with economic theory relations. But, because Tinbergen needed to combine theories to form the model, it was not really possible to test the individual theories separately. Instead, Tinbergen specified the individual equations in his model of the USA in accordance with one or more of the economic theories concerned with those variables. He then estimated each equation and examined these statistical relationships between the economic variables in the light of the various theories. He used his normal iterative approach to estimation and model choice so that in the process of building the model he was also 'testing' the theories, combining some and rejecting others not supported by his applied work.

The completed model of business cycles in the USA incorporated 71 variables, 48 equations and covered the period 1919 to 1932. It was a considerable advance on the Dutch model not only in size but also in economic interest. He exhibited considerable skill as an applied econometrician in juggling so many different partial verbal theories, different variables and other pieces of information. For example, he paid particular attention to the peculiar difficulties of the period, notably the Great Crash of 1929, with crafty modelling of cash hoarding and the stock market boom.

Tinbergen relied on two different types of assessment at this second stage test: one used economic criteria and the other relied on historical explanation. The use of economic criteria involved examining the sizes (both absolute and relative) and signs of coefficients in the measured relations compared to those expected from the theories. A good example of this was on an equation involving the marginal propensity to consume. Here he rejected cases where the propensity was greater than unity and where it was lower for low income earners than for those with high income. In this same section he also rejected negative coefficients where positive were expected and occasionally retained coefficients for theoretical reasons when they proved statistically insignificant. Although standard errors of the coefficients and multiple correlation coefficients were reported, Tinbergen carried out no independent tests of the model on other data, nor did he subject his equations to the battery of tests used in the first report for the League.

The other criterion used was to see whether the individual equations offered reasonable and adequate explanations of the historical record for the US for 1919 to 1932. This entailed using the stacking graphs to trace which were the important variables causing variation (turning points, rises or falls) in the dependent variables. Tinbergen proffered some explanations about the specific turning points on the basis of this examination of the graphs, but of course these results could not be generalised to other countries or time periods but were specific to time and place.

In the third stage of evaluating the model, the interrelated equations of the model were then combined to make the final equation representing the system. This derived final form equation was examined to see whether the model as a whole would generate a cyclical pattern. Tinbergen was now very much more articulate about why he was doing this. His rationale was as follows: the model consists of a network of causal connections or equations between a number of economic variables. Although these variables fluctuate over time, none represents the business cycle itself. It is the causal connections, he argued, which form the mechanism of the business cycle and must be able to explain and represent the cycles. He demonstrated what he meant with a small three variable, three equation, dynamic model and showed, with worked examples, that different coefficient values would lead to different patterns in the single final form equation for the system. Some were cyclical and some not.[13] Tinbergen reasoned from this example, that

> In fact, it seems difficult to prove by pure reasoning alone – i.e., without knowing anything about the numerical values of the coefficients – whether or not any given theory explains or does not explain cyclic movements.
>
> (Tinbergen (1939), II, p. 18)

---

[13] In his later discussion (1940) of the mathematical structure of the models, Tinbergen emphasised the importance of knowing not only the constant coefficients of the model but

This in turn explained why the second stage of testing was so very important: you needed to have some confidence that the coefficients were reasonably correct before you could tell whether the causal connections would result in the cyclical pattern required of a business cycle theory. But, Tinbergen also warned later that different estimated equations which seemed to fit the data equally well under the second testing stage could lead to different period and damping ratios in this third stage. In this case, he said, the choice between the models would have to depend on other considerations.

In practical terms, the simplicity of a model was regarded as being an advantage at this stage. If the model was too complicated, the necessary elimination process to get to one final equation could not be carried through. On the other hand, the model had to be sufficiently complex to reflect the most important relationships in the economy in a form which provided a workable system of equations. As Tinbergen later described it:

> The performance of the elimination process exhibits very clearly one fundamental difficulty in business cycle theory. In order to be realistic it has to assume a great number of elementary equations and variables; in order to be workable it should assume a small number of them. It is the task of business cycle theory to pass between this Scilla and Charybdis. If possible at all the solution must be found in such simplifications of the detailed picture as do not invalidate its essential features
>
> (Tinbergen (1940), p. 78)

These were the practical implications of the trade-off between simplicity versus realism. In addition, since there were always a number of different ways of deriving the final form equation, it was important to choose the correct place to start so that the elimination process could take place smoothly.

Faced with the large US model, Tinbergen was forced to indulge in a certain amount of approximation of the individual equations in order to be able to carry through the elimination process. This process resulted in a group of several equations which he called the 'strategic relationships' forming the

> kernel of relations which can more easily be treated. It is, of course, not by chance that we are left with these equations and these variables. The logical structure of our system of equations, which after all is nothing but a reflection of the structure of the business-cycle mechanism, is such that they play the central role.   (Tinbergen (1939), II, p. 133)

also the lag structure in order to determine whether a model would generate a cyclical pattern from its final form equation.

Having derived the final form equation (a difference equation in one of these strategic variables), he then went on to examine the characteristics of that equation and the solution path of the single strategic variable under different regimes (such as the presence or absence of cash hoarding).

It is worth examining in more detail Tinbergen's explanation of one of these cases: the final equation in the case of absence of a stock exchange boom or cash hoarding (Tinbergen (1939), II Equation 6.31, p. 137):

$$Z_t^c = \sum_{i=1}^{4} e_i Z_{t-i}^c + (AU + HO + F + R)_t$$

where Z_t^c was the net income (profits) of corporations. The other four variables represented external (exogenous) factors in the system; each had its own explanatory equation, except for R, which was a conglomerate of little disturbances and regarded as random. AU represented influences from changes in the gold stock and central bank policy. HO represented developments in the housing market which showed almost autonomous cycles. F stood for external (climatic) influences on crops.

The first four coefficients (e_i) of this derived final equation depended on all the regression coefficients of the individual elementary equations of the model (because the final equation had been obtained by substitution and elimination from the individual equations). The coefficients

> describe in an abbreviated form the structure of the economic mechanism with regard to business cycles; they will be different in other countries, or under another regime, where the economic structure of society is different.
>
> (Tinbergen (1939), II, p. 137)

The second consequence of the elimination process was that, since each elementary equation contained a group of unsystematic influences (treated together as one random variable), the final equation contained a great number of these random terms originating in the individual equations. These, of course, were the 'shocks' of Frisch's model. In this case, the four external forces were more or less indepndent of the general position of the business cycle and therefore had the same effect as shocks on the path of Z_t^c.

Tinbergen illustrated how Z_t^c depended on earlier values of the exogenous and random forces using another of his distinctive visual aids,[14] reproduced in Figure 11 (where R here represents the

---

[14] Tinbergen's arrow scheme had made its first appearance in his small book on statistics in 1936. It was not absolutely new to econometrics, for it had appeared in Sewall Wright's

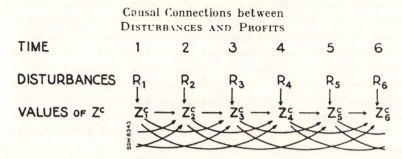

Figure 11   Tinbergen's arrow chart showing the role of disturbances
Source: Tinbergen (1939), II, p. 138, Graph 6.31

sum of the four external variables and the shocks) with the commentary:

> The arrows indicate causal connections. Each value of Z^c depends immediately on certain disturbances, but it depends also on the earlier ones through its connection with the Z^c-values for one, two, three and four years back. (Tinbergen (1939), II, p. 138)

The diagram showed how the internal and external forces of the business cycle mechanism came to be woven together and how the shocks (already cumulated into the final equation) are carried along affecting future values of the systematic variable. It was the disturbances from the external variables and the cumulated shocks (and perhaps, conceded Tinbergen, non-linearities) which

> make it possible that one cycle is completely different from another, and that it is yet, in both, one mechanism that links the variables together. (Tinbergen (1939), II, p. 162)

Tinbergen's careful discrimination between the role of internal and external forces meant that he could categorise policies into those which attempted to change structure (through changing the relationships or their coefficients), or those which tried to change the average level of variables (for example, minimum wage legislation) and those which affected shocks. Policy could be addressed to stabilising one elementary equation or to act on the strategic equations at the kernel.

Tinbergen's critical appraisal of the theories of business cycles surveyed by Haberler was a little disappointing following the richness

discussion of corn and hog cycles in agricultural econometrics in 1925. However, Wright's work was not well known, and Tinbergen has only recently (1979) recognised the similarities.

of his model building. But there were several difficulties in the way of making any very definite inferences. First, there was the problem of assessing economic theories which mostly failed to pass Tinbergen's first test: that of completeness and determinateness. The lack of explicitly specified dynamic relationships in the theories formed a second serious drawback, since these, together with the structure and coefficients of the model, were paramount in determining whether the model passed the final test of providing a cyclical pattern. Thirdly, the appraisal was considerably limited by the shortness of the estimation period of only 13 years.

Tinbergen's general conclusion was that a depression would result from prior 'disproportionalities' (Haberler's term) in the economic system, provided there was unchanged economic structure and no exogenous shocks. Policy changes or shocks might both, according to Tinbergen, intervene to prevent the continued rise of a boom or the continued fall of a depression. This conclusion at least refuted the claims of the periodic models of Moore and Jevons and at most suggested that government policy might have successfully intervened to halt the Great Depression. Tinbergen also used the statistical results that he had found in working with his Dutch, his US and his UK models (see below) to carry out a more direct appraisal of Haberler's theories; this appeared later in 1942.[15] But by this time, war had vanquished the economic depression and business cycle theories were fast going out of fashion.

One further work completed Tinbergen's large-scale macroeconometric modelling programme. This was his model and report on business cycles in the UK covering 1870–1914. The work had been carried out in 1939 and 1940, but the volume was not published until 1951. It followed a similar format to his work for the League of Nations, but by the time the report came out, Tinbergen had new competitors using more sophisticated statistical techniques provided primarily by the work at the Cowles Commission in the 1940s. The econometricians at the Cowles Commission were great admirers of Tinbergen's econometric work and at one stage they thought of applying their methods to Tinbergen's own US model. Instead, they hired L. R. Klein to formulate a new model and this step began the post-war generation of macroeconometric models. The title of Klein's book, *Economic Fluctuations in the United States 1921–1941* (1950) signifies the continuity of thought from Tinbergen's earlier econometric work on business cycles.

---

[15] But this exercise proved no more definitive because Haberler's theories were grouped into categories which Tinbergen (like Mitchell) viewed as providing complementary rather than rival explanations of the cycle.

4.4   The critical reaction to Tinbergen's work

In contrast to his work on the Dutch model which had made little impact on his fellow economists, Tinbergen's first report for the League of Nations proved highly controversial. It was circulated in 1938, prior to publication, and provoked an interesting and long-lasting discussion on the role of econometrics in theory testing. The second report containing the US model was received more calmly. Because of the differences in content of the two reports, it is important when considering the arguments which follow, to bear in mind which volume is being discussed.

It was J. M. Keynes' (1939) famous critique of Tinbergen's first League of Nations study, 'Professor Tinbergen's Method', which sparked off the debate about the role of econometrics.[16] It was unfortunate that, while Keynes attacked the subject with his ususal rhetorical flourish, he had clearly not read the volume with any great care. Some of his criticisms also revealed his ignorance about both the dynamic economic models of the business cycle developed in the previous decade and the technical aspects of econometrics. For example, Keynes supposed that business cycle theory was still at the stage of Jevons' sunspot theory and he failed to see how cyclical patterns could occur except through periodic causes, and certainly not through a system of linear relations.[17] In another example, Keynes supposed wrongly that trends were measured by joining up the first and last observations of the series, whereas Tinbergen had used a moving average trend or a linear trend term in the multiple correlation. (It is perhaps just a little surprising that Keynes should have been so unaware of the econometric literature in question since he had been on the editorial board of *Econometrica* from its first issue and had been a member of the Council of the Econometric Society since 1935.[18] To those economists who failed to read Tinbergen's report for themselves and who remained ignorant of the developments of econometrics since the mid-1920s, Keynes' criticisms of Tinbergen's first volume must have been devastating. This was a pity since Tinbergen's econometric work demonstrated how much more advanced the subject had become.

[16] The Keynes–Tinbergen debate remains a popular topic (see, for example, Stone (1978), Hendry (1980), and Pesaran and Smith (1985). The account here deals not only with the immediate criticism and reply but the contemporary debate which followed.

[17] It is clear also from Keynes' correspondence with Harrod about Tinbergen's work (Keynes (1973), pp. 284–305) that Keynes did not recognise the dynamic mathematical models or Frisch's shock model which Tinbergen used.

[18] Of course, editorial board members are not necessarily aware of everything which appears in their journal. Keynes remained on the Council until his death, and was the Econometric Society's President in 1944–5. It is worth pointing out that many economists had joined the Society at its formation who were not sympathetic to the statistical side of the econometric approach; Robbins was another case in point.

In fact, most of Keynes' specific points of criticism proved invalid since, in his model building and applied work, Tinbergen had dealt with the particular problems raised and carried out the various tests or procedures which Keynes criticised him for omitting.

Keynes also made a number of weightier criticisms of the methods and methodology of econometrics. These points were not new but were already the subject of concern to thoughtful econometricians like Tinbergen. For example, Keynes complimented Tinbergen on his discussion of the method of multiple regression, but he felt strongly that the prior 'logical problem' had not been worked out; that is, Tinbergen had not explained

> fully and carefully the conditions which the economic material must satisfy if the application of the method to it is to be fruitful.
>
> (Keynes (1939), p. 559)

These conditions, according to Keynes, were that econometric techniques could only be applied where there is a correct and complete list of causes, where all the causal factors are measurable, where these factors are independent, where the relationship is linear and where problems such as time lags and trend factors are adequately dealt with. Keynes claimed that these conditions had not been satisfied in Tinbergen's work.

Tinbergen defended his work against the general difficulties raised by Keynes, not only in direct reply but in an additional paper in 1940.[19] Tinbergen argued that provided the list of explanatory variables held the most significant or important ones, this was sufficient for the method to provide good measurements of relationships. Further, as econometricians knew, for statistical purposes explanatory factors did not need to be statistically independent of each other but only reasonably uncorrelated. Tinbergen distinguished this statistical dependency from his idea of economic dependency which he represented by an arrow scheme, showing the immediate causes and the secondary causes (the causes of the first causes) which made up a causal chain system of relations. This arrow scheme is reproduced in Figure 12. Tinbergen argued that for estimation purposes, each elementary equation (or statistical explanation) should only represent one level of causes; the economic dependency between the different levels of causes was inherent in the relationships between the equations in the system. Tinbergen used these arrow schemes as a pedagogical tool to represent his model and to help readers understand the logical structure of his

---

[19] Tinbergen's direct reply (see Keynes and Tinbergen (1940)) and his introduction to (1939), II dealt with many of the issues Keynes had raised, and tried to correct some of his errors. (But Tinbergen's modesty softened the force of his defence (see Magnus and

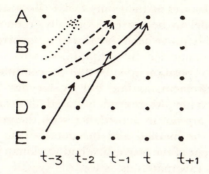

Symbolic representation of logical structure of dynamic economics (sequence analysis).

Figure 12   Tinbergen's arrow scheme showing causal structure
Source: Tinbergen's reply to Keynes in Keynes and Tinbergen (1940), p. 144, Graph 1

models and their lagged schemes.[20] Keynes had also quibbled about where the time lags in equations come from and wanted to insist that their specification came from the theorist. But theorists gave no help on such matters, so Tinbergen was forced to choose the time lags between causes and effects from a process of estimation by trial and error.

There was a second major area of methodological criticism which followed on from Keynes' concern that the necessary conditions be fulfilled. This was the issue of inductive claims. Keynes wrongly supposed that Tinbergen was primarily interested in measuring the strength of various factors. This was because Keynes believed that the method of multiple correlation

> is one neither of discovery nor of criticism. It is a means of giving quantitative precision to what, in qualitative terms, *we know already as the result of a complete theoretical analysis* – provided always that it is a case where the other considerations ... are satisfied.   (Keynes (1939), p. 560; my italics)

Keynes, like so many economists, was unwilling to concede to econometricians any role in developing theory and regarded the measurement

Morgan (1987)). In addition, following his debate with Keynes, Tinbergen was invited by the editors of the *Review of Economic Studies*, to give further explanations of his method. In the resulting article (1940), Tinbergen explained at greater length many of the points which contemporaries had found difficult to understand.

[20] Tinbergen's arrow schemes and discussion indicate he thought in terms of recursive models, but as the equation on p. 118 above shows, his systems could not always be reduced to one single difference equation, suggesting non-recursiveness of some parts of the system. To discuss the topic in these terms is to leap ahead to the later 1940s when the idea of recursiveness was proposed by Wold as an alternative to the simultaneous equations model of Haavelmo (see Chapter 7, Letters 12 and 14).

of already known theories as their only task.[21] Because Keynes 'knew' his theoretical model to be correct, logically, econometric methods could not conceivably prove such theories to be incorrect. Therefore, if a theory was not confirmed by the applied work, then the reason according to Keynes' position must be that the conditions necessary for econometric measurement, as laid out by Keynes (and referred to above), had not been met. More crudely stated, this common argument runs: if the results are not in accordance with theoretical preconceptions, then blame the method and the data but not the theory (an argument reminiscent of the proverb: a bad workman blames his tools, and in this case his raw materials as well).

Keynes had rejected the possibility that econometrics could be innovative about theory or claim to test theory, and regarded Tinbergen's work as 'a piece of historical curve-fitting and description' (Keynes (1939), p. 566). So when Keynes criticised Tinbergen for his lack of inductive claims, it was for lack of foretelling the future. But, Tinbergen had, as a matter of course, forecast two periods ahead with many of his equations as a test of the model. Keynes had also warned, quite correctly, that in order to forecast from the model, the periods must be homogeneous and recommended Tinbergen to investigate this matter by testing the model on different subperiods of the data series. Again, this is precisely what Tinbergen had done, and had found evidence of changes in structure in his comparison of the regression coefficients! Tinbergen believed that changes in structure did not necessarily invalidate the usefulness of the whole model since the changes might be localised or might be subject to estimation. Alternatively, the changes might be in the values of variables rather than in the functions themselves. In any case, he thought that the more interesting problems were the variation problems (tracing the effect of alternative policy changes) rather than the problem of short-term forecasting.

Tinbergen, in his reply to Keynes, defended the wider inductive claims that he made for his own work. For Tinbergen, econometrics was concerned both with discovery and criticism, as should be clear from the discussion of this chapter. He believed, contrary to Keynes, that if the theory was not confirmed by the results, then the inference was that the theory was wrong or insufficient. Thus, for example, statistical work might result in the introduction of new variables, or

[21] Tinbergen has a delightful example of this attitude in which Keynes 'knew' the numerical value of the parameter in his theory. I have not discussed details of the model content in this account, but Neil de Marchi points out that one of the reasons Tinbergen found Keynes' comments peculiar was that he was influenced by Keynes' macroeconomic ideas. On both points, again, see Magnus and Morgan (1987).

forms of variables, not previously considered as important by theory. Theory might also be criticised by statistical evidence, if, for example, little or no influence was found in the regression relationship for a variable considered important in the theory. It is clear that Tinbergen saw econometrics as a way of evaluating different theories; a much wider frame than that viewed by Keynes.

There was another very important criticism of Tinbergen's first report not published at the time though it was distributed in mimeographed form: this was a memorandum written by Frisch for a conference held in 1938 to consider Tinbergen's first League of Nations' volume.[22] Frisch's memorandum discussed the relationship between the economic relations of theory and those obtained by fitting curves to data. He suspected that there was a considerable gap between Tinbergen's applied results and economic theory, due to a large measure of arbitrariness in the solutions to his final equations. Frisch argued that in finding the component solutions of time-series data, the values found for amplitudes and timing of phases were only relative; they were fixed absolutely only by the initial conditions. A further element of arbitrariness was due to the model chosen: different choices of lags, for example, would give different solutions. In general, the solutions were not unique and different equations could give the same solutions. Those equations which were not 'reducible' (that is, those equations with the lowest element of arbitrariness) for the system as a whole were the only ones which could actually be discovered from the data.

Unfortunately, according to Frisch, these 'coflux' (irreducible) equations often had a low degree of 'autonomy'. Autonomy is a concept concerned with economic behaviour and theory: relations with a high degree of autonomy were defined as ones which remain unchanged when other relations alter. There is thus a sort of 'super-structure' in the economy consisting of those relations with a high degree of autonomy. These relationships are more fundamental and give deeper insights into the behaviour of the economic system than ones of low autonomy. If they can be found, they are closest to being a 'real explanation' of the economy. Frisch gave the following example to illustrate his concept:

[22] Although both volumes were officially published by the League of Nations in 1939, the first volume was circulated in advance in 1938 and evaluated at a special conference in Cambridge (England) in July of that year. Neither Keynes nor Frisch attended this meeting but Frisch produced a written critique which arrived after the event. This memorandum, Frisch (1938) (to be published for the first time in Hendry and Morgan (forthcoming)) gave a new stimulus to the work on identification by Koopmans and others at the Cowles Commission in the 1940s (see Epstein (1987)), and was crucial in the development of the concept of structural relations which is my concern here (and see Aldrich (1989)).

> The coflux relations that can be determined by observation of the actual time shapes may or may not come near to resembling an autonomous relation, that depends on the general constitution of the phenomena studied. To give two extreme examples: the demand function for a consumers commodity as depending on price and income and perhaps on some secondary variables will, if the coefficients can be determined with any degree of accuracy, come fairly near to being an autonomous relation. It will not be much changed by a change in monetary policy, in the organisation of production etc. But the time relation between the Harvard A, B, and C curves is a pure coflux relation, with only a small degree of autonomy.
>
> (Frisch (1938), p. 17)

Frisch accused Tinbergen of finding only coflux equations, which could not be used to refute theory since they did not necessarily express the autonomous structural system which was equivalent to theory.

Tinbergen, in immediate reply to the 'Autonomy' Memorandum, interpreted Frisch's criticisms as being concerned with multicollinearity. It is important to note that this term had been earlier defined by Frisch to mean the existence of linear dependence between variables (including the explanatory variables of an equation), other than the relationship of interest. Multicollinearity could also therefore in Frisch's definition denote identification problems; and indeed in the 1930s these concepts were not separate but interlinked principally because of Frisch's work on confluent relationships. For example, in the context of business cycle work, multicollinearity might mean that the structural relationships were obscured by parallel cyclical movements in all the variables. Tinbergen interpreted Frisch's view of the problem as being that

> all business cycle curves are more or less sines or waves, and that therefore the danger of multicollinearity is permanently present,
>
> (Tinbergen, 1938, see Frisch (1938/48), p. 20)

and argued that in this case, bearing in mind his model, parallel data series were not particularly a problem.

In a further response to Frisch (at the beginning of his second report to the League), Tinbergen pointed out that he had started out from theoretical relationships, and the individual equations he estimated reflected the direct causes (rather than the secondary causes). He believed this would give his relationships the maximum degree of autonomy, that is,

> relations which are as little as possible affected by structural changes in the departments of economic life other than the one they belong to.
>
> (Tinbergen (1939), II, p. 14)

He thought that his relationships would have high autonomy compared to the observed A-B-C relationships found by the Harvard method. Further, Tinbergen argued that the use of economic theory put a constraint on the choice of lags, reducing the danger of arbitrary solutions. So, although Tinbergen took note of Frisch's criticisms in his second report, he did not view them as seriously undermining his work on the US model.

Because of the controversial reception accorded to the first report, there was some anxiety at the League of Nations about publishing the second. In fact, Tinbergen's second volume received less critical attention, possibly because its publication was overtaken by the outbreak of war. The most critical of these reviews was by Freidman (1940), who also discussed the issue of testing. He complained that no statistical tests had been carried out, and that none could be, because the estimated equations were all the result of correlation hunting (using trial and error to obtain high values of the multiple correlation coefficient). Friedman went on to quote Mitchell in support of his view that the only way to test such an empirically derived model was to see how it performed on other data sets. (At this point, it must be remembered that Friedman was reviewing the second report, and that it was in his first report that Tinbergen had tested his model on other time periods and on data from other countries.) Friedman himself experimented in this direction by using Tinbergen's final equation to forecast five years ahead. He described the result as 'unimpressive' ($R^2 = .68$ between actual and forecast amounts) but the cyclical pattern was reasonably good.

Friedman's closing statement was that

> The methods used by Tinbergen do not and cannot provide an empirically tested explanation of business cycle movements. His methods are entirely appropriate, however, for deriving tentative hypotheses about the nature of cyclical behavior; and from this viewpoint students of business cycles may find Tinbergen's volume of considerable interest.
>
> (Friedman (1940), p. 660)

Tinbergen had provided a statistically verified explanation of the business cycles in the US for a particular period and had checked to see that the model would generate cycles in the absence of shocks. He had not made a test of the model against new data, so Friedman's judgement is justified. But, Friedman, unlike Keynes, was willing to see Tinbergen's work as a useful source of further theorising.

A more technical criticism was advanced by Haavelmo (1940).[23] In

---

[23] A further technical problem was pinpointed by Orcutt (1948) who argued that Tinbergen had a serious problem of autocorrelation in the data used for his US model. This criticism

this paper he dealt only with the final testing stage of Tinbergen's work and criticised him (and others) for neglecting the effect of the errors in determining the time path of the system. He showed that it was possible for a system of equations with a non-cyclical solution to explain observed cycle movements once the effects of the errors were taken into account. (This was a reminder of Slutsky's result that cycles can occur solely through the summation of random error terms.) It therefore followed, according to Haavelmo's work, that a cyclical solution to the economic system part of a business cycle model could not be taken as test of adequacy for business cycle models, as both Frisch and Tinbergen had proposed. This, of course, was a serious problem for Tinbergen's testing programme, but, like Keynes' criticisms, Haavelmo's observations had little effect on the practice of econometrics in this case because the business cycle programme of study was near its end, at least for the time being.

Tinbergen's work had aroused strong criticism, but he also had many staunch supporters who joined in the debate about the role of econometrics. Some, like Allen (1940), used their own reviews of Tinbergen's League of Nations reports to defend him. Marschak and Lange (1940) wrote a stronger reply than Tinbergen's for the *Economic Journal*, but it was not published at the time.[24] Particularly important is Haavelmo's (1943) response to the critique of Keynes. This paper provided a highly articulate discussion of the role of econometrics in testing theory. Haavelmo defended the econometric approach (and Tinbergen's work) but he also wanted to insinuate probability theory as the essential missing component which would make the approach fruitful. (This had not, by any means, been thought a necessity by econometricians, as we shall see later.) Haavelmo stated:

> When we speak of testing theories against actual observations we evidently think of only those theories that, perhaps through a long chain of logical operations and additional hypotheses, lead to *a priori statements about facts*. A test, then, means simply to take the data about which the a priori statement is made, and to see whether the statement is true or false.
>
> Suppose the statement turns out to be true. What can we then say about the theory itself? We can say that the facts observed do not give any reason for rejecting the theory. But we might reject the theory on the basis of other facts or on other grounds. Suppose, on the other hand, that the

---

marks the start of new developments, which are not treated in the present study, but see Gilbert (1988).

24 Keynes, as editor of the journal, perhaps felt enough had already been said. The paper is available in Marschak's papers, (UCLA Special Archive Collection), and is to be published in Hendry and Morgan (forthcoming).

statement turns out to be wrong. What we can then say about the theory depends on the characteristics of the theory and the type of a priori statement it makes about the facts.   (Haavelmo (1943), pp. 14–15)

For example, Haavelmo argued, no economist would work with a theory which implied that next year's national income would be exactly $X million, since this theory would always be rejected. That is,

> If the statement deduced is assumed to be one of necessity, we would reject the theory when the facts contradict the statement. But if the statement is only supposed to be true 'almost always,' the possibility of maintaining the theory would still be there . . . If the statement is verified, should we accept the theory as true? Not necessarily, because the same statement might usually be deduced from many different constructions. What we can say is that an eventual rejection of the theory would require further tests against additional facts, or the testing of a different statement deduced from the same theory. Each test that is a success for a theory increases our confidence in that theory for further use.
>
> (Haavelmo (1943), p. 15)

Haavelmo's position had two implications. One was that, in answer to Keynes, simple models were legitimate, since if the

> simplified theory also covers the facts, the discovery is an addition to our knowledge   (Haavelmo (1943), p. 15)

and might provide constraints additional to a priori knowledge. The second implication was that a stochastic formulation was necessary for workable and fruitful econometrics because otherwise inference would mean that we would either always reject a theory or never reject a theory, depending on whether it was sharply or broadly specified. Haavelmo clearly differentiated Tinbergen's pioneering macroeconometric models from previous statistical work on business cycles and approved of his work. But he criticised him for not going far enough in his use of statistical reasoning to warrant the description of 'deriving relations with "inductive claims" ' (as Keynes had described the aim) versus the alternative of 'historical curve fitting' (Haavelmo (1943), p. 17). The proper formulation of the problem required to assess these inductive claims was still lacking in econometrics. That was the role, Haavelmo argued, of probability theory. This important development is discussed in Chapter 8.

Abstracting from the immediate debate enables us to evaluate Tinbergen's achievements and put them into perspective. When the work of Tinbergen is compared to that of Mitchell, Persons, Jevons and Moore, it is clear that there had been real advances in the quantitative treatment of the business cycle. First, like Moore, Tinbergen relied on quantitative theory, but he had the advantage of Frisch's general mathematical model designed especially for business cycles. Tinbergen used this model to develop complex multi-equation econometric models to represent the cycles of the whole economic system.[25] In the process of building and using his models, Tinbergen increased econometricians' understanding of the nature and properties of econometric models and of associated concepts such as the structure of the system and causal chain models. Second, this was not a period of technical progress in statistical techniques. Correlation and regression analysis (in various guises) were still the main analytical methods; but a comparison points up the greater skill and finesse in Tinbergen's econometric work compared to that of Moore. His development of testing procedures for theory evaluation entailed a broadening in scope and clarification of purpose rather than the introduction of new techniques. Tinbergen's contributions to econometrics came through his practical work: he developed best practice for applied econometrics, and he deepened econometricians' understanding of their approach to economics.

[25] In this context, we should note that Tinbergen's models are generally regarded as the first macroeconometric models. This is undoubtedly correct, but to see them only in this light is to ignore the general structure of his models (and particularly his concern with dynamics) and the historical and theoretical business cycle context from which they sprang. Tinbergen's models owed more to the development of dynamic cycle theory, both by the econometricians themselves (and particularly Frisch's shock model) and by the Stockholm school of economists (for the development of sequence analysis), than it did to the development of macroeconomic theory. Conventional accounts of the development of macroeconomic theory and data in the 1930s often neglect the business cycle theory context from which they emerged and ignore econometrics entirely. Patinkin (1976), for example, concentrates on the advent of national income accounting (for which, see Kendrick (1970)) and Keynesian macroeconomics as the two great achievements of interwar economics. The renewed interest in business cycles may lead to some revision of this view (see, for example, Lucas (1980) whose brief historical account supports my view of the importance of Tinbergen). We should also note that it was for developing and applying macrodynamic models that Tinbergen and Frisch were awarded the first Nobel Memorial Prize in Economics in 1969.

Part II

Demand analysis

Introduction to demand analysis

The idea that price varies negatively with quantity demanded and positively with quantity supplied is a long-established one, although Hutchison (1953) has suggested that classical economists' ideas on supply and demand schedules were neither well defined nor consistent. Nevertheless, or perhaps because of this fuzziness, the desire to make economics more scientific (both to express the theories more exactly and to provide a stronger empirically based knowledge) found expression particularly early in the field of demand. It was one of the first areas of economic theory to receive graphical and mathematical representation. This is generally believed to have been at the hands of Cournot in 1838, although his contributions to the development of economics were not appreciated until later in the century.[1] The Victorian polymath Fleeming Jenkin developed the mathematical and geometric treatment of demand and supply further in a series of articles between 1868 and 1871.[2] He even included variables to represent the other factors which cause the demand curve to shift back and forth. Although the use of mathematics was resisted at the time, it gradually became more acceptable since graphs and equations were good media in which to display the new 'marginal' theory.

The 'marginal revolution' of the 1870s is usually portrayed as changing the basis of the theory of value from the classical concentration on the production side to a new analysis based on the individual consumer. Blaug (1968) has described how this theory developed along two paths corresponding to the ideas of Marshall and Walras. Walras

---

[1] Antoine Augustin Cournot (1801–77) was regarded by the early twentieth-century econometricians as one of the founders of their movement, particularly for his use of mathematical analysis in economic theory. He was the subject of an article in the first issue of *Econometrica* and a special session in honour of the centenary of the publication of his book was held at the December 1937 meeting of the Econometric Society.

[2] Fleeming Jenkin was a notable engineer (specialising in bridges) who made contributions to literary and dramatic criticism as well as publishing five papers in economics. His work has been reassessed by Brownlie and Prichard (1963).

followed Cournot's earlier work and used quantity as the dependent variable. He represented the price/quantity relationship as the quantity demanded or supplied for a given price (other things held constant) and the adjustment to disequilibrium in the market was made by a change in prices. Marshall, on the other hand, switched the determining factor in the system and characterised price as the dependent variable. His system was based on the price consumers and sellers were willing to pay or accept for a given quantity and adjustment to disequilibrium was made on the quantity side. Their formalisation of demand theory provided models to which both mathematical reasoning and statistical evidence could be easily applied.

Cournot and Jevons had both believed that numerical laws of demand could be empirically determined. Jenkin had also discussed the possibility of experimentally determining the laws of demand and supply from year to year variations in prices and quantities. Yet none of these three had tried their hands at such work, although as G.J. Stigler (1954) notes, other economists had begun to do so by the 1870s. At the end of the nineteenth century, J. N. Keynes was still optimistic about the possibility of successfully measuring demand schedules, but he was not unaware of the problems econometricians would have to face in matching theory to measurements. Keynes described these difficulties, with help from Cournot:

> With improved statistics of consumption, towards which valuable contributions might be afforded by shopkeepers' books and the great co-operative stores, it might be possible to draw up empirical demand-schedules representing approximately the actual variation of demand with price for certain commodities in general use. As Cournot remarks: 'If we suppose the conditions of demand to remain the same, but the conditions of production to change, because the expenses of production are raised or lowered,... then prices will vary, and corresponding variations in demand will give us our empirical tables'. (*Principes de la Théories des Richesses*, § 56). But, as is also recognised by Cournot, the conditions of demand rarely do remain the same for any considerable length of time. There are constantly in progress independent changes, such as changes in fashions and habits, in the purchasing power of money, in the wealth and circumstances of consumers, and the like, which cause the demand at a given price itself to vary. Since therefore the statistical calculation would have to cover a more or less prolonged period of time, it would always be liable to be vitiated by the effects of such changes as the above, except in so far as these effects could themselves be estimated and allowed for.   (In Palgrave (1894–8), I, pp. 540–1)

It was some while before econometricians fully understood how to deal with the difficulties foreseen by Cournot and so clearly stated by Keynes.

Early statistical demand analysis started with a strong body of generally agreed theory, and the perceived role of econometrics was to measure the laws of demand and find the numerical parameters of these relationships. This is in complete contrast to the statistical analysis of business cycles, where much of the early work concentrated on defining and isolating the cycle in the data. The presence of many cycle theories was associated with the development of many different models of the cycle and different approaches to cycle analysis; and this ultimately led to the exploration of important issues of theory testing in econometrics. The general agreement on theory in the case of demand was associated with less diversity in statistical approach and revealed a different set of problems. These problems of correspondence, or the matching of measured relationships to theoretical models, are dealt with in two chapters. Chapter 5 deals with the attempts to reconcile the requirements of theory with the conditions under which the data had been collected. This interaction between theoretical models of demand and their measured counterparts stimulated considerable developments in econometric modelling. Chapter 6 is concerned with another area of correspondence, namely the ability to identify an empirical relationship as a demand curve rather than some other relationship. This entailed both the isolation of identification as a separate problem from other correspondence problems and its solution.

CHAPTER 5

Narrowing the data-theory gap in demand analysis

The first attempt at measuring a demand function was probably by Charles Davenant in 1699 (but generally attributed as Gregory King's Law) and consisted of a simple schedule of prices and quantities of wheat. By the late nineteenth century, simple comparisons had given way to mathematical formulations of such demand laws. For example, Aldrich (1987) discussed how Jevons (1871) fitted 'by inspection' an inverse quadratic function to the six data points of Gregory King's Law. Wicksteed (1889) disagreed with Jevons' function and found that a cubic equation fitted the data exactly.[1] Although this sort of function fitting was possible with six data points, it was obviously inappropriate for large data sets, and by the beginning of the twentieth century investigators had turned to the field of statistics for help in measuring demand relationships.

It quickly became clear that simply applying statistical methods to the price and quantity data did not necessarily lead to sensible results and the work of econometricians in the first two decades of the twentieth century reveals both insight and confusion about why this should be so, as we shall see in the first section of the chapter. The ways in which econometricians formulated the difficulties they faced and then tried to solve them first by adjusting their data and then by developing more complex econometric models of demand are discussed in the following two sections. Other aspects of the difficulties raised in this early work are held over for discussion until Chapter 6.

5.1   Difficulties in early statistical measurements of demand

Statistical methods were initially used in demand analysis to organise observations and reduce them to manageable form. Methods such as averaging, ranking and taking mean deviations of the data were applied

---

[1] Wicksteed (1889) used a trial and error method but his cubic equation was 'confirmed' by a correspondent using the 'method of differences'.

before comparing price and quantity data series to find their relationship. Such methods are illustrated by the work, again on harvest data, of Engel in 1861 and Laspeyres in 1875; both discussed by G. J. Stigler (1954). A. B. and H. Farquhar (1891) were marginally more sophisticated in their attempts to confirm the simple price–quantity demand relationship; they standardised their data for changes in population and then compared year to year changes (both in absolute terms and in percentages). Much of this early work in the field has been admirably surveyed, from the point of view of the history of economic thought, by G. J. Stigler (1954), but his analysis terminates at around 1914, precisely the point where a number of very interesting econometric problems had been raised.

The development of correlation analysis in biometrics in the late nineteenth century by Galton and Karl Pearson had yielded a new measure which proved very used for econometricians.[2] The correlation coefficient both averaged the data and provided a single simple measure of the strength of a relationship. Correlation analysis was applied to economic time series in the early twentieth century in the search for statistical relationships in economics. As Chapter 2 showed, by 1920 it was a commonly used tool in trade cycle research; but it was also used in the early work on demand. In his 1905 paper Hooker, working with price and quantity data for maize, correlated the mean deviations of their levels and found a low correlation coefficient of $-.28$. Plotting each series against time, he observed that there were no strong secular (long-term) movements similar to both series, but that short-term movements appeared to be connected. So he correlated first differences of the data and found a high correlation coefficient of $-.84$. Hooker suggested that this higher correlation coefficient gave an indication of a causal relationship between the two series. It is interesting to note Hooker's confusion between correlation coefficients as a measure of the strength of an empirical relationship and a high coefficient as being indicative of a causal relationship. He was influenced in this by Bowley who, in his statistics textbook of 1901, had suggested that if the correlation coefficient were more than six times the probable error of the coefficient, then a causal connection between the two data series might be inferred.[3]

---

[2] The development of correlation and regression analysis in the context of genetics is described by Mackenzie (1981). For more general accounts, see the references given in the Introduction.

[3] Bowley's causality condition (p.320 in his textbook) was, if: $r > 6 \{ 0.67 \ (1-r^2)/n \}$ then causality exists. The question as to whether correlation and related measurements are only measures of association or can also be taken as indicators of causality is a long-running debate. In econometrics, King (1917) gave an early view in the argument which goes

Correlation provided a more systematic way of relating two data series than the simple comparisons or function fitting of the earlier years. In its turn, correlation gave way to more sophisticated curve fitting methods such as least squares regression. In the context of demand studies, this raised an immediate problem of which regression to choose: the regression of quantity on price or price on quantity? The problem of regression choice was treated in Edvard Mackeprang's doctoral thesis (1906).[4] Mackeprang carried out a substantial amount of statistical work in demand, for example, estimating the demand for sugar in nineteenth-century Britain. He failed to find an adequate answer to his initial question of which regression to use, and ended up computing and using both. In another example, Persons (1910) (the inventor of the Harvard Business Barometer, discussed in Chapter 2) took Hooker's work on maize data a step further by calculating both the regression equations. Thereafter, two different solutions to the problem of regression choice developed, characterised here as the 'statistical' and the 'economic'.

One solution to the regression choice question was based on the presence of measurement errors in the data, a situation in which the application of statistical reasoning was generally accepted. If there were measurement errors only in price data, then the appropriate regression to choose for statistical purposes was one in which these errors were minimised by regressing price on quantity. The presence of measurement errors in both price and quantity variables presented a more difficult problem. The solution to regression choice in this case was the subject of considerable discussion in econometrics in the 1930s and is discussed at more length in Chapters 7 and 8.

Most early econometricians unconsciously adopted an economic theory decision rule in their choice of regression: their choice of economic theory dictated which regression they used. In a brief review of the status of demand theory given earlier, it was suggested that there were two alternative economic models which applied workers could adopt: either quantity was dependent on some given price, or price was dependent on some given quantity. These models were characterised as Walrasian and Marshallian models respectively. Such characterisations involved considerable simplification and distortion of the original theories, nevertheless, they were the sort of

through to more sophisticated recent work on the subject of causality tests. Some of the arguments are discussed further in Part III and see Cartwright (1989).

[4] Edvard P. Mackeprang (1877–1933), a Dane who studied economics and statistics and worked in the insurance business. He failed to obtain a university position, but continued his econometric work which is discussed in Wold (1969a) and at greater length in Kærgaard (1984).

models actually used in early applied work since they could be translated directly into simple regression equations with one or two independent variables. (The time-consuming nature of doing least squares regressions by hand, or later by simple mechanical calculator, was the primary reason for the very small number of variables handled.[5]) A third model in which price and quantity are jointly determined was more complex and it did not prove so easy to translate this into a simple regression model.

G. J. Stigler's (1954) survey shows that in the first decade of this century, Benini and Gini both adopted the Walrasian model. Benini in 1907 estimated the demand for coffee while Gini in 1910 estimated demand functions for a number of goods using a semi-log function borrowed from psychophysics known as the Weber–Fechner law:

$$Q = a + b \log P$$

where P was termed the 'stimulus' and Q the 'response' term.[6] Both Benini and Gini used estimation techniques based on averaging of groups of data rather than the least squares method. Early users of the Marshallian model included J. M. Clark (1913) who estimated the demand for gold (also using non-least squares regression) and Henry Ludwell Moore (1914), who calculated a number of different equations for the demand for agricultural goods as part of his work on economic cycles.[7]

Applied work carried out using these simple models and methods was generally thought successful. But the criteria for success in applied work were rather weak, economic-theoretic, rules rather than statistical ones. These rules involved some idea of 'reasonableness'. Initially this meant simply: is the estimated demand parameter negative and does it have a reasonable value? If the answers were yes, then the inference was that the 'true' demand curve had been found. The problem of measuring demand curves was actually more complex, as quickly emerged in work by Moore, Marcel Lenoir and Robert Lehfeldt in the years 1913–14.

Along with his 'successful' (by the economic-theoretic criteria) work on agricultural goods, Moore (1914) estimated the demand curve for

[5] Some papers in the statistics literature were solely concerned with providing computation methods. The development of graphic methods of correlation in the 1920s was initially to deal with non-linear demand functions (Ezekiel (1924)), but later versions (e.g. Bean (1929)) were proposed to short-cut the standard methods of calculating correlation and regression coefficients. Certain times are given for calculating regression equations; Bean (1929) suggests eight hours for a four-variable multiple regression.

[6] This law was well known in psychology as one of the earliest empirical laws derived from statistical tests in the 1860s (see the discussion in the Introduction).

[7] Moore and his cycle work are discussed in Chapter 1.2.

pig-iron (raw steel). He claimed to have found a brand new type of demand curve, namely the positively sloped demand curve applicable to all producer goods. Moore believed that econometrics could be used to derive new theoretical laws from empirical results, as well as to find numerical parameters for existing economic laws. This perhaps accounts for his interpretation of the positive demand curve as a new law. But his contemporaries thought the positive demand curve sufficiently 'unreasonable' to reject it. A critical review by Lehfeldt (1915) suggested that Moore had estimated a supply curve for pig-iron because the data indicated a moving demand curve (due to the business cycle) and a relatively stable supply curve; and P. G. Wright (1915) demonstrated the same point using a graph. Judged by the economic criteria, Moore's positive demand curve was unacceptable. This, perhaps even more than his Venus theory of the business cycle, devalued Moore's real contributions to econometrics in the eyes of his contemporaries (see G. J. Stigler (1962)).

At the same time that Moore advanced the positive demand curve, the more complicated model involving demand and supply relationships was brought into use in econometrics. Although the underlying model involved two relationships between price and quantity, only one of them was estimated. In a little known doctoral thesis in French, Marcel Lenoir (1913) discussed demand and supply factors and showed how the dominance of supply or demand influences in a particular market would dictate whether an estimated relationship was the supply or the demand curve.[8] He drew diagrams with shifting demand and supply curves to illustrate this point. He analysed the markets for four goods: coal, corn, cotton and coffee. The statistical relationships between their prices and quantities (production/consumption) were examined and cyclical or trending factors (in the form of indices of prices and consumption and the quantity of money) were also introduced into the correlation analysis. In addition, he computed regression equations, such as a demand equation for coffee using quantity as the dependent variable and including a linear time trend.

Robert Lehfeldt (1914) was another economist who tried to deal with interdependent supply and demand relationships.[9] Although his short

---

[8] Little is known about Marcel Lenoir, whose promising career as an econometrician was cut short by his death in the First World War, see Marchal (1952). A short part of his thesis will appear in translation in Hendry and Morgan (forthcoming) and see further discussion in Chapter 6.1.

[9] Robert A. Lehfeldt (1868–1927) was initially a physicist, holding positions as Professor of Physics at Sheffield and later at the South African School of Mines and Technology. He then turned to economics and from 1917 was Professor of Economics at the University of Witwatersrand.

paper, 'The Elasticity of Demand for Wheat', contained little formal theory compared to Lenoir's, it is worth describing in some detail. Lehfeldt proposed to measure the elasticity of demand for wheat and believed that if he could find the quantity supplied under constant demand conditions, then movements in the supply curve would trace out points along the constant demand curve. To achieve a constant demand curve he corrected the quantity figures for changes in demand due to population growth, by standardising his quantity data for 1888–1911 to a static 1900 population level. He then considered the possibility that the demand curve shifts (for which he had already corrected) were not parallel due to changes in taste, quality of the wheat or the prices of other goods. He tested out these three possibilities and made the necessary corrections to the data. Finally he analysed the timing of the relationship between the changes in quantities and prices by looking at the correlation coefficients between differing lagged values of his adjusted data. He chose the highest valued coefficient which was the correlation between prices and quantities lagged one year. Only then did Lehfeldt consider whether this measured demand relationship was valid in terms of economic theory and he concluded that it was reasonable for the harvest of wheat one year to determine the prices paid by consumers for wheat in the following year.

Lenoir and Lehfeldt showed a deeper understanding of the problems of relating data to theory than Moore with his controversial positive demand curve. Lehfeldt was perhaps the first econometrician seriously to test that the assumptions made in the theoretical demand model were actually fulfilled in the statistical data. He grappled with the problem of interdependence of supply and demand with considerable success. Lenoir used a more formal analysis to deal with the same problem. He considered which model (the demand or the supply) would occur empirically for different types of goods. He chose his model, based on this theoretical and statistical analysis, before estimating the relationship. Moore's approach was a mixture. At its worst, it involved both the unthinking application of theory to data and the adoption of empirically derived relationships without reference to theory. Though Moore's boldness and imagination were sometimes regrettable, they were also the qualities which made him a true pioneer of econometrics.

The work of all three taken together, Lehfeldt, Lenoir and Moore, had exposed a number of problems in the econometric treatment of demand curves. First, in dealing with an interdependent system of demand and supply, both demand and supply curves were likely to be shifting backwards and fowards over time. To estimate one of the parameters, it was necessary to pre-adjust the data in such a way that one of the two curves was stable. This in itself introduced a number of questions: why were the curves shifting, how could the shifts be measured and how could the data be preadjusted to remove them? Secondly, Moore's positive demand curve had demonstrated that a simple single-equation model for demand could equally well describe a supply curve; there was a need to differentiate the economic theory models being used. Thirdly, the critical reaction to Moore's work had illustrated that if the economy generated data from a fixed supply and moving demand curve, then, at most, only information on the supply parameter could be gleaned from the data and nothing could ever be learnt about the demand parameter. These problems were exacerbated by the lack of adequate criteria to judge applied results. The success criteria which allowed a 'reasonable' parameter estimate to be accepted as a 'true' parameter were sufficient to judge that Moore's positive demand curve was 'wrong', but they were not sensitive enough to differentiate between different 'reasonable' estimates of the 'true' parameter. Finally, there was the additional, but generally worrisome, problem of measurement errors in the data, on which more will be said in Part III of this book.

Whereas in modern econometrics these problems are separated out and dealt with individually, this was by no means true in the 1920s and early 1930s when these issues were seen either as a set of overlapping problems or even lumped together into one subsuming problem of a mismatch between theory and data. So much so, that by the late 1920s some econometricians began to view statistical demand curves as only 'approximations' to the 'true' demand curve. These approximations were thought to be good enough for policy and forecasting purposes even if they were not the 'true' curves.[10] Econometricians' attempts to solve the questions raised in their demand analysis can be broadly divided into two parts. Efforts to develop a better match between theory and data concentrated on reducing the gap by making adjustments to both; the rest of this chapter deals with these developments. A second area of problem solving was concerned with whether a demand relationship could be estimated, given the data available; such issues of identification are dealt with in Chapter 6.

5.2 Static theory and time-series data

Econometricians were interested in measuring the elasticity of demand for various goods but were faced with a basic conflict between theory and data. Demand theory was concerned with a static relationship

[10] See, for example, the discussions in E. J. Working (1927), P. G. Wright (1929) and Gilboy (1930).

under *ceteris paribus* conditions whereas the data available were single point realisations of demand and supply interactions over a long time period, when other things were not constant.[11] Moore stated the problem thus:

> Two fundamental defects in the current theoretical method of treating economic questions are exemplified in the case of the theory of demand: first, the assumption is made that *all other things being equal* (the old *cæteris paribus*) ... The 'other things' that are supposed to remain equal are seldom mentioned and are never completely enumerated; and consequently the assumption that, other unmentioned and unenumerated factors remaining constant, the law of demand will be of a certain type, is really tantamount to saying that under conditions which are unanalyzed and unknown, the law of demand will take the supposed definite form.
>
> (Moore (1914), p. 66)

The *ceteris paribus* conditions were not the only problem as far as Moore was concerned; demand theory also came complete with a defective 'static' method:

> According to the statical method, the method of *cæteris paribus*, the proper course to follow in the explanation of the phenomenon is to investigate in turn, theoretically, the effect upon price of each factor, *cæteris paribus*, and then finally to make a synthesis! But if in case of the relation of each factor to price the assumption *cæteris paribus* involves large and at least questionable hypotheses, does one not completely lose himself in a maze of implicit hypotheses when he speaks of a final synthesis of the several effects? We shall not adopt this bewildering method, but shall follow the opposite course and attack the problem of the relation of prices and supply in its full concreteness.
>
> The fruitfulness of the statistical theory of correlation stands in significant contrast to the vast barrenness of the method that has just been described, and the two methods follow opposed courses in dealing with the problem of multiple effects. Take, for example, the question of the effects of weather upon crops. What a useless bit of speculation it would be to try to solve, in a hypothetical way, the question as to the effect of rainfall upon the crops, other unenumerated elements of the weather remaining constant? The question as to the effect of temperature, *cæteris paribus*? How, finally, would a synthesis be made of the several individual effects? The statistical method of multiple correlation formulates no such vain questions. It inquires, directly, what is the relation between crop and rainfall, not *cæteris paribus*, but other things changing according to their natural order.
>
> (Moore (1914), pp. 66–7)

---

[11] The additional gap between the *ex ante* concept embodied in theory and the *ex post* nature of the data was rarely considered at this time, although Gilboy (1930) did perceive that the distinction has implications for measuring demand curves.

Moore's strident rejection of the standard method was somewhat premature, if only because early econometricians could not necessarily cope with all the other changing factors in one multiple regression.

Somehow, econometricians needed to make the theory and the data compatible so that the statistical curve would correspond with the true demand curve. The most important point of difference between theory and data was perceived to be the element of time. Initially applied workers dealt with time by trying to eliminate its effects from the data before measuring the elasticity. They believed that by eliminating certain effects (influences) which changed over time, they could estimate the static demand curve which corresponded to economic theory. Simple methods of data adjustment gradually gave way to more complex methods which involved the measurement and removal of time trends from the data.

In the early twentieth century, statisticians with no particular economic models in mind had experimented with economic time-series data, in order to find out what sort of data adjustments removed what sort of time components from the data. For example, Hooker (in 1901 and 1905) experimented with time-series data to try and separate out long-term secular movements, periodic movements and short-term oscillations. He also advocated the methods of measuring deviations from a moving average trend to remove the effects of periodic (cyclical) movements. Persons (1910) suggested the removal of short- or long-term influences by taking first differences of the data or by fitting a mathematical function or 'growth curve' to the data and taking deviations of the observations from this trend. These methods were soon applied to isolate the business cycle component, as already discussed in Chapter 2.

Economists also applied these ideas in the context of their work on demand. Norton, in a study of the New York money market (1902), had fitted a growth curve by interpolation and taken deviations from it to remove long-term changes. Mackeprang had used data in logarithms of the deviations from a 5-year moving average trend for the same reason. Methods of data adjustment were popularised in econometrics by Moore to eliminate trend or cyclical disturbance factors which caused demand curves to shift over time. He discussed the need for the techniques in his 1914 book on cycles:

> The chief difficulties in the computation of statistical laws of demand are due to changes that occur in the market during the period to which the statistics of prices and quantities of commodities refer ... But in case of staple commodities, such as the agricultural products with which we shall have to deal, the effects of those changes in the condition of the market

that obscure the relation between prices and amounts of commodity may be largely eliminated. As far as the law of demand is concerned, the principal dynamic effects that need to be considered are changes in the volume of the commodity that arise from the increasing population, and changes in the level of prices which are the combined result of causes specifically responsible for price cycles and of causes that produce a secular trend in prices. The effects of these two fundamental changes may be eliminated approximately by a single statistical device.

(Moore (1914), pp. 68–9)

Moore's 'single statistical device' was the use of first differences (which he termed 'link relatives') of the data, measured either in percentage or absolute terms:

By taking the relative change in the amount of the commodity that is demanded, instead of the absolute quantities, the effects of increasing population are approximately eliminated; and by taking the relative change in the corresponding prices instead of the corresponding absolute prices, the errors due to a fluctuating general price level are partially removed. (Moore (1914), p. 69)

Later, Moore (1917 and 1922) applied alternative methods such as removing trends by taking 'trend ratios' (the ratios of prices and quantities to their trend values).

Moore's work in this area proved influential. His data adjustment methods (link relatives and trend ratios) were naturally used by his disciple Henry Schultz, but they were adopted by many other econometricians, particularly in agricultural economics. The price of this popularity was that the methods were sometimes used thoughtlessly. Later, Ferger (1932) showed that the methods were dangerous if used indiscriminately because they measured different phenomena and implied different models.[12] In a carefully constructed experiment using one set of price and quantity data, Ferger obtained correlation coefficients of opposite signs for the two different methods; the correlation of link relatives was positive, while the correlation of trend ratios was negative. He claimed this as proof that the methods implied different models; the use of link relatives modelled the relationship between changes in prices and changes in quantities, whereas trend ratios gave a model of the relative levels of prices and quantities. Ferger suggested that consumers' markets should be modelled using relative levels while dealers' or speculators' demand could be better modelled by using price changes or expected price changes (using past price changes as a measure) and quantity levels.

---

[12] In this case Ferger was repeating a point made by Irving Fisher (1925) in the context of business cycle measurement.

Economists also sought to remove the effects of specific trending variables rather than general cycles or trends. For example, both the Farquhars (1891) and Lehfeldt (1914) used per capita quantity data, equivalent to the removal of a population growth trend. In another early example, J. M. Clark (1913) adjusted his data for changing population and consumption standards by ascertaining a 'normal' growth curve, based on eight other commodities, and used the percentage differences between the actual and the 'normal' adjusted quantities. Whatever the level of sophistication, the basic idea behind all the methods was to pre-adjust the data in line with the *ceteris paribus* conditions of static demand theory in order to estimate the statistical equivalent of the theoretical demand law.

From the middle of the 1920s to the early 1930s the assumption that received economic theory was in some way immutable – and therefore that any adjustment towards making theory operational must be made on the data side – gradually gave way to the realisation that economic theory had little to say about dynamic elements such as the course of economic change and the timing of economic reactions. Econometricians began to think that if the 'true' demand curve were never constant, they should instead perhaps incorporate dynamic elements into their models and estimate the changing or 'dynamic demand law'. So they gradually switched from data adjustment to attempts to deal with the time element inside the estimation equation; first by using a time trend variable and then by incorporating into the relationship the specific variables which influenced demand over time and finally by dynamic modelling.

One of the first to discuss these ideas was an agricultural economist, B. B. Smith (1925), who suggested that the removal of disturbances by pre-adjustment of the data was a serious error. He advocated the inclusion of a time trend variable inside the estimation equation (rarely done up to this point, though Lenoir's use was an early example) in order to capture omitted independent variables and in order not to remove possible important trending influences. He wrote:

> Should these two, dependent and independent, series chance to have approximately similar trend or seasonal movements, and should these latter be extracted from the two series prior to their correlation, one might under the name of seasonal and trend extract much of the variation by which these two were related, and thus obscure their true relationship. The unconsidered practice of eliminating trend and seasonal from series prior to their correlation is to be looked upon askance, therefore. It is often a serious error.   (Smith (1925), p. 543)

Smith argued further, that leaving trend factors in the regression led to better fit and, he claimed, was less work:

correlation coefficients secured by *simul-*
methods will be as high or higher, and
from any possible sequence of *consecutive*
dependent factors from the dependent, of
ating seasonal variations *before* correlat-
ials of the two methods the writer has
tion for trend and seasonal regression
rs always gave markedly higher corre-
nsiderably less labor involved in the
raction of trend and seasonal from each
eliminated.[13]

(Smith (1925), p. 545)

ore's (1929) book, supported Smith's
ta was equivalent to throwing infor-

tistical Laws of Demand and Supply with
was also especially concerned about
the problem of dealing with time inside the model:

in order to bring the theory of consumption into closer agreement with the
facts of our experience it is necessary to show how the demand curve *moves*
– how it changes its position from time to time.   (Schultz (1928), p. 27)

He defined his statistical law of demand as:

$$P_1 = F(Q_1, P_2, \ldots, P_n, t)$$

(where t is a time trend) and believed that the important long-term
disturbing variables were not the other prices in his model but those
variables that t represented, such as population changes. He discussed
the desirability of dealing with disturbing variables within the equation
by multiple regression or by pre-adjustment of the data and concluded:

[13] Whether or not it took greater time to do a multiple regression compared to pre-adjusting
data depended on what sort of pre-adjustments were used and the number of variables in
the regression. For example, a trend fitted by least squares would require more work than
simply taking the link relatives.
[14] Henry Schultz (1893–1938) was born in Poland and educated in New York. He studied at
Columbia University with Mitchell and Moore and briefly at the London School of
Economics and Galton's laboratory. He joined the University at Chicago in 1926 and,
inspired by Moore's work, developed a research programme in the econometric analysis
of demand. Schultz used Moore's methods of data adjustments and some of his models, but
he was much more careful and pedestrian about his applied work. His 1928 book is an
extended version of his thesis on the demand for sugar, completed (and also published) in
1925. His best known book *The Theory and Measurement of Demand* (1938) was virtually an
encyclopaedia of the subject, covering demand theory and applied practice (and its
history), though the econometrics it contained were little changed from those of his 1928
book. See Christ (1985) for a survey of his econometric work.

> it would seem as if the method of multiple correlation were expressly
> invented for the purpose of deriving dynamic laws of demand.
>
> (Schultz (1928), p. 30)

Despite this statement, he decided that a time trend variable (t) could
be dealt with by using Moore's data adjustment methods just as
successfully as by multiple correlation.

One reason for the comparatively rare use of time trends in demand
equations of the 1920s was because econometricians were unsure of the
validity of such a technique in dealing with the *ceteris paribus* conditions.
The reason for using data adjustment techniques was to remove the
disturbing influences of other factors and find the 'true' constant demand
curve, but econometricians did not know whether the inclusion of time
trends in the equation had the same effect. Econometricians were also
unsure whether the estimated demand curves represented static or
dynamic laws. Schultz, for example, claimed that the equations resulting
from data adjustment methods were dynamic laws of demand:

> The law of demand derived in this study is a *dynamic* law; it describes in
> summary form the 'routine of change' of an important economic phenom-
> enon. It is the dynamic law of demand in a simple form ... It is quite
> different from the static law of demand of the classical writers.
>
> (Schultz (1928), p. 94)

Ferger (1932) was not so convinced. He pointed out that 'dynamic'
meant change and was not to be directly identified with 'time', and that
static laws which were constant over a certain time period should not be
regarded as dynamic purely because they were measured over time or
because there were variations in the conditions. On the other hand, he
felt there was a problem in the way 'time' was used by applied workers as
an all-purpose variable to represent complex changes in other independent variables. He proposed that instead of using a time trend variable,
dynamic changes should be divided into those which were regular and
predictable (first order dynamics which could be modelled by the statistician), and those which were unpredictable (second order dynamics
which could not be modelled). Ferger then discussed whether data
adjustment methods or multiple correlation methods were better at
dealing with these first order dynamics. He decided in favour of the
method of multiple (or partial) correlation and then considered its
implications:

> Finally we must consider the bearing of the multiple and partial corre-
> lation technique for demand curve derivation on the dynamic or static
> character of the results. The method is basically related to the scatter-
> diagram or simple correlation method, but with refinements which are of

extreme theoretical and practical importance. In none of the methods thus far considered has the fundamental condition of the classical definition of the static demand curves been realized – *that all other things remain unchanged*. This requirement has been approached in some measure by the adjustments which have been made on the data before being correlated, such as deflating the prices, using per capita quantities, and removing the trends of prices and quantities.   (Ferger (1932), p. 59)

He believed that the method of multiple correlation (or partial correlations) measured the relationship between price and quantity while effectively holding constant the other variables in the equation. The method was therefore equivalent in his view to the economist's *ceteris paribus* condition and would yield

> *substantially the classical static demand curve of economic theory.*
>   (Ferger (1932), p. 60)

In the first volume of the new journal *Econometrica*, Schultz (1933) reported an experiment to test whether there was any technical difference between an equation using detrended data (data treated by either of the two methods of trend ratios or link relatives) and one incorporating a time trend variable. He drew three-dimensional diagrams of the regression equations and compared the elasticity of demand and degree of correlation between the observed and fitted values of the dependent variable for each of the equations. He found that trend ratios and time trend methods produced very similar parameter results with little difference between linear and log-linear models. The parameter results for the link relatives method were more erratic, but in some cases were very close to the others. Since, in some cases, all methods gave similar parameter results (leaving no way of distinguishing between them on the basis of economic theory), Schultz turned to a statistical criterion to choose the model specification. He concluded that one should usually choose the method that resulted in the best fitting equation for a given dependent variable.

Frisch and Waugh (1933) considered the same problem later in the first volume of *Econometrica*. They disagreed with what they saw as a blanket recommendation by Smith to include time trends and seasonal variations in the equation rather than to pre-adjust the data. They discussed a number of issues concerning the significance of the regression coefficients obtained using the two methods, which they thought had been rather generally misunderstood. In particular they believed that

> there exists a misconception as to the meaning of these coefficients as approximations to the underlying 'true' relationship between the variables.   (Frisch and Waugh (1933), p. 388)

They illustrated these misconceptions using the example of sugar consumption and its relation to price. They stressed that some trends were important variables which must be left in the relationship. For example, if an increase of sugar consumption had occurred because of a population increase then this trend should be eliminated before measuring the demand elasticity. If on the other hand, the increase in consumption was due to a fall in the price (not mentioned but presumably because of the supply curve shifting to the right), then this trend variation should be left in the price and consumption material and allowed to influence the regression coefficient between consumption and price.

The point was that econometricians had to think first exactly what they were trying to measure; they had to decide which 'true' relationship they were looking for:

> Proceeding now to a more exact statement of the problem, we must first consider the meaning of a 'true' relationship, and in what sense such a 'true' relationship can be approximated by various empirical methods.
>
> When comparing the results of different methods in time series analysis one must keep clearly in mind the *object* of the analysis. It must be specified which sort of influence it is desired to eliminate, and which sort to preserve. Unless this is specified it has no meaning to say that a certain method will yield a 'truer' relationship than another.
>
> Such an expression has a meaning only if it is referred to a given theoretical framework. An empirically determined relation is 'true' if it approximates fairly well a certain well-defined *theoretical* relationship, assumed to represent the nature of the phenomenon studied. There does not seem to be any other way of giving a meaning to the expression 'a true relationship.' For clearness of statement we must therefore first define the nature of the *a priori* relationship that is taken as the ideal.
>
> (Frisch and Waugh (1933), p. 389)

Frisch and Waugh called the theoretical or ideal relation which they postulated the 'structural' relationship.[15] An empirical relationship could then be considered 'true' if it approximated the postulated theoretical relationship. So they stated quite clearly how they thought econometricians should view the relationships between the real world, theory, and applied results. This view implied a separation of the activities of defining the model of interest (choosing the model) and finding its empirical counterpart (estimation).

Frisch and Waugh then demonstrated, both analytically and for a numerical example, that for a given structural relationship:

---

[15] Frisch's terminology was adopted, via Haavelmo, by the Cowles Commission in their label 'structure'. Frisch and Waugh's (1933) usage is the first, and is relatively close to its modern meaning (see Aldrich (1989)).

$$Y = B_1 X + B_2 t$$

where t is a time trend, the regression coefficients
(1) b_1 from the fitted equation $\quad Y = b_1 X + b_2 t$
(2) b_1' from the fitted equation $Y' = b_1' X'$

(where Y' and X' are in deviations from trend values) were identically equal. They explained why the generally higher correlation coefficient (R^2) obtained for the equation which included a time trend (equation (1)) was not indicative of a truer result; after all they argued, both b_1 and b_1' were identically equal approximations to the true structural coefficient (B_1), therefore one could not be closer to the 'true' parameter than the other. Frisch and Waugh's analysis confirmed Schultz's experimentally obtained results and resolved the technical issue of time trends versus data adjustment.

Frisch and Waugh also made a clear distinction between the interpretation of the regression coefficient between price and quantity and the interpretation of the law to demand referring to the whole relationship (and measured by the degree of multiple correlation). Their analysis had shown that the elasticity parameter would be the same even though the equation and fit were different. An equation with a time trend explained more of the variation in the dependent variable and, it was argued, more of the movements in the demand curve and was thus closer to being a dynamic law of demand. The understanding of the behaviour of coefficients in the presence of other factors from the work of Ferger (1932) and of Frisch and Waugh (1933) paved the way for a more generous use of the other factors in the demand equation. In fact the incorporation into the equation of specific variables causing changes in the demand curve through time was already underway by the 1930s, though the computing constraint still meant that regressions with many variables were not to be undertaken lightly.

This section has described how econometricians initially believed theory correct and tried to verify and measure that theory. The realisation that static economic theory was an inadequate description of the real world and that the 'true' demand curve was constantly shifting over time led to attempts to clear the data of these shifting influences. This in turn led to an examination of how demand curves did move over time and to models of demand which would incorporate the shift factors. (The development and use of dynamic demand theory in 1930s is considered next.) The idea that theory was inadequate had a further important implication: while theory was immutable, the use of criteria based on reproducing certain features of that theory had seemed quite sensible but once theory had been toppled from its pedestal, such criteria could no longer be the sole arbiter of applied success. This paved the way for the infiltration into econometrics in the 1930s of additional, non-economic, criteria – namely statistical criteria – for testing econometric models. But full use of statistical criteria based on the Neyman–Pearson testing procedures (developed in the late 1920s) was dependent on the probability model which, as Chapter 8 reveals, was not accepted into econometrics until the 1940s.

5.3   Econometric models of demand

The late 1920s and 1930s saw advances both in model choice, where more sophisticated theories were developed and applied to a wider range of goods, and in testing the specification of these new models. The increasing complexity and widening applicability of models of demand in the 1930s were due to two basic factors: first, developments in the economic theory of demand and its mathematisation (in which, as in the field of business cycles, econometricians played a leading role), and secondly, to the impact of the economic events of the interwar period.

There were three areas of advance in demand theory which in particular fed through into applied econometric work of the 1930s. Developments in the economic theory of the household went hand in hand with renewed interest in cross-section studies of demand and in the role of substitute and complementary goods in market demand studies. Advances in the theory of imperfect competition turned attention to the supply side of price determination and its econometric modelling. But perhaps the most important development was the mathematical formulation of dynamic theories of demand and the consequent development of a set of dynamic models whose applied performance could easily be compared.

In the early twentieth-century work on demand, econometricians had focussed their interest almost exclusively on market demand data (with few exceptions such as Pigou (1910)). Yet some of the earliest applied economics to use statistical data, dating back to the eighteenth century, had been budget studies (see G. J. Stigler (1954)), and the 1930s saw a considerable revival of interest in this field. The important theoretical work of Hicks and Allen (1934) in 'rediscovering' the role of income in the individual's demand decisions was linked with an applied study of budgets by Allen and Bowley (1935) and Bowley's statistical analysis of prices (1933).[16] Staehle wrote not only on the theoretical aspects of budget studies (covering the assumptions made about the

---

[16] See the preface to Allen and Bowley (1935) which suggests that these three works were part of the same research programme.

sample, the distribution of the data and the relationships between the theory of demand and budget studies) (1934), but he also carried out an applied study (1934a) in which he compared the budgeting behaviour of three samples of consumers (Americans in the US, Swedes in Sweden and Swedish immigrants in the US) and made a survey of data sources (1935). Marschak also tried to combine market demand analysis with budget studies in two papers (1931 and 1939).[17] Finally, both Tintner (1938a) and Lewis (1939) developed mathematical economic models based on the Hicks–Allen theory as part of the econometric development of demand models and Tintner's particular concern was to create a dynamic version of the theory for applied work.

The incorporation of a single complementary or competing good's price in estimated market demand models had been fairly common in the work on agricultural commodities of the 1920s. But the interest by theorists (particularly Hotelling (1932), according to Schultz) in the properties of the individual's demand curve stimulated a further consideration of the role of other products and prices in market demand analysis by econometricians. For example, Ezekiel (1933) compared the properties of models where the competing product entered the demand equation through its price or through its supply quantity. He estimated four different single equation models for two goods, beef and pork:

(1) $P_1 = f(Q_1, P_2, Z)$
(2) $P_2 = f(Q_2, P_1, Z)$
(3) $P_1 = f(Q_1, Q_2, Z)$
(4) $P_2 = f(Q_2, Q_1, Z)$

where subscripts refer to the two goods, and Z is an index of payrolls to capture the effects of changes in consumers' income. He used nine data points and left one for a forecasting test. He then compared the models on the basis of their coefficients of determination ($\bar{R}^2$) and their errors of forecast for the tenth observation. Ezekiel rejected models (1) and (2) even though they had higher $\bar{R}^2$ and lower forecast errors because he thought the results were spurious due to two-way causal influence between P_1 and P_2. He preferred models (3) and (4) as he believed any causal relationship involving P_1 as a cause of Q_1 would be lagged, that is

---

[17] Jacob Marschak (1898–1977) was born in Kiev, studied engineering (and statistics with Slutsky), fought on the Menshevik side in the Revolution and left Russia in 1919. He studied economics, statistics and philosophy in Germany and embarked on a career of academic teaching, research and journalism before being forced to flee Germany in 1933. He became director of the Oxford Institute of Economics and statistics in 1935 but moved to the USA in 1939. He directed the Cowles Commission in 1943–8; the period of its intense and influential work on theoretical econometric problems.

previous year's price determines present supply. Unfortunately, his quantity data were consumption figures which somewhat undermined his lagged supply theory.

In another example, Gilboy (1932) examined the case of markets where the supply of two goods, as well as their demand, were interdependent.[18] She considered that the two dairy products, milk and butter, competed on the supply side and were connected on the demand side. In addition she believed that supply factors were not independent of demand factors. She used a data-based modelling technique to derive models of the economic relationships between milk and butter from graphs of monthly data series for the two goods. She estimated her models by orthogonal regressions (minimising the sum of squares of the perpendiculars to the line), which she suggested was a first step to dealing with the problem of interdependent relationships or simultaneous causality in the equation. (An interesting idea which was not taken up: simultaneity and the orthogonal regression are both discussed in Part III.) Schultz (1938) also dealt with the theory and practice of modelling related demands in his massive book on econometric demand analysis.

Tinbergen was one of the few economists to apply econometric techniques developed in demand analysis to test separate models of supply.[19] In a 1930 paper, he was interested primarily in the supply side of the market although he used various two-equation demand and supply models. He examined a number of different models of the structure of the supplying industry:

> the assumptions of static competition, static monopoly, limited competition under static conditions, dynamic competition and dynamyc [sic] monopoly are used successively. It is argued that under the prevailing conditions Cournot's formula of limited competition provides the best explanation of the empirical data.   (Tinbergen (1930), pp. 798–9)

Tinbergen's work on the two-equation model has a special place in the history of the identification problem and is discussed in detail in the next chapter.

Tinbergen was also one of the earliest proponents of dynamic models. In (1933) he analysed the path of supply curve shifts over time

---

[18] Elizabeth Waterman Gilboy, of the Harvard Committee on Economic Research, also worked on business cycles. She was particularly responsible for developing applied work on the short 40-month cycle found in the US data.

[19] Other economists in the 1920s who modelled the supply side mostly drew on the simple lagged models put forward by Moore (discussed in Chapter 6.2). An example is that in Schultz's (1928) book, which dealt with the demand and the supply side of the sugar industry. Schultz was planning to extend his work on supply when he was killed in a car accident in 1938.

for several commodities. He outlined a model where economic agents made plans based on their expectations of future demand and supply. Some of the plans were realised and some were revised in succeeding time periods and this affected stocks which also entered the model. His applied work covered several markets in order to determine the average planning horizon of suppliers in particular markets.

Another early enthusiast for the dynamic treatment of demand was the mathematical economist G. C. Evans. His theoretical paper on the dynamics of monopoly (1924) also dealt with demand and he suggested a cobweb model in a later paper of 1931. Evans influenced Charles Roos, who, like Moore, was insistent on the importance of building dynamic economic theories.[20] Both men attempted to produce dynamic versions of Walras' general equilibrium theory (Roos (1927) and Moore (1929)). Both also aimed to produce dynamic models of demand. Moore used data in the form of trend ratios to introduce time into his models. Roos, on the other hand, introduced dynamic elements into his mathematical models of demand theory and production theory by the use of differential and integral terms.

Roos developed his ideas further in two papers (1933 and 1934) which dealt with the theoretical aspects of demand: dynamic theory, the role of past, present and future prices, the functional form of demand equations, the form of time lags and a discussion of factors often ignored such as obsolescence, repeat buying, monetary conditions, etc. His models of demand seemed to him to be very different from the rather pedestrian econometric models of the 1920s. He concluded his 1934 paper with the following reflection:

> It might be said that the theory of demand has progressed to a point where it is questionable that further theoretical work should be done until statistical studies have been made to verify or disprove the hypotheses and conclusions so far reached. This statistical investigation is, in itself, a tremendous task. A new type of mathematical statistician will be required to make the studies. Nevertheless, there are reasons to be optimistic regarding the possibilities of the discovery of statistical laws of demand.
>
> (Roos (1934), p. 90)

It is not surprising that Roos was optimistic, for in the same year the first of the Cowles Commission Monographs was published under Roos' authorship with the title *Dynamic Economics* (Roos (1934a)). It was a theoretical and statistical study of demand and supply covering

[20] Charles F. Roos (1901–1958) was one of the founders of the Econometric Society and research director of the Cowles Commission from 1934 to 1937. He directed economic research for the National Recovery Administration (1933–4) and set up an econometrics consulting firm in the late 1930s. He wrote on mathematics and statistics as well as economics.

consumer, agricultural and producer goods and incorporated cyclical effects, joint demand and many aspects of supply. Theoretical mathematical models were extensively developed, but the applied work did not match up to the advances in theory. His ability to carry out statistical work on his models was limited by the lack of data, the statistical techniques and procedures available, and by the ever-present computing constraint.

The improvements in econometric modelling in the 1930s can be illustrated by two further examples. The first of these is a paper by Whitman (1934) on the demand for steel. He considered six different dynamic single-equation demand models, of which five were drawn from the work of Roos and Evans. These equations contained various combinations of lagged and differential price terms (and in one case an integral term covering all previous prices). He discussed the theoretical implications of the models and their expected parameter signs. He estimated five models (rejecting the equation containing the integral of prices as impractical from the computation point of view); compared the results: the parameter signs and sizes, their standard errors and $\bar{R}^2$; and then considered the reasons why the parameter estimates differed in the models. He chose his final model on the basis of three criteria: the 'rationality' of the model, the statistical measures and the stability of each model when it was fitted for three different time periods. He decided in favour of the model:

$$Q = aP + b + h(\mathrm{d}P/\mathrm{d}t) + cI + dt$$

(where t is a linear time trend and I an index of industrial production).

Though Whitman had studied with Schultz, he estimated more interesting models and his testing procedures were far more sophisticated than those of his teacher. For example, Schultz (1938) considered ten different models (including Whitman's six), but in his applied work he fitted only the two elementary regressions and the orthogonal regression: the three regression models he had estimated from the start of his career in 1925. The applied econometric work on demand had developed so rapidly in the meantime that Schultz's book, which incorporated his previously published applied work of the 1920s and 1930s, was already outdated in some respects by 1938.

Another example of the trend to more sophisticated dynamic modelling, but using theoretical ideas from other disciplines, was the paper by de Wolff (1938) on the demand for cars.[21] He treated demand as being composed of new demand and replacement demand and modelled them separately. Replacement demand was modelled with the help of

[21] See also Solo's criticism and de Wolff's reply (both 1939).

an empirical function calculated from the figures for the lifetime of cars and new demand was modelled with a 'saturation curve'. The residual elements were modelled using the price variable and cyclical indicators.

With its primary emphasis on model specification and testing using statistical and model stability criteria, Whitman's article exemplifies the best of the 1930s' applied work. Although statistical tests were being gradually adopted in econometrics throughout the 1930s, there was variation in the tests carried out and no ground rules for reporting the results. Whitman's procedures of specifying a number of different economic models and choosing the best model by comparing the estimated models with the use of statistical and stability tests were unusually rigorous. Unfortunately, his work is typical in that he ignored the supply side of the model and the consequent identification issue. The problem of identification, so popular in the late 1920s (as we shall see in Chapter 6), was virtually ignored in applied work by the middle of 1930s: the search for the 'true' demand curve had shifted to focus on model specification to provide the answers.

The improvements in econometric modelling, illustrated by both Whitman and de Wolff were becoming more common by 1940, but not all applied work was of this quality. Much showed little advance over the work of the 1920s, and as econometrics became more fashionable it attracted some who had little understanding of the problems involved. This led to some very poor work; for example Broster (1937) claimed to have devised a new method of obtaining demand curves. This consisted of simply ranking price and quantity data in inverse order while ignoring the time dating of individual observations. Of course, this produced a meaningless but well-defined negative (i.e. demand) relationship between the variables.[22]

The generally increasing level of sophistication in econometric models was noted by E.J. Working (1934) in a general review of demand studies. He drew links between the developments in theory, the developments in econometrics and the events in the real world. The early demand studies had ignored the years of the First World War because of the violent price changes in those years. The post-war years witnessed similar unexpectedly sudden economic changes. Improved models were needed not only to explain the dramatic price changes of the interwar period but also because of the growing importance of demand in the analysis and modelling of economic cycles. Economic

[22] This paper was published in a reputable British journal and was rightly criticised by the young Milton Friedman (who had been helping Schultz with his statistical work) in the following year (see Friedman (1938)).

events were also important in changing policy. In the 1920s policy concerns had influenced applied economists in the USA to concentrate on agricultural goods; in the 1930s policy concerns had widened, in the US and elsewhere, to cover demand for consumer and capital goods and the role of demand in cycle policy. Events had also brought to the fore certain problems often ignored in earlier demand studies, namely, the issue of real versus money prices, the lack of independence of data series which included cyclical factors, as well as structural trends, and the importance of time relationships in forecasting during periods of cyclical change.

Although econometric model building was in the ascendancy in statistical demand studies, it certainly did not have a monopoly position. For example, Mills (1936), like Working, recognised the importance of demand and supply studies for policy purposes and for the explanation of cycles, but he advocated a descriptive approach involving analysis of the frequency distribution of price changes, levels, and their variability, etc. Mills believed that this descriptive approach would throw light on speculative demand and would increase the knowledge of the interrelationships of prices with other economic variables ·necessary for the explanation of cycles. Examples of this approach can be seen in the work of the NBER, of Bowley (1933) and of H. Working (1935).

The progress made in various aspects of modelling in the 1930s was primarily due to developments in mathematical economics, but stimulation from outside events also played a role. There were personnel factors which linked these influences and aided this progress. Many of those active in econometrics in the narower statistical sense were also active in developing mathematical economic models because this was how they conceived econometrics; and some, like Roos, were also very active in policy making. The second factor was that the Econometric Society (formed in 1930) provided a new forum for discussion. The membership of the Society in its early years was unusually mixed for such an institution, including not just academics but a considerable number of businessmen and government officials. Through its journal, *Econometrica*, which first appeared in 1933, the Society encouraged communication within this disparate group.[23]

---

[23] Few businessmen or government officials actually wrote for the journal apart from trained economists who worked in those spheres (such as those in company research divisions). An obvious exception to this was Alfred Cowles (founder and funder of the Cowles Commission and *Econometrica*) who contributed econometric analyses on stock market prices. His involvement was probably one reason for the broad appeal of the Society.

5.4   The data-theory gap under review

There is no doubt that by 1940 considerable progress had been made in narrowing the gap that existed between formal economic theory and the data available for applied work. This chapter has described how initially data were adjusted to theory to enable econometricians to measure theoretical relationships. Later, applied workers adapted theory to suit their data. Finally, formal theory made some advances useful to econometricians.[24] Despite these undoubted advances, econometric work still met with considerable antagonism from economic theorists, for econometrics remained a minority interest in economics and continued to suffer from a credibility problem in the eyes of non-mathematical economists. For example, Robbins satirised econometric demand work and described the methods used in such work as 'judicious doctoring'. He attacked econometric work as 'doomed to futility from the outset' (Robbins (1932), pp. 101 and 102). Robbins rejected quantitative work based on the econometric approach.

A compromise between econometricians and theorists was advocated by G. J. Stigler in his 1939 review of statistical demand work. He analysed what advances were necessary to abolish the discrepancies between theoretical and statistical demand curves and suggested that theorists had a duty to meet the econometricians part way. He criticised theory for being either too general in scope (such as the general equilibrium approach) or too narrow (for example, in ignoring variables and dynamics in an attempt to get formal results for a simple system). However, the detail of his discussion concentrated on pointing out the shortfalls of applied practice in relation to theory, with only minor attention to aspects where he felt theoretical advances could be made. The discussion centred around the problem of changes over time, but Stigler regarded the work of mathematical economists (such as Roos and Evans) as empirical theory rather than pure theory and doubted whether a 'theoretical solution of economic dynamics' was in fact possible (G. J. Stigler (1939), p. 475). Stigler concluded that the gap between theoretical and applied models would never be bridged but, unlike Robbins, he was in favour of econometric work because it represented a scientific approach to economic problems:

> the inconclusiveness of the present statistical demand curves should not be taken as an excuse for lapsing back into the use of 'commonsense' and 'intuition.' These are indeed powerful tools, but unless they are tempered

---

[24] Blaug's (1980) survey of methodology in economics suggests that at the beginning of our period, economic theory would be assumed correct and verification would be the order of the day. By implication then, to close the data-theory gap the data would have to be

by a scientific methodology, their fruits will be few and lacking in nutrition. The methodology (although not the methods) of the present statistical studies, rather than a resort to empiricism, seems to hold most promise for future progress in a field whose importance is excelled only by its difficulties.   (G. J. Stigler (1939), p. 481)

So much for the views of economists.

Econometricians were not uncritical of theorists. For example, Gilboy discussed the failure of theorists to deal with the dynamic aspects of demand theory in the 1920s:

> Most of the attempts to reconcile orthodox theory with statistically derived curves have been concerned with the modification of static theory so as to fit the actual data, or with an attempt to modify the data, primarily through the elimination of time so as to fit the theory. There has been, for the most part, no question that orthodox theory could be applied successfully to the interpretation of statistical curves. And yet it has been repeatedly remarked that the theoretical analysis does not include time and statistical data do. What is more, it is admittedly impossible to eliminate time completely from statistical series. It seems strange that so few attempts have been made to attack the problem theoretically with the element of time left in.   (Gilboy (1930), p. 608)

In another criticism of the role of pure theory, Schultz (1938) advocated that economists make use of the operational approach expounded by the physicist and philosopher Percy Bridgman in 1927.[25] Instead of defining the meaning of demand in terms of its properties (such as utility) the operational procedure would define demand in terms of the set of operations needed to measure it. Roos and von Szeliski adopted this idea and urged mathematical economists to be more specific about their models in the interests of verifying theory:

> In modern days econometrics has contributed a little, to the extent that it has made the deductive process more rigorous, but papers have given too much attention to purely formal mathematical exercises. To be of practical value economic hypothesis and theory must be sufficiently precise to be capable of verification.   (Roos and von Szeliski (1939), p. 652)

Econometricians had reacted to the inadequacies of standard economic theories by building up their own models based on an analysis of the industry or market in question. By the end of the 1930s,

adjusted to the theory. Later, as the verificationist school retreated under the influence of operationalism, the process would reverse. This is what seems to have occurred in demand analysis.

[25] Schultz (1938), pp. 10–12 (and one or two others), made direct reference to the influence of Percy Bridgman (and his 1927 book). He is almost the only contemporary philosopher of science to have been referenced by the econometricians (see Morgan (1988)).

then, progress had been made towards translating demand theory into usable models and the data-theory gap was considerably reduced in this respect. Attention is now turned to other correspondence difficulties, particularly identification problems as raised in the early work by Lenoir, Lehfeldt and Moore.

CHAPTER 6

The evolution of identification questions

It is no accident that the standard economic model used in textbooks to illustrate the identification problem in econometrics is the simple market demand and supply model, for it was while attempting to estimate demand elasticities that pioneering econometricians first discovered the identification problem and related correspondence problems.

In a general sense identification is concerned with the correspondences between economic activity, the data that activity generates, the theoretical economic model and the estimated relationship. In early econometric work on demand, these correspondence problems were attacked in various ways. In some cases, investigators examined their data to see which relationships could be estimated and then sought to interpret these relationships in terms of economic theory. This involved two ideas of identification: one of identifying as 'interpreting' an estimated relationship in terms of economic theory, and secondly, one of identifying as 'locating' a relationship in the data. This notion of locating a relationship in the data has its closest modern counterpart in economic time-series analysis, which is concerned with finding a model which characterises the data given certain criteria. In other early work, investigators started with economic theory models and examined the circumstances under which these models could be estimated. This latter approach is nearest to the present-day scope of 'the identification problem', which deals with the question of whether the parameters of a model can be uniquely determined, given that the model is known (that is, assumed to be the 'true' model).

To equate the early econometric work on identification entirely with modern views and practice would be false. Model choice, identification and estimation are now treated as separate activities, and tests of the extent to which the theoretical model has been correctly chosen (model specification tests) constitute a fourth separate activity. In early econometrics, these tasks were jumbled together. The early views on identification are consequently less well conceptualised, but they are also richer in that they cover a wider range of correspondence problems than presently defined by the phrase 'the identification problem'. The last chapter dealt mainly with developments in model choice and specification. This chapter traces the evolution of other correspondence problems and how early workers in the field tried to deal with them.

6.1 The emergence of correspondence problems

Correspondence problems were clearly visible in the early work by Lehfeldt, Lenoir and Moore, though their approaches to the problems differed. Their work was discussed briefly in the previous chapter (Chapter 5.1), but warrants further examination.

Robert Lehfeldt in 1914 wanted to calculate the elasticity of demand for wheat. He stated the problem as follows:

> The coefficient of elasticity is defined by
>
> $$\varepsilon = \frac{-p.dq}{q.dp} = \frac{-d(\log q)}{d(\log p)}$$
>
> where p is the price of wheat and q is the supply [quantity], subject to constant conditions of demand. Now the supply fluctuates from year to year, according to the state of the crops; in order to make the statistics of supply [quantity] available, they must first be corrected for the annual change in demand. (Lehfeldt (1914), p. 212)

(His work is confusing to read because he uses 'supply' to mean quantity as well as the conditions of supply, so I have added [quantity] where necessary.) Lehfeldt operated on the data to try and obtain a fixed demand curve in the belief that fluctuations in the supply curve would trace out the constant demand curve.

Despite this fairly clear argument about locating a demand curve, it is not immediately clear, from his procedures, whether his resulting estimate could be interpreted as a demand curve. He estimated the demand elasticity by the ratio of standard deviations of his price and quantity data which were in the form of mean deviations of the logs. This ratio (equal to 0.6) was naturally positive, but Lehfeldt also computed the correlation coefficient between the two series (prices and quantities lagged by one year) and reported a coefficient of .44. But he had omitted the sign of the correlation, which was negative (computing the Marshallian model least squares coefficient gives $-.72$).[1]

[1] Lehfeldt's measure of the ratio of standard deviations with the negative sign of the cross-products of the data is equivalent to the diagonal mean regression for the two-variable case as proposed by Frisch in 1928, used by him in his critique of statistical demand studies (1933a) and by Tinbergen in some of his League of Nations' work.

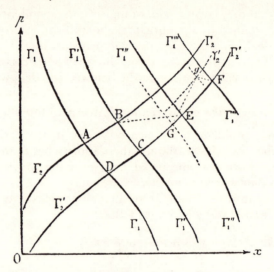

Figure 13   Lenoir's identification diagram
Source: Lenoir (1913), p. 58, Figure 44

According to the view of the time, Lehfeldt had successfully identified a demand curve, for neither H. Working (1925) nor Schultz (1928) found anything particularly amiss with his approach or method of calculation (although Schultz was concerned about the implied functional form).

Marcel Lenoir's thesis on demand, *Etudes sur la formation et le mouvement des prix*, in 1913 suggested a similar appreciation of identification issues. He asked whether supply factors would dominate demand factors or vice versa. He illustrated his answer with a graph (reproduced in Figure 13) and by examples:

> This price depends: on the general economic situation (always supposed constant, in all of this study), on supply and on demand. Now these three elements are never fixed, and, during the course of time, the price follows their variations. In the second part of this study an attempt is made to distinguish by observation these complicated influences. But we are able to anticipate here the direction of the variation that will tend to produce a change in each of the two last factors, supply and demand ...
>
> One sees now [Figure 13] that, supply being constant, to any growth of demand corresponds an increase in production-consumption and a rise in price. The representative point in *p*, *x*, passes from A to B or from D to C. The price and the consumption vary in the same direction – If demand is constant, an enlargement of supply corresponds to an increase in production-consumption, and a fall in price. The representative point passes from A to D or from B to C. The price and consumption vary in this case in

different directions – If supply and demand increase simultaneously (from A to C), production-consumption will increase, the price could vary in one or the other direction, or remain constant. If the supply grows, while the demand diminishes (from B to D) the price will fall, the production-consumption could vary or remain constant.

For certain goods the influence of one of the two factors seems likely to be dominant. For an article of food of common use, produced by cultivation, such as corn, one can admit that in a given country, the curve of demand varies only slowly and remains nearly the same during many years. In contrast, the supply curve dependent on the state of the harvests varies from one year to another. The representative point moves along the same demand curve, the price varies in inverse direction to the supply, rises when the harvest is abundant, sinks when it is poor – with reservation, in addition for the influence which can be exerted by the general economic condition.[2]

If we consider, on the contrary, a good, such as coal, or cast iron, produced by industry, consumed, at least for the most part by industry, it seems that it would be the demand which rises more rapidly. The supply curve only rises here in consequence of a change in the means of production, a change which only takes place under the pressure of demand, rather slowly, and always or nearly always, in the same direction, tending to enlarge the supply. Demand, in contrast, is very capricious, and its influence, in the short time periods, is predominant. Price and production-consumption will change therefore in the same direction.   (Lenoir (1913), pp. 56–8, translation by this author)

Of course, the applied work was more difficult because the general economic situation did not remain constant, as assumed in the theoretical discussion. The coffee market proved relatively easy to analyse and Lenoir estimated a demand curve for the good. In the case of coal, he had predicted that demand factors would dominate in the short term (changes in supply would be gradual and over the long term), and thus prices and production-consumption (as Lenoir called quantity) would vary positively. Although he found that prices and consumption did vary positively he also found that price and production were inversely related:

That suggests the idea that the movement in average price, during a long period, is in inverse relation to the increase in production. It will be in that case the supply which, as well as the demand, will determine price.

                                        (Lenoir (1913), p. 101)

Lenoir was able to reconcile his results with his expectations by further study of the general economic situation, using graphs, simple and partial correlations, and regressions as analytical tools. He concluded:

---

[2] Lenoir seems to have made a genuine mistake in writing his ideas down in the last sentence of this paragraph, rather than a failure of understanding, since it is clear that he is discussing the case of movements between say A and D on his diagram.

three kinds of relationships have appeared in the course of this study: In the short period the price of coal varies with the quantity consumed, the oscillations in price follow the oscillations in demand, set off by the economic cycles.

In a long period the movement of price seems subject to two influences: it varies with the production of metallic money, and in a direction inverse to the increase of production, follows the variation of supply.

(Lenoir (1913), p. 104)

The short-term movements in the coal market were, for example, equivalent to movements between A and B on Lenoir's graph; while in the long term, supply increased and prices consequently fell, so that the short-term variation was between D and C.[3]

Identification problems were exposed most clearly in this early work by Henry Ludwell Moore's positive demand curve of 1914. When the context of the positive demand curve is examined, it becomes easier to understand why Moore was led astray. In order to explain how economic cycles were generated, Moore sought an empirical link between the harvest cycle and the industrial cycle. He correlated the trend ratios (deviations from trend) for crop yields per acre with pig-iron production (taken as a proxy for industrial output and trade). The maximum positive correlation (and inferred relationship) was found to be between an increase in crop yields and an increase in pig-iron production lagged by one to two years. But Moore wanted to find not just a correlation but also a causal link between the harvest cycle and the general cycle of prices. The conventional negative demand curve did not seem to provide the link that he was seeking. Constant demand conditions with supply shifts appeared to be incompatible with the evidence that he observed of the relationship between general prices and crop yields:

> In consequence of the decrease in the yield per acre, the price of crops would ascend, the volume of commodities represented by pig-iron would decrease, and upon the hypothesis of the universality of the descending type of demand curves, the prices of commodities like pig-iron would rise. In a period of declining yield of crops, therefore, there would be a rise of prices, and in a period of increasing yield of crops there would be a fall in prices. But the facts are exactly the contrary. During the long period of falling prices from 1870–1890, there was a decrease in the yield per acre of the crops, and during the long period of rising prices from 1890 to 1911, there was an increasing yield of crops. It is obviously inadmissible to assume that in a dynamic society there is one law of demand for all commodities. The dogma of the uniformity of the law of demand is an idol of the static state.   (Moore (1914), pp. 112–13.)

[3] A similar sort of analysis, though I think less explicit, seems to have been made by Warming (1906) in his review of Mackeprang's book (1906). Kærgaard (1984) gives a translation and analysis of the relevant part of the review.

So when Moore estimated the relationship between prices and quantities of pig-iron and it turned out to be positive, he presented this result as a new type of demand curve: the positive demand relationship which was applicable to producers' goods (as opposed to the negative relationship applicable to agricultural goods).[4]

Moore's critics were very confident in their diagnosis: his positive demand curve was to their minds a supply relationship for pig-iron. P. G. Wright wrote in his 1915 review:

> Professor Moore's studies in demand curves illustrate the principle that the need of checking statistical inductions by abstract reasoning is quite as great as that of verifying abstract reasoning by statistics. The demand curves for crops harmonize perfectly with theory: the conditions of demand remain approximately constant; there is an increased output of crops (very probably due to heavier rainfall); with the diminishing utility due to this increased supply, the marginal utility and hence the price falls. But how about the 'new type', the ascending demand curve for pig-iron, is it so hopelessly irreconcilable with theory? Not at all. The conditions of demand are changed (very probably by improved business conditions) in the direction of a rapid and continuous increase. This would be indicated, conformably to theory, by shifting the entire demand curve progressively to the right. The ordinates to this shifting curve, corresponding with the lagging supply, will yield Professor Moore's 'new type'.
>
> (P.G. Wright (1915), p. 638)[5]

Lehfeldt's views were even clearer:

> The author thinks he has discovered a new type of demand curve, sloping the opposite way to the usual kind! But the curve (for pig-iron) ... is not a demand curve at all, but much more nearly a supply curve. It is arrived at by the intersection of irregularly fluctuating demands on supply conditions that, on the whole, may be regarded as steady but for a secular growth, whereas the whole line of argument with regard to crops is based on considering the intersection of irregular supply (due to fluctuations of weather) with a steady demand.   (Lehfeldt (1915), p. 411)

One way to look at the episode of Moore's positive demand curve is simply to see it in terms of the correct model choice. His was the wrong

---

[4] It is possible to reconcile Moore's 'facts' with demand theory in different ways. For example, one problem could lie in his use of crop yields as evidence of supply changes. Standard US data sources show that in the first period (1870–90) corn acreage doubled and it increased by a further third in the second period (1890–1911). Such increases in grain supply were not incompatible with the changes in yields per acre that Moore observed; but in these circumstances, yields would not have portrayed supply conditions adequately.

[5] Wright's contention that the demand curve was shifting to the right was criticised by E. J. Working (1927) who pointed out that if this were true, Moore's use of relative changes of the data (link relatives) would tend to eliminate this factor. After discussing the point with him, Wright agreed with Working that the demand curve must have been shifting backwards and forwards for Moore's result to be obtained.

choice of model because he had found a positive relationship. Moore's mistake made this point in a negative way; working with a 'demand' model he had estimated a supply curve according to the criteria of the time. There is a second way of looking at the problem: in the circumstances where the demand model correctly describes economic behaviour, can the empirical counterpart to the model be isolated from the data? The instant reaction by contemporary economists and their explanation as to why Moore must have estimated a supply curve suggests that they saw the problem in this latter light. It seems reasonable to claim this sort of understanding of identification since Lehfeldt (1914), in grappling with the problem of both supply and demand curves shifting, had realised that in order for the moving supply curve to trace out (identify) the demand curve, the demand curve itself would have to be stable or fixed. Lenoir's work also showed considerable understanding of this problem. He had understood the necessity for one of the functions to shift and one to be stable in order to identify the stable curve. He had made a pre-estimation examination of whether a statistical curve would approximate a demand or supply curve. His procedure dealt neatly with model choice and identification problems. Unfortunately Lenoir's ideas were not taken up by his contemporaries in the field.[6] Lehfeldt's work was well known to his contemporaries but his solution to identification, though discernible with hindsight, was perhaps opaque at that time.

Identification problems are concerned with economic models in relation to economic data. A purely empirical approach to the estimation of relationships does not involve the same problems of identification. Moore could estimate a positive relationship between price and quantity without causing offence, it was calling that relationship a demand curve which was controversial. To economists it stuck out like a sore thumb. It is significant that statisticians who criticised Moore's book did not react in the same way; Yule ignored the positive demand curve, Persons remarked that it confirmed his own empirical results.[7] The possibility that an empirical relationship with no direct theoretical counterpart might result instead of a demand curve did not seem to have occurred to these early econometricians or turned up in their empirical work; this was to be a later development.

---

[6] G. J. Stigler (1954) claims that Lenoir's work was rediscovered in the 1920s, but it does not appear to have formed part of the common knowledge in discussions of identification in the late 1920s. For example, Schultz (1938) did reference Lenoir, but only in respect of the economic theory contributions.

[7] Similarly, in the earlier statistical work, Hooker (1900) had presented a graph which showed an inverse relationship between prices and production of wheat as a supply relationship.

6.2   Identifying the demand curve

The estimation of single equations of demand threw up little in the way of problems in the 1920s. This was probably because most applied work was on agricultural commodities, for which, as Lehfeldt had suggested, demand shifted relatively slowly and steadily in response to factors such as population growth, while supply was likely to be much more unpredictable due to the influence of factors such as the weather. Adjustments for changes in demand conditions were carried out, ostensibly to remove the disturbing elements and find the 'true' demand curve. Applied workers initially concentrated on measurement aspects of data-theory correspondence, trying to match the data closely to the requirements of demand theory. The desire to adjust the time-series data to match the static nature of theory was discussed in the last chapter. There were other, less pressing problems. For example, theory dictated that the data should apply to a well-defined geographical market, a well-defined group of buyers at a particular stage of the marketing process (e.g. wholesale or retail) and a sensibly defined time unit (e.g. from one harvest season to the next rather than calendar years). These problems, like the problem of time, were dealt with by making adjustments to the data wherever possible. These adjustments, in effect, helped to provide a 'fixed' demand curve and moving supply curve which allowed the demand curve and elasticity parameter to be identified.

Identification problems re-emerged in the later 1920s when the investigators began to develop econometric models of demand. Whilst seeking to estimate a static curve, econometricians had tried to remove shifts from the demand curve and had mostly ignored shifting supply. During the 1920s, they became more sophisticated in their treatment of the *ceteris paribus* clauses of economic theory and started to model shifting demand curves (by incorporating time-related disturbing factors in their demand equations). At this stage, econometricians also began to consider demand shifts in conjunction with shifts in supply. Thus the incorporation of time elements into models of demand led to the re-emergence of identification as an issue in econometric analysis.

Once workers thought about estimating a dynamic rather than a static demand function, it became more difficult to ignore the supply side of the model. This did not necessarily mean that econometricians seriously attempted to estimate separate supply relationships in the 1920s, for they did not (the examples of Tinbergen discussed in the previous chapter dated from the 1930s). The first econometrician to begin to model demand and supply jointly was Moore. He began experimenting with two-equation models in 1919, using alternative data to estimate the supply function. In 1925 he proposed a model in which both demand and supply parameters could be estimated from one set of price and quantity data:

(1) demand equation $\quad P_t \;=\; a_0 + a_1 Q_t^{\mathrm{D}}$
(2) supply equation $\quad\;\; Q_t^{\mathrm{S}} = b_0 + b_1 P_{t-1}$
where $\qquad\qquad\quad\;\; Q_t^{\mathrm{S}} \equiv Q_t^{\mathrm{D}}$

This cobweb model enabled Moore to 'identify' both demand and supply parameters in a way which avoided any question of simultaneity by lagging the supply relationship.[8] Moore's exposition was easy to understand and his model soon became well known and applied. But, as we shall see, certain of its features later came under criticism and doubts were expressed as to whether the two estimated relationships could be interpreted as those of demand and supply.

Nowadays, the earliest theoretical treatment of the identification problem is believed to be that by Elmer J. Working (1927). It is almost the only paper on identification (or on any other aspect of econometrics) prior to 1940 which is referred to in econometric textbooks. In fact, his paper was only one contribution in a wide-ranging discussion of the problem and it was pre-dated by a paper, 'The Statistical Determination of Demand Curves' by his brother Holbrook Working in 1925.[9] Holbrook Working posed the problem as:

the extent to which statistically determined demand curves may be identified with theoretical demand curves,

and he believed the answer was:

one of statistical rather than theoretical economic interpretation.
(H. Working (1925), p. 526)

By this, Holbrook Working meant that it was a data problem not a theory problem. His analysis began with the regression choice question: he drew out three regression lines using Lehfeldt's data (the two elementary regressions and Lehfeldt's regression line) and found that they gave different demand elasticities. He suggested that the elementary

---

[8] Though his model was formulated with previous price as the independent variable in the equation, he actually regressed previous prices on current quantity in his estimation of the supply relationship.
[9] Holbrook Working (1895–1985), the elder of the two brothers, spent most of his working life at the Stanford Food Research Institute undertaking statistical work on food commodities. This has included some interesting work on modelling stock market prices as random events. Elmer Joseph Working (1900–68) also worked in agricultural econometrics; his career spanned both university and government positions.

regressions could be used for forecasting (for example, forecasting price for a given quantity from the regression of price on quantity), but that further assumptions had to be made to determine the 'true' demand curves. Holbrook Working's first solution was based on the statistical treatment of measurement errors, that is, if price observations were accurate but quantity observations were measured with error, then these errors could be minimised by regressing quantity on price to give the true demand curve. But he believed that in practice there would be errors in both data sets and therefore neither of the two elementary regression lines would represent the 'true' relationship.

Secondly, Holbrook Working suggested that the observations were scattered from the 'true' demand curve because of disturbing elements which shifted the demand curve either horizontally or vertically from its true position. The direction of displacement of the demand curve (horizontal or vertical) would indicate the correct measurement method to fit the curve. His statistical solution to the identification problem was therefore equivalent to the statistical solution to the choice of regression problem. He failed to see that a shift in the demand curve would normally result in a displacement of both price and quantity observations along a fixed supply curve which was not necessarily horizontal or vertical, implying a weighted regression technique. Schultz (1925) similarly treated the identification problem as an estimation question divorced from the demands of economic theory.

Holbrook Working did not get very far with the identification problem because he sought a solution solely in terms of the characteristics of the data. In contrast, his brother, E. J. Working, provided an analysis which successfully united data characteristics with economic theory. His analysis gave the clearest presentation of the problem during the 1920s; he explained not only what the problem was, but provided a statement of the solution as far as it was known and understood at that time. The paper was both stimulating and influential in challenging the profession to work further on the problem, and was widely referenced by contemporary econometricians.

Elmer J. Working's famous paper, 'What do Statistical "Demand Curves" Show?' (1927), started with a two-equation supply and demand economic model and demonstrated, graphically, the effects of shifts in supply and demand curves over time on the likely scatter of observations. He showed that shifts in one curve were necessary to trace out the other. He introduced the term 'variability' to measure the tendency of a curve to shift backwards and forwards because of changes in demand and supply factors. He assumed initially that shifts in demand and supply were independent and random. If the demand curve had greater variability (shifted relatively more) than the supply curve, then the resulting fitted line would approximate a supply curve and *vice versa*. Like Lenoir, E. J. Working also considered the results which were likely to be obtained in different markets. He concluded that agricultural commodity markets were likely to have stable demand and shifting supply curves and the fitted curves would therefore approximate demand curves; manufacturing goods' markets would be the reverse. He also showed that if the relative shifts in the two sets of curves were approximately equal, no satisfactory line of fit could be obtained (one line would fit as well as any other). He postulated that, by correcting the same data separately for supply and demand shifts, it would be possible to get an approximation to both supply and demand curves:

> whether we obtain a demand curve or a supply curve, by fitting a curve to a series of points which represent the quantities of an article sold at various prices, depends upon the fundamental nature of the supply and demand conditions ...
>
> Whether a demand or a supply curve is obtained may also be affected by the nature of the corrections applied to the original data. The corrections may be such as to reduce the effect of the shifting of the demand schedules without reducing the effect of the shifting of the supply schedules. In such a case the curve obtained will approximate a demand curve, even tho the original demand schedules fluctuated fully as much as did the supply schedules.
>
> By intelligently applying proper refinements, and making corrections to eliminate separately those factors which cause demand curves to shift and those factors which cause supply curves to shift, it may be possible even to obtain both demand curve and a supply curve for the same product and from the same original data.
>
> (E. J. Working (1927), pp. 224–5)

He did not actually try to apply this novel suggestion.

E. J. Working's systematic treatment also covered the problem of correlated shifts in demand and supply curves. Assuming that the demand curve's variability was less than the supply curve's variability, he showed that the elasticity of the line would be either lower or higher, depending on whether the correlation was positive or negative, than that of the 'true' demand parameters. He argued that provided no structural changes occurred, such as the imposition of tariffs, these empirical curves could be used for prediction purposes. He did not attempt to deal with the particularly knotty problem of equal variability and correlated shifts.

Both E. J. Working's analysis of the problem and its answers were clearly laid out. Much of what he stated was already well understood (as is shown by the work of Lehfeldt, Lenoir and the reviews of Moore) but he did make substantial contributions of his own, first in defining the problem of equal variability but uncorrelated shifts in demand and supply, and secondly in dealing with the problem of correlated shifts. It is interesting to note that he seemed not to think of statistical relationships in the first instance as being direct counterparts to theoretical relationships, instead he used theory to help interpret what he had observed in his experiments. His approach was rather one of identification as locating relationships in the data, which he believed might have counterparts in economic theory or might not.

Mordecai Ezekiel, in 'Statistical Analyses and the "Laws" of Price' (1928), believed that E. J. Working was using the wrong economic model and that if the theoretical model were correctly chosen then the parameters could always be identified[10] He justified the use of a single-equation models by broadening the usable economic theory to include not only Marshallian demand curves but also the Wicksteed demand curve. In a much quoted passage, Wicksteed (1914) had denied the existence of the Marshallian supply curve and advocated instead the demand curve of all those who wished to possess the commodity. The Marshallian supply curve in Wicksteed's analysis became part of the 'total demand curve'. In Ezekiel's discussions, then, the 'Marshallian cross' referred to a consumers' market with a con-sumers' demand curve and a supply curve of goods or stocks onto the market. The Wicksteed demand curve was the curve of the demand by all possible holders of the good: producers, whosesalers, speculators and consumers. Ezekiel argued that in most markets, supply adjust-ments to market conditions were not instantaneous and therefore a lagged supply model, such as Moore's two-equation system, could be used. If they were instantaneous, then the supply curve could be treated as the producers' reservation demand curve and the total demand curve of all possible holders of the good (the Wicksteed demand curve) could be estimated instead. So, Ezekiel argued, by careful analysis of the market, the correct economic model could be chosen prior to any empirical work and the identification problem created by the two-equation supply and demand model could be avoided.

By defining the problem as one of theory choice, Ezekiel, like Holbrook Working missed the point. In E. J. Working's analysis, identification of either the Marshallian demand curve or Wicksteed's demand curve depended on the shifting of the supply curve. In the

---

[10] Mordecai Ezekiel (1899–1974) worked on economic problems for the US Government Department of Agriculture and its agencies, see Fox (1989). He published articles on econometrics and was well known for his practical textbook, *Methods of Correlation Analysis* (1930). Later he turned to development economics and to work for the international agencies in that field.

Wicksteed case (which, by the way, E. J. Working thought was only applicable to non-durable goods in the short term), the supply curve is the total stock of the good available and when this shifts over time it is highly likely that producers' demand schedules will also shift so that shifts in demand and supply curves will be correlated. Ezekiel seemed to think that, in case of such correlations, the necessary adjustments for the factors affecting one of the curves could be made without affecting the other. (He also suggested that use of the orthogonal regression method would help to get around the problem of correlated shifts.) But, again, as E. J. Working's work had suggested, although some empirical relationship might be located, the presence of correlated shifts made the interpretation of this as a demand curve doubtful.

In contrast to the well-defined theoretical analyses of the identification problem conducted by the Working brothers and Ezekiel, Philip Green Wright's (1929) criticism of Schultz's (1928) book used simulated experiments to demonstrate, simply and effectively, the nature of the identification problem.[11] The approach he criticised was the Schultz–Moore method of using simple single or two-equation models with pre-adjusted data. Wright drew out a stable supply curve of known constant elasticity and a set of parallel demand curves of known elasticity. He extracted observations on the points of intersection of the curves. To these data points he applied Schultz's estimation methods and attempted to reconstruct his original curves and known information on the elasticities. Of course, Wright failed, and managed to obtain only the supply curve and its elasticity. He repeated the experiment for a fixed demand curve with moving supply curve and for a third case of both curves shifting. He found respectively his original demand curve and a horizontal trend line which gave him neither his demand nor supply elasticities back again. The results of two of these experiments are reproduced in Figure 14. Wright had shown here what was clearly latent in Moore's positive demand curve and the critical reaction to it, namely that if the economy generated data from a fixed supply and moving demand curve, then, at most, only information on the supply parameter could be gleaned from the data and nothing could ever be learnt about the demand parameter.

[11] Philip Green Wright (1861–1934) trained as an engineer and later studied economics under Taussig at Harvard. He taught mathematics, economics and literature at a small-town college in Illinois for much of his working life. A man of many parts he wrote poetry and ran a small publishing press from his basement. (His proudest achievement was to have taught the American poet Carl Sandburg, and to have published his first volumes of poems.) In middle age, he returned to Harvard as an instructor and thence went to Washington to undertake economic research for the US Tariff Commission and then the Brookings Institution. His trenchant criticisms of econometric practice appeared for the most part in book reviews (see Chapters 1.2, 5.1 and 6.1).

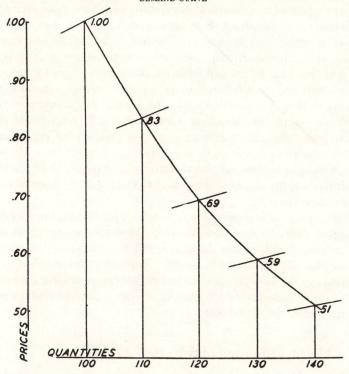

DEMAND CONDITIONS STATIONARY: SUPPLY CONDITIONS CHANGE; DATA REVEAL
DEMAND CURVE

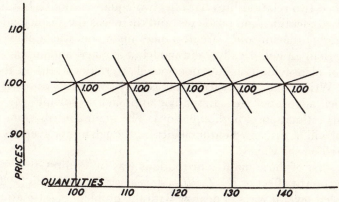

DEMAND AND SUPPLY CONDITIONS BOTH CHANGE; DATA AFFORD NO EVIDENCE
OF EITHER SUPPLY OR DEMAND CURVE

Figure 14   Results from Wright's identification experiments
Source: P. G. Wright (1929), pp. 212–13, Charts II and III

If more proof of the existence of the problem was needed following E. J. Working's treatment, Wright's experiment certainly provided it.

Wright's second criticism was concerned with the parameter results that Schultz had obtained. Schultz's results showed that the coefficients of demand and supply approached equal value but opposite signs as the price–quantitiy correlation approached unity. Wright suggested that this happened because the specification of the model (Moore's two-equation cobweb model) produced two correlations for the same data series first without, and then with, a lag; it was not because the supply and demand parameters really were equal and of opposite signs. Schultz was aware of this problem of equal valued parameters with opposite signs and was more careful than Moore (of whom Wright later made the same criticism) in deciding first whether the industry supply response was likely to be lagged, by how much and in which direction.

Wright's criticisms show the way in which problems of model choice overlapped with those of identification. Moore's two-equation model could be identified from the data, as could Wright's trend model; they were empirically identifiable models. But they did not necessarily correspond to the underlying behavioural processes or have parameters which could be interpreted in terms of economic theory or which would be of interest to the economist.

6.3   The identification of two relationships

Up to this point, most of the discussion had been concerned with identifying (in the senses of locating and interpreting) the demand relationship in the presence of the supply relationship. Moore had identified two relationships with his two-equation model, but had not discussed identification problems, and there was the suspicion (voiced by Wright) that in some circumstances his model was a convenience rather than an empirically valid model of demand and supply. Other ways of identifying two-equation models were developed in the later 1920s. Wright and Tinbergen extended E. J. Working's analysis, while Leontief advocated an alternative approach involving the simultaneous estimation of both equations. The main contributions to this subject will be discussed chronologically, though minor avenues will be explored on the way.

The first of these main contributions was by Philip Green Wright, writing on the effect of *The Tariff on Animal and Vegetable Oils* (1928). He suggested several ways of dealing with the problem of estimating both demand and supply curves:

Elasticity of supply/demand can be computed only when assurance is obtained that the cost/demand curve remains fixed while the demand/cost curve is changing its position. Such assurance may come from an intimate knowledge of the industry or from statistical methods introducing additional data.   (Wright (1928), pp. 310–11)

Wright believed his first idea would be applicable when it was reasonable to assume that demand variability was high and random and supply shifts were small and in one direction. In this case a slope coefficient for each successive pair of observations could be obtained. By taking only the positive slopes and finding their median, he argued that an approximately 'true' supply elasticity could be found (and negative slopes would give a demand elasticity).

Using a similar approach to this idea of Wright, a paper by A. C. Pigou (1930) deserves brief attention here. Pigou complained that econometricians sought the 'most probable' demand curve without giving any idea of the probability attached to their results. He attempted to apply the ideas of probability and statistical distributions to identification of the 'true' demand parameter. Pigou assumed that demand shifts were independent of supply shifts and his method depended crucially on a further assumption of equal shifts of the demand curve in each time period. Taking logs of successive observations in threes, he derived sets ('triads') of equidistant parallel lines.[12] He rejected those triads which had a positive slope (which he did not try to interpret as supply curves), and those which were based on very small movements in the price and quantity data. He then considered the distribution of the remaining slope coefficients. He believed that errors in measurement were unlikely to be normally distributed and decided to take the median of the slope observations as a measure of the elasticity of demand.

Unfortunately Pigou's new method proved useless since, as Ferger (1932a) and Cassels (1933) pointed out, it gave the correct result only under the very unlikely conditions implied by Pigou's assumptions of parallel and equal shifts in the demand curve and uncorrelated shifts in the supply curve. Moreover, Ferger showed that Pigou's method would fail to identify the demand curve if the demand curve were stable since the observation points would be collinear giving no result at all. Both Pigou's and Wright's methods also suffered from the drawback that they magnified the effect of measurement errors in the data.

[12] Pigou also assumed that for any three successive time points, the demand shifts were parallel as well as of equal length. His method was based on the fact that through any three points, three sets of equidistant parallel lines can be drawn, but only one set if they are ordered (i.e. numbered so that the line through the second observation $t = 2$, in the time sequence $t = 1,2,3$, lies in the centre).

Wright's other suggestions for estimating demand and supply curves were applicable in situations where the 'intimate knowledge' of market conditions required for his first method was lacking. In these cases, Wright claimed, other statistical data would have to be substituted since the ability to estimate both supply and demand curves depended on additional information:

> In the absence of intimate knowledge of demand and supply conditions, statistical methods for imputing fixity to one of the curves while the other changes its position must be based on the introduction of additional factors. Such additional factors may be factors which (A) affect demand conditions without affecting cost conditions or which (B) affect cost conditions without affecting demand conditions.
>
> (Wright (1928), pp. 311–12)

He suggested two (or rather three) ways of using this additional information. The first way was to eliminate separately from the price and quantity data all factors influencing demand or supply (E. J. Working's suggestion):

> A complementary process would obviously be to find the relation between output and price, after eliminating the effects of all factors (A) which affect cost conditions or after eliminating the effects of all factors (B) which affect demand conditions. This may be possible by the method of partial correlation.   (Wright (1928), p. 312 n. 13)

(Note the extra idea in the last sentence.) Wright's proposed alternative to data adjustment methods was to make direct use of additional factors in the estimation process, but it was the way he decided to use this extra information that was completely new. He demonstrated, with a treatment which was part graphs and part algebra, how the additional factor (A), uncorrelated with supply but correlated with demand (for example, the price of a substitute good), could be used to find the elasticity of supply (and similarly how a supply factor (B), uncorrelated with shifts in demand, could be used to find the demand elasticity). He used these conditions of correlation and non-correlation of the additional disturbing factors in each relationship to derive instrumental variable estimators of the elasticities of demand (e_D) and supply (e_S):

$$\hat{e}_D = \frac{\Sigma B_t Q_t}{\Sigma B_t P_t} \qquad \hat{e}_S = \frac{\Sigma A_t Q_t}{\Sigma A_t P_t}$$

Wright's new method allowed the identification of both demand and supply parameters. Finally, he also showed that the method of path analysis, a sort of causal chain model and method of estimation, developed by his son Sewall Wright, would give the same result as his instrumental variable method.[13] P. G. Wright's applied work used various of the methods he had discussed. For example he calculated the elasticity of demand for butter using the 'successive slopes' method ($-.53$) and by the instrumental variables method ($-.62$). Wright's treatment of identification questions did not make much impact: the method of path analysis was developed in biometrics and genetics but rarely applied in econometrics, and the general idea of instrumental variable estimators was not really 'discovered' and developed until the 1940s (see Chapter 7).

Another important contribution to the debate on identification and estimation of demand supply curves was Wassily Leontief's (1929) paper. Leontief assumed that the economy was an equilibrium system and so demand and supply curves could not be measured separately but must be derived together from the same data. He viewed each observation as the mean of a group of points which themselves were the intersection points of a number of static instantaneous demand and supply curves. The fitted demand and supply curves were then the average curves for the whole period. He made the usual assumptions of constant elasticity along the curves and over time (he used log data), so that shifts in each curve were parallel. (These simplifying assumptions were fairly standard in econometric work on demand since they enabled linear demand functions to be fitted to the data.) The difference of any point from the average supply or demand curve (measured in a direction parallel to the other curve in each case) was then due to the movement or shift at that time point from the average position. But although he assumed an equilibrium world, his most important assumption, the one upon which his method depended, was that shifts in demand and supply curves were independent of each other. The method itself consisted of arbitrarily splitting the data set into two and fitting both demand and supply curves to both sets (by minimising the deviations in a direction parallel to the other curve), and imposing the condition that they have one pair of curves in common. (Schultz (1938) gives further details of the method.) Leontief considered that pre-adjusting data to eliminate trend effects was an empirical approach and therefore undesirable. He mostly worked with

[13] Sewall Wright (1889–1987) (son of P. G. Wright) had developed path analysis for his own use in genetics in the period prior to 1920. He applied it to the problem of corn and hog cycles in agricultural economics (not published until 1925) and carried out the path analysis for his father's book. Henry Schultz knew Sewall Wright quite well (they were both at the University of Chicago and used to go hiking together) and occasionally used his method of path analysis (e.g. in his 1928 book). Further description of path analysis and a discussion of the methods used by P. G. Wright can be found in Goldberger (1972).

unadjusted data (though he sometimes used moving averages of the data) and estimated demand and supply curves for 46 different data series on seven commodities.

Leontief's paper appeared in a German journal and was immediately taken up and discussed by American econometricians. Both Gilboy (1931) and Schultz (1938)[14] gave examples comparing Leontief's method with the standard Schultz method (that is, single regression of pre-adjusted data series) for specific commodities. Gilboy preferred Leontief's method in theory but concluded that it was useless in practice because the assumption of complete independence in the shifts in supply and demand was unlikely to be realised in unadjusted data. Schultz concluded that Leontief's elasticities were 'numerical accidents' since there was nothing in the method to prevent both slopes being negative or both positive. Despite the validity of these criticisms, Leontief's paper marked an ingenious and challenging attempt to estimate a two-equation demand and supply model simultaneously and without resorting to Moore's methods of lagging data.

The solution to the two-equation model problem used in econometrics today was first found by Jan Tinbergen in a 1930 paper; 'Bestimmung und Deutung von Angebotskurven',[15] Tinbergen stated clearly at the beginning of his paper that the problem of identifying demand and supply functions with variable price and quantity observations was insoluble unless information additional to price and quantity data was available. To start with, he rejected the solution proposed in Moore's work on the two-equation lagged model because of the implications of such a simple cobweb model:

> This assumption, however, can only be accepted if the supply really only depends on the price of the previous year and is independent of e.g. natural factors such as doubtlessly are operative in the case of agricultural products. Moreover, it can be seen, ... that a continued movement of prices and quantities is possible only if the value of b_1 [supply parameter] approximately equals that of $(-a_1)$ [minus the demand parameter]. As soon as b_1 is different from $(-a_1)$, the mechanism ... leads either to increasingly violent fluctuations, or to a rapid restoration of the equilibrium position.
>
> (Tinbergen (1930), p. 2, parentheses added and terms changed to preserve consistency with text)

[14] The discussion of Leontief's work in the text of Schultz (1938) was taken from his publication in German of 1930. This was not published in English but was in limited circulation under the title 'Meaning of Statistical Demand Curves'. Gilboy (1931) also relied on Schultz's unpublished 1930 paper.

[15] In English: 'Determination and Interpretation of Supply Curves'. The translation quoted here is Tinbergen's own (but the mathematical notation has been changed to the same as that used in this chapter). The full translation appears in Hendry and Morgan (forthcoming).

Tinbergen explained with the help of diagrams, just why econometricians should be suspicious of the parameter results found with
Moore's model. P. G. Wright (1929) had earlier tried to explain the
problem; Tinbergen was the first to analyse the cobweb model properly
and expose its dangers.

Tinbergen's proposal for identifying demand and supply parameters
also relied on the use of additional factors, but instead of using the extra
information to pre-adjust the data (E. J. Working's solution) or to use
as instrumental variables (as P. G. Wright had done), he derived what
is now known as the reduced form model. Most unusually for the
period, Tinbergen made a clear distinction between the latent theoretical economic variables and the observed data outcomes. He demonstrated his ideas with the following model:

Demand function $d(\pi) = a_0 + a_1\pi$
Supply function $\quad s(\pi) = b_0 + b_1\pi + b_2B$

(where π is any possible price, and B is a supply variable). He solved for
the reduced form:

$$Q = \frac{a_1 b_2 B}{a_1 - b_1} \quad \text{and} \quad P = \frac{b_2 B}{a_1 - b_1}$$

(now ignoring the intercept terms and where Q is the actual quantity
and P the actual price) to show that only a_1 and therefore the demand
function could be identified while the supply parameter (b_1) remained
indeterminate. In order to identify the supply curve in his model, he
added a further variable, A, to the demand function:

$$d(\pi) = a_0 + a_1\pi + a_2A$$

solved for the reduced form, and showed that both demand and supply
parameters could be identified. Tinbergen also suggested that the two
equations could be separately estimated in their original (i.e. structural) form and the parameters would be identified.[16]

Although the use of the reduced form method of deriving these results
was new to econometrics, the mathematical solution to the problem of
simultaneous equations was of course well known. But it is emphasised
that Tinbergen was not concerned with the problem of simultaneity in
the statistical relationships, nor was his own model discussed in such

[16] Tinbergen used neither of the terms 'reduced form' or 'structural form'. Structural
relationships were defined by Frisch and Waugh (but not until 1933) as relationships
derived from theory to represent, in ideal form, some empirical phenomena. It is
interesting to note that Tinbergen referred to the parameters of the reduced form as
determining 'the structure of the variations' in the two endogenous variables. Neither term
was generally used until the 1940s.

terms. The role of the reduced form in his work was primarily to provide a way of checking and demonstrating that the parameters of interest (the demand and supply parameters) were identifiable. The secondary use of the reduced form as an estimation device was perceived by Tinbergen to be no different from the use of ordinary least squares on the two individual equations (which he called the 'direct method').[17]

Not content with this neat theoretical solution to the identification problem, Tinbergen also applied his method to the market for potato flour, a product for which Holland was the main exporter in the 1920s. So, in the model above, the variable B was production of potatoes plus stocks at the beginning of the production year, and A was the domestic potato crops of France and Germany (the main importers of Dutch flour). He estimated the parameters of the reduced form model and solved back to find the structural form parameters ($a_1 = -6.9$, $b_1 = 12.2$); and he also estimated by the 'direct method': estimating the structural form equations separately (giving $a_1 = -6.2$, $b_1 = 11.2$). He noted, without explaining, the slight difference in the results (which were presumably due to simultaneous equations bias in the structural form estimates). All this theoretical analysis and estimation was in fact only background to the main purpose of Tinbergen's paper which was an investigation into the structure of the supplying industry. This involved modelling and estimating supply curves based on different assumptions about the extent of the competition (discussed in Chapter 5.3) and the dynamics of market adjustments.

Tinbergen's approach was distinctly different from that of E. J. Working. Tinbergen wanted to find the parameters of a given theoretical model. Before undertaking his applied work, Tinbergen worked out (using the reduced form derived from the theoretical model) the conditions for the unique determination of his model in terms of the presence, and absence, of explanatory variables in each of the equations. This was very different from E. J. Working's examination of the situations in which relationships could be determined from the data and when these could be interpreted as economic relationships. Despite the remarkable features of Tinbergen's paper, the initial section on identification with its stress on incorporating additional information

---

[17] Tinbergen at this stage did not understand the statistical estimation problem of simultaneous equations models, as he makes clear in Magnus and Morgan (1987). This was possible because he, like all other econometricians of the period, wrote down his econometric models without error terms and made no explicit probabilistic statements about his estimation (see Chapter 8 for further discussion). The reduced form method of estimation as a solution to bias in estimating the simultaneous equations model was not formally introduced in econometrics until Haavelmo's work of the 1940s (see Chapter 7 Letter 14).

into the model and its reduced form solution appears to have made no impact on other econometricians. For example, Marschak (1934) discussed Tinbergen's paper but did not mention the reduced form method while Ezekiel (1938) referenced the paper only for its use of the cobweb model. Schultz (1938) strangely, considering his wide knowledge of the literature, did not reference the paper at all. Frisch (1933a), who was next to tackle the subject, did not reference the paper either; he did derive a reduced form model along with many other algebraic formulae but he did not use it in his own solution to the problem.

The last of the papers requiring examination is Ragnar Frisch's (1933a) article, 'Pitfalls in the Statistical Construction of the Demand and Supply Curves', which had three aims. It formed a critique of 'careless methods' of demand analysis, a general examination of identification problems and finally a response to Leontief's (1929) work. Frisch wrote of the problems of demand analysis:

> In this field we need, I believe, a new type of significance analysis, which is not based on mechanical application of standard errors computed according to some more or less plausible statistical mathematical formulae, but is based on a thoroughgoing comparative study of the various possible types of assumptions regarding the economic-theoretical set up, and of the consequences which these assumptions entail for the interpretation of the observational data. (Frisch (1933a), p. 39)

Note once again Frisch's desire to create a 'new type' of analysis; and he believed that he had introduced this in this paper.

The first section of Frisch's paper provided a cogent criticism of the sort of method adopted by Pigou, which Frisch described as the case of

> fictitious determinateness created by random errors.
> (Frisch (1933a), p. 7)

He warned that when two data series were both subject to errors of observation, measuring the relationship between them by taking slopes of successive pairs of observations would often result in incorrect measurement. This was because, in cases where successive observations were approximately equal, the observed slope was entirely a function of the measurement errors and a nonsense result would be obtained. Although Frisch did not reference Pigou's work, it is clear that Pigou's methods was his target here.[18]

---

[18] Allen (1934) reconsidered Pigou's method in the light of Frisch's work. Allen carried out some applied work using Pigou's method to estimate both demand and supply parameters from the same data set. Allen preferred Pigou's method to Leontief's on the ground that its relatively simplicity made it easier spot and reject cases where errors caused the determination of the value and because it was more flexible in its assumptions.

Next Frisch carried out a more general analysis of the identification problem and referred favourably to the 'fundamental paper' of E. J. Working (1927) on this topic. Frisch attacked the problem by assuming that only one set of data on prices and quantities was available, and then considered the assumptions and circumstances under which the parameter estimates obtained from the data could be taken to represent demand and supply elasticities. He set up the problem and obtained its solution in a formal manner and proved analytically the results obtained graphically by E. J. Working in 1927. Frisch specified the following model:

$$\text{Demand function } Q = aP + u$$
$$\text{Supply function } \quad Q = bP + v$$

(where a and b are constant demand and supply elasticities, u and v are time-series shifts which are not directly observable and Q and P the logs of directly observed time-series data on quantities and prices). Frisch then examined the distribution of the observed data set (Q, P) under certain assumptions about the distribution of the unobserved data (u, v). His method used a mathematical analysis of the variances and covariances of the variables in his model.

He considered three limiting cases when the shifts in demand and supply were uncorrelated, that is: $r_{uv}^2 = 0$. Frisch's analysis gave him the following results:

(1)   Demand curve stability implies that $\Sigma u^2 = 0$ and, for a real solution for a to exist, that $r_{QP}^2 = 1$. In this situation, the regression gives the demand relation and the supply parameter b is indeterminate.

(2)   Supply curve stability implies that $\Sigma v^2 = 0$ and again that $r_{QP}^2 = 1$. In this case b is determined and a is indeterminate.

(3)   Bilateral but uncorrelated shifts in demand and supply imply that $\Sigma v^2 \neq 0$ and $\Sigma u^2 \neq 0$. Then the appearance of the (Q,P) set will depend on the relative variances of u and v. Frisch argued that unless reasonable assumptions can be made about these relative variances, then a and b are both indeterminate in this case (and therefore he did not go so far as E. J. Working in his analysis of this problem).

Frisch also gave a similar analysis of the data distributions in the more complicated case where shifts in supply and demand are bilateral and correlated (due to cyclical, trend or other effects). He then summarised his whole analysis from the opposite view point to answer the question:

What underlying assumptions are implied by the observed data characteristics?

Lastly, Frisch turned his attention to Leontief's problem. In Frisch's terminology this amounted to two (Q, P) data sets with the assumptions that a and b are the same in each and u and v are uncorrelated in each. He analysed the features that would be required in the two observed data sets for Leontief's method to determine correctly the demand and supply parameters. The features he considered were the degree of correlation and the relative variances of Q and P in each data set. He argued that if these features were the same for both data sets then only one regression slope (not two, as Leontief hoped) would be determined, and the conditions under which this one relationship would be a demand or supply curve or trend effect would be as already discussed in the case of the single data set.

The analysis necessarily became more complex when the data sets exhibited different features. In the earlier part of his study, Frisch had shown that with one data set, two equations and two parameters to determine, the parameters cannot be determined uniquely unless there is further information. Thus, Leontief can be interpreted as trying to double his data information by splitting his data into two sets. Frisch showed, in the second part of his paper, that if such doubling is spurious – in other words the data sets show similar characteristics – then Leontief is no better off, in fact probably worse off, because he is able to obtain the nonsense or arbitrary results (referred to by Schultz) which would have been indeterminate in the single data set. If the two data sets really do contain different information about the true relationships, then Frisch argued this information could be used to estimate both parameters but only under very restrictive conditions on the error variance matrix which he believed very unlikely to occur in practice.[19] In nearly all cases, then, Frisch believed that Leontief's method would give meaningless or indeterminate results.

Frisch's analysis of identification problems was important not because it provided new results but because he showed other ways of obtaining them. He used the observed data to make informed assumptions about the distributions of the unobserved data (the shifts or error terms) and in turn used this information to achieve identification. It is clear from his analysis of the relationship between observed and unobserved series that Frisch had grasped an idea that is now standard, namely that information (or assumptions made) about the error

---

[19] The error variance matrix must be diagonal and must have $\Sigma u_1{}^2 \gg \Sigma v_1{}^2$ and $\Sigma v_2{}^2 \gg \Sigma u_2{}^2$. In terms of observable variables, Frisch wrote down the conditions as: $r_1{}^2 \neq r_2{}^2$ where r_i is the correlation between P_i and Q_i; and: $\Sigma Q_1{}^2 / \Sigma P_1{}^2 \neq \Sigma Q_2{}^2 / \Sigma P_2{}^2$

variances and covariances is important in determining whether parameters can be identified. It was an essentially different solution from Tinbergen's, who had used additional observed information to identify his parameters.

Like Tinbergen's reduced form notion, Frisch's ideas were not immediately used in applied econometrics, though they did receive some attention and were used by others in their analysis of identification problems.[20] Frisch's ideas were more widely known because his criticism of Leontief led to an acrimonious debate in the pages of the *Quarterly Journal of Economics* in 1934 (see Frisch (1934a), Leontief (1934 and 1934a)). One of the main points of contention was Leontief's assumption of independence in the supply and demand shifts. Leontief's belief in the assumptions of his economic theory was overriding, as is clear in his reply to Frisch:

> the assumption of independence *is really the common foundation of all the statistical attempts at supply and demand analysis*. If there exists a definite interdependence between the two kinds of shifts, i.e. if every upward movement of the demand curve is systematically associated with a proportional upward (or downward) shift of the supply curve, then all the theoretically possible price-quantity combinations necessarily have the tendency to be distributed along a definite single curve. This, however, would be neither the supply nor the demand curve. The cases of pure demand or pure supply shifts (Professor Frisch calls them stability cases) would be not only practically improbable but theoretically impossible. The whole theory of supply and demand would then become vitiated and useless, and would have to be replaced by a theory of the uniquely determined paths of price-quantity variation.
>
> The only real danger to which every statistical supply and demand analysis is exposed is the possibility of a purely accidental (spurious) correlation between the independent shifts of the two curves.
>
> (Leontief (1934), p. 358)

This brought forth a very short-tempered riposte from Frisch (1934a), who pointed out that the root of Leontief's failure to identify supply and demand curves by his method lay in his refusal to consider the theoretical model in relation to the data at hand:

> It is flagrantly incorrect to say ... that the common foundation of all the statistical attempts at demand and supply analysis is the assumption that the shifts of the curves are independent. Those who have followed the actual work in this field will know that the main efforts are at present just concentrated on the study of how the shifts are intercorrelated. When the demand and supply curves are considered in the form used by Dr. Leontief, one of the most important problems, which is nearly always taken up in a modern analysis, is to investigate the *routine of change* of the

[20] Apart from Allen (1934) (see n.18), Metzler (1940) also drew extensively on Frisch's work.

curves. Dr. Leontief's method is fundamentally unsuitable for any such analysis just because he assumes independent shifts ... In general terms this objection may be formulated by saying that frequently the nature of the data at hand will contradict one or more of the assumptions underlying the method, particularly the assumption of independent shifts.

Dr. Leontief does not yet seem to have perceived this aspect of the criticism. He seems to have the idea that he is *in salvo* simply because he can say that independent shifts are amongst his theoretical premises ... No discussion of *premises*, however detailed, can of course ensure that a given set of *data* will have an assigned observable feature ...

Anybody who makes a hypothesis – as, for instance, the one of independent shifts – has of course a *duty* of trying to make sure that there is nothing in his data which contradicts his hypothesis. He must investigate the various possibilities and try to obtain criteria that can guide him in his estimate of the fit between hypothesis and data. Nothing of that sort was done regarding the hypothesis of independent shifts in Dr. Leontief's first study, and now he even tells us that he does not want to do it.

(Frisch (1934a), pp. 749–50)

Leontief and Frisch could not agree and it was left to Marschak to try and calm the debate and suggest compromises. For example, Marschak (1934) suggested that Leontief split the data set according to the assumptions laid down by Frisch as necessary for the method, rather than split the data set in an arbitrary fashion.

6.4   Back to the single demand curve

Reviewing the advances made on the theory of identification in the 1920s and 1930s it seems clear that considerable progress had been made. 'The identification problem' of uniquely determining parameters of a known model was quite generally understood and the basic conditions for its solution, although not codified into rank and order conditions, had been put forward. These conditions involved the presence of additional information on observed variables (shift factors required in one equation and excluded from the other) or on unobserved variables (the less well-known and understood variance and covariance features of Frisch's unobservable shifts). In addition, the reduced form model had been derived and used to investigate and check the identification of a two-equation system.

Despite these theoretical advances, applied work on demand in the 1930s stuck to single-equation models. These models incorporated additional demand factors, which it was hoped were not highly correlated with supply shifts. By the 1930s it was recognised that the incorporation of these additional factors stabilised the demand relationship between prices and quantities, and was equivalent in effect to E. J. Working's solution of separate adjustments, or the partial correlations solution suggested by P. G. Wright. Providing the unacknowledged supply curve continued to shift, such a demand relationship was identified in the sense that a price-quantity curve could be located and, if negatively sloped, the curve could be interpreted as a demand relationship, even though there was no 'proof' that the demand curve was uniquely identified.

For a representative example of this late 1930s view of identification problems there is perhaps none better than Schultz's (1938) book. His discussion of identification drew only on the explorations of E. J. Working (1927) and P. G. Wright's review (1929) of Schultz's earlier book. He defined four possible configurations: a fixed demand curve, a fixed supply curve, shifts in both and both curves fixed. He believed that it was unlikely that shifts in the curves would be totally uncorrelated, but his treatment of the subject was not rigorous. Schultz referred to Frisch's work on identification only in a footnote (for its criticism of Leontief) and failed to reference Tinbergen's (1930) paper at all, despite his familiarity with the European literature.

The failure to take up the new solutions proposed by Frisch, Wright and Tinbergen for identifying and estimating two-equation models or checking the indentification of single demand equations accounts for the historical importance and influence of E. J. Working's widely read and easily understood paper. But the failure itself requires explanation. Wright's use of additional information in the form of instrumental variables appears to have remained unrecognised, as did Tinbergen's derived reduced form model. This may be because Wright's ideas were tucked away in a book devoted to tariff problems and his use of instrumental variables, though easy enough to follow in his particular example, was not perhaps easy to grasp and apply as a general idea. Tinbergen's identification work was published in German; but this is not a compelling reason, for, as we already noted, Tinbergen's paper was referenced. In particular, Marschak (1934) noted that Tinbergen's work was unusual because he estimated a two-equation supply and demand model, but he noticed nothing unusual about the method. In any case the leading English speaking econometricians typically kept up with the continental European literature.

A more compelling reason in Tinbergen's case may be that the reduced form proposed by Tinbergen had no equivalent in the comparative statics diagram which E. J. Working had used to show how shifts in the demand or supply curves can identify one of the curves. The economic meaning of the reduced form equations remained obscure (as did the similar final form equations in Tinbergen's business cycle work). Tinbergen himself used the reduced form as a way of showing Working's results using algebra, not because he regarded it as having any important meaning in itself. When faced with a similar problem of interdependent equations in his work for the League of Nations, he did not use a straight reduced form but alternative 'mongrel' equations (a sort of modified reduced form) in which he estimated separately a demand or supply equation and a price equation which could be interpreted in economic terms.[21] In addition, the predominant styles of explanation and reasoning in statistical demand analysis were still words and diagrams. Mathematically expressed and argued treatments of general problems in econometrics were rare, for there was as yet little that could be called econometric theory. So even though the reduced form solution to a simultaneous equations problem was familar in mathematics, such manipulation in statistical economics as in Tinbergen's or Frisch's treatments was very unusual.

Frisch's results on identification suffered from some of the same difficulties as Tinbergen's. In the first place, they were presented in a highly technical mathematical form which, as noted above, was unusual in econometrics at that time. Both Frisch's general approach and his new two-equation solution used the formal errors-in-equations model which was not usually fully specified in applied work in the 1930s. This unfamiliarity probably acted against the application of his ideas. Secondly, his treatment of E. J. Working's ideas on single-equation models involved the use of unobservable factors but no new results on observable factors. Frisch's paper was more influential in stressing the pitfalls of the new methods of measurement proposed at that time than in providing new ideas for standard econometric work on demand; consequently his paper had little influence on ordinary applied work.

After this work of the late 1920s and early 1930s, the theoretical problem of identification was not taken up again until the work of Koopmans and others at the Cowles Commission in the 1940s. This work, stimulated by Frisch's (1938) paper on autonomous relationships and business cycles, led to the codification of the rank and order conditions for identification of linear models involving several equations (see Qin (1989) and Epstein (1987)). Their other advance was in dealing with the problem of overidentification, whereas the work of the 1920s and 1930s had dealt with the cases of just-identified and underidentified models (see Koopmans (1949 and 1950)). This codification and formalisation of the identification problem transformed it into a technical problem divorced from the other correspondence problems of location, interpretation and even model choice, of which in the 1920s and 1930s it was seen to be a part.

[21] An example of this is discussed in Tinbergen (1939), II, pp. 52–3.

Part III

Formal models in econometrics

Introduction to formal models

The last part of this book examines how econometricians formalised and generalised their ideas on the relationship between economic theory and economic data. We see that they developed three formal models of the way in which observed statistical relationships might correspond to their expected theoretical relationships. Each model provided an explanation of the data-theory gap and a rationalisation of the approximate, rather than exact, fit found in measured economic laws. One model explained these approximations in terms of measurement errors: the errors-in-variables model. Another explanation rested on variables omitted from the measurement equation: the errors-in-equations model. The third model provided a more general explanation of the relationship between empirical results and economic theory by treating the theoretical relationship as probabilistic. Each of the three models was associated with an appropriate statistical analysis.

So far, this history has concentrated on the development of econometrics within its applied context. Econometricians have been portrayed as responding (not always successfully) to problems thrown up in their applied work. These last chapters provide a more integrated history of the field. They draw both on the applied work of the period (discussed in the earlier chapters) and on the theoretical discussions of econometricians, which began in earnest only in the 1930s. In particular, Chapter 7 offers a synthetic reconstruction of the development of the ideas involved in formal models. It concentrates on the development of the errors-in-equations and errors-in-variables models and brings in the probability model only briefly. Chapter 8 returns to the narrative style to interpret the change in thought, and in practice, associated with the introduction of the probability approach into econometrics.

CHAPTER 7

Errors-in-variables and errors-in-equations models

The evolution of formal models of the data-theory relationship is complex and intertwined with other important issues in theoretical econometrics such as identification, simultaneity and causality. The tale of how these models developed is recounted through a series of letters which I imagine to have been written by econometricians of the period 1900 to 1950. these letters provide both a synthesis of the history of the ideas involved and a rather personal internal account. The imaginary authors of these letters (named with Greek letters) represent the composite views of a number of econometricians; none consistently represents the views of any single writer. Following Lakatos (1976), the actual history (authors, dates and sources) is told in the notes following each letter. These notes are brief, for most of the literature and ideas involved either have already been discussed in the context of the applied work or will be discussed in detail in the final chapter. Although some letters bear a close resemblance to articles cited in the footnotes, others elucidate less explicit views. The growing formality of the model representations in the letters, and the increasingly technical nature of the discussions, also reflect the real literature.

The chapter is divided into two major parts and a substantive postscript. The first part is concerned with the development of a data-theory model for single relationships and the second with models for interdependent relationships; there is no real break in the history intended here, more a change into a higher gear as the problems become more complex and the treatment more technical. The last part of the chapter, a postscript to the main story, is concerned with the development of instrumental variable estimators within the errors-in-variables programme.

7.1 Errors and the single equation

Letter 1   From Alpha to Beta

Dear Beta,

I have spent some time recently experimenting with ways of measuring economic laws and now find myself in a quandary; I was advised that you might be able to help me. I began using regression methods because they seemed appropriate to the task but now I am not so sure. For example, I have collected the data for the consumption of sugar over the last century with a view to measuring the elasticity of demand for that good. I have price and quantity data, and I could measure the elasticity by regressing price on quantity data or vice versa, by regressing quantity on price. This will give me two different demand elasticities, one from each regression. Can they both be true? Surely there is only one true elasticity for each good – but how am I to find out which one? Do I use both in some way (for example, by taking the average) or are there established grounds for making the choice?

Can you shed any light on this problem for me please? I should mention that I am directing the same enquiry to Gamma who I believe has also been dabbling in this field.

Yours Alpha

The problem of regression choice in economics was posed by Mackeprang, a Dane, in his thesis (1906) though it is unlikely that his work was well known. The existence of two regressions was also pointed out by Persons (1910) in a more widely circulated form, and by Lenoir (1913).

Letter 2   From Beta to Alpha

Dear Alpha,

Thank you for your letter regarding the choice of regression problem. The question has a straightforward solution. As an economist, I believe in certain deterministic relationships or causal laws in economic behaviour. Economic variables do not just occur of their own free will, but are determined in the marketplace. So, if I write down the linear demand equation:

(1) $Q = a_0 + a_1 P$

(where Q is the quantity demanded of a good, P is the price of the good) then I am stating my own particular belief that prices determine quantities (that is, quantities depend on prices). Another economist might believe a different hypothesis: that prices depend on quantities demanded:

$$(2) \quad P = A_0 + A_1 Q$$

Your theoretical beliefs will decide which way you write down the demand relationship and therefore which regression equation to use to measure the demand elasticity.

This seems to me the obvious answer to your question and one which I believe has been adopted generally. I hope it makes sense to you.

Yours Beta

Economists chose different versions of the demand relationship to form the basis of their measurement equations. For example, Moore (1911 and 1914) was reasonably explicit about his theoretical beliefs which he translated directly into an equation representing the causal relationship which then formed his regression equation. There was no conscious choice of regression, only a conscious choice of economic theory.

Letter 3   From Alpha to Beta

Dear Beta,

Thank you for your explanation and highly practical solution to my problem of regression choice. Perhaps you could advise me further on one point? You have suggested that the choice of economic relationship decides which regression you use. But the data do not lie on the measured curve whichever regression is chosen, so how can it be the true law of demand? My experience suggests that it is very difficult to get a high correlation when working with simple demand models and data. What does it mean if the correlation between the price and quantity data is low and what should I do in such a case?

Regards Alpha

The problem of lack of exact fit in the measured economic relationship was discussed by, for example, Moore (1917) and King (1917).

Letter 4   From Beta to Alpha

Dear Alpha,

I have to admit that my own experience tallies with yours in as much as exact correlations are rarely achieved. But, I do not think you should throw out your initial hypothesis unless the degree of correlation is very low. If it is low then you should first try fitting a different function to the two variables (a quadratic instead of a linear function), or use the observations in a different form. If this makes the fit reasonably good, then I think you can feel that your measurements are not too far away from the true ones.

There is a second way of improving the fit. We know quite well that there are many factors which cause variations in the demand schedule for a good apart from its price: namely the prices of other goods, changes in tastes, in population, in the quality of goods and other economic factors. If we can remove the effects of all these factors before measuring the price–quantity equation we should observe an exact relationship. In practice it is impossible to account for all the disturbing factors, but adjustment for even the two or three most important ones will usually cause a considerable increase in the degree of correlation.

As you rightly point out, unless the fit is exact, the measured equation can not be equal to the true equation. However, a high degree of correlation suggests that the most important factors disturbing the relation have been taken account of (by pre-adjusting the data before regression) and so justifies the claim that the measured equation is approximately equal to the true one.

Yours Beta

The suggestion of trying different functions if a poor fit was obtained was made by Moore (1914); in 1917 he expressed the view that omitted variables cause lack of exact measurement of demand curves. Early workers, including Moore, preferred to try to exclude the effects of the disturbing factors before regression took place (other examples: Lenoir (1913) and King (1917)). The idea of an exact underlying relationship was standard; economists maintained a non-stochastic view of the world.

Letter 5   From Gamma to Alpha (in response to Letter 1)

Dear Alpha,

In response to your enquiry about the regression choice question, let me first lay out the problem as I see it. An exact linear relationship exists in the real world between the variables (in this case between the price and the quantity demanded of a good) and this economic relationship can be measured to give the true demand elasticity. The problem is that the standard regression method provides two alternative

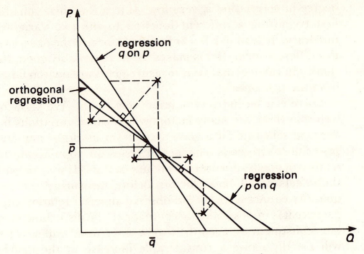

Figure 15   Elementary and orthogonal regressions

measurements. Do I understand you correctly? If so, then the answer depends on the presence of measurement errors in the data. These errors account for the scattering of the points which mask the underlying exact relationship. The two different regressions apply according to which variable contains the measurement errors. So, the choice of regression has nothing to do with economic theory (as Beta would have you believe), which only defines the general relationship that you are trying to measure.

To elaborate: if you know (or can reasonably assume) that the price data are correctly observed but that the quantity data have been measured with error then you should regress quantity on price. This is because, in this case, the regression method minimises the measurement errors in the quantity data. It does so by minimising the sum of the squared deviations between the observed quantity values and the fitted line (in a direction parallel to the price axis). If, on the other hand, you believe that prices are measured inaccurately but that there are no errors in the quantity data, then you should choose the other regression of price on quantity. Then the least squares method will minimise the errors of measurement in the price data. You can see the two regressions in the diagram [Figure 15].

In economics, most of our variables will be subject to errors of observation or measurement. Certainly, in the demand model discussed here, it would seem to me more reasonable to assume that both variables (price and quantity) are measured with error. If that is the case, then neither of the two elementary regressions I have mentioned will be correct in the sense of giving the true measured relationship, for each will ignore the errors in one of the variables. But there is a way of allowing for measurement errors in both variables, known as the orthogonal regression. This regression minimises the shortest distances from the observations to the fitted line (the normals to the line). The orthogonal regression line (also in my diagram) will always lie between the two elementary regression lines.

Of course the orthogonal regression is not the perfect solution. Like the elementary regression, its coefficients will change if the scale of the variables changes. This is not a very satisfactory state of affairs. A more interesting problem arises when we do know something about the errors and would like to use this information in taking the true measurement. Unfortunately, as yet, we have no general method to accommodate this information.

I trust you will find this helpful.

Yours Gamma

The errors-in-variables model was the standard one for statisticians and scientists of the nineteenth century: see S. M. Stigler (1986). In economics, we find that, for example, Clark (1913) blamed his failure to obtain an exact curve on measurement problems. The idea that inexact results were obtained because of the presence of measurement errors in the data was formally introduced into econometrics by Gini (1921) and more forcefully by Schultz (1925). both writers also suggested using the orthogonal regression, Gini using a graph like the one used here to explain the idea. Schultz (1928) noted that it made particular assumptions about the measurement errors which might not be correct. He also noted the problem of scale dependency and thought it made the orthogonal regression unreliable to use. The diagonal mean regression was developed by Frisch (1928) in an attempt to find a regression which was not scale dependent.

Letter 6   From Gamma to Beta

Dear Beta,

I have been corresponding with Alpha regarding the interesting problem of regression choice in measuring economic relationships. As you probably know, I favour the measurement error approach whereas I understand that in your view, economic theory determines the choice of regression. I feel certain that such superficial statements do credit to neither of our viewpoints. I would like to ask a couple of questions about your approach; in return I would be most interested in your views on my own ideas.

I expect you are fairly familiar with my views, but a restatement does no harm and the questions that I have spring from them. I believe that there exists an exact linear relationship between the true variables of a given economic relationship (I do not insist on linearity except as a simplifying device). These economic relationships would manifest themselves in exactly defined empirical relationships, were it not for the presence of measurement errors in the observations. In order to find the true relationship it is necessary to have knowledge (or failing that to make some informed assumptions) about the presence and size of the measurement errors. The differences between the observations and the fitted line (the residuals of the regression) are due to the presence of these measurement errors.

For me, the choice of economic relationship is an entirely separate question from the choice of regression. Like you, I think of economic laws as involving cause and effect relationships. The choice of variables in the causal relationship of interest and the form of the relationship are determined by economic theory. But the choice of statistical method we use to measure the relationship must be determined by the statistical characteristics of the variables, otherwise we will not accurately measure the empirical relationship that exists. Whether these empirical relationships are the result of causal forces in the economy or whether they are correlations which occur, so to speak, naturally, does not alter the way we measure the data relationship.

The method I have outlined for measurement of economic relationships stems directly from the views I have of those relationships (that they are exact but the variables are subject to measurement error) and of the relationship between economic models and data. You, on the other hand, do not appear to differentiate between an economic theory model and the regression or measurement equation: you translate the theory model directly into the regression equation. Do you then believe that there is an exact correspondence between them? I have also failed to find in your published work any real explanation as to the meaning of the residuals of the regression. Are they due to measurement errors, and if not, what is your interpretation?

I would be grateful if you could clarify the points that I have raised.

Yours Gamma

The separation of the economic theory equation from the regression equation can be seen quite clearly in Schultz (1928) and Frisch (1928). The underlying views on the correspondence between theory and measurement equation were expressed more obliquely.

Letter 7   From Beta to Gamma

Dear Gamma,

I am glad that you wrote to me, since I was on the verge of asking you to clarify one or two points in your own views. Let me try to answer your questions first.

In my view the main reason that our results are not completely accurate is because we are using simplified regression models to represent more complicated economic theory. In most cases theory suggests that one economic variable is determined by a large number of other variables, some economic and some not. Ideally all these determining variables should be included in the regression equation to get as close to the true equation as possible. In practice, first it would create a considerable computational burden to deal with more than two or three independent variables (although we have been able to get around this problem to some extent by pre-adjusting the data to remove the effects of these variables from our dependent variable before we carry out the regression). And as you may have noticed in your own work, the addition of the other factors which are considered most important adds greatly to the degree of correlation, while the addition of the less important factors usually has very little or no effect on the correlation coefficient. Secondly, assuming we could put in all the variables we could measure, there would still be left out all those unmeasurable or even unobservable variables such as changes in fashions or tastes. In order to find a simple economic model that we can calculate, we have to omit some variables which we think have little influence in the relationship and those which we cannot measure. The omission of these explanatory variables means that the measured relationship can never be more than a good approximation to the true law, and the errors caused by omitting these variables are represented by the regression residuals.

I can almost hear you saying: 'Aha, so he does believe in an exact underlying relationship?' The answer is, I think, 'No.' Let me make use of a typical example. We know that the demand curves we try to measure shift about from one time period to the next and we view the true demand curve as some underlying stable curve. You have interpreted the deviations from the stable curve as measurement errors. I have preferred to interpret the deviations as due to omitted variables which disturb the underlying relationship. While I am prepared to accept that the theoretical law of demand which we are trying to measure may be an exact relationship, the fact is that the measured law which we find is a statistical law of demand which is not exact: it is an aggregate of individuals' behaviour and an average over a considerable time period. I think that even if we included all the economic variables of the theoretical relationship we would still only get a measured law which was an average in some sense. So strictly speaking the residuals of the regression include not only errors due to omitted variables but also some random type errors of aggregation or averaging as well as measurement errors. Yes, I am willing to admit the presence of inaccurate data, but I remain convinced that the major component of regression residuals is error in the relationship due to omitted variables. I therefore choose to ignore measurement errors, which I believe to be a much smaller component.

Perhaps a direct explanation of the way I work is needed. I start with a very general relationship from economic theory, which I regard as a causal relationship with many determining variables and one dependent variable. As far as possible I adjust the data for the disturbing effects of some of the main variables and all the minor variables are omitted. I then have the relationship I am interested in measuring (the demand curve would be the relationship between price, quantity and perhaps one other variable). This is a simplified version of the economic theory that I started with. If this simple model does not fit the data very well and the errors in the relationship are large, then I would include more regressors (that is, make the equation more general) in an attempt to improve the fit of the relationship.

You have accused me of not differentiating between the theoretical model and the regression equation and of not defining the relationship between the two. I view the theoretical relationship as a causal relationship and regression equations as involving an implied dependency; this dependency in the two levels of relationship must always match. (The regression residuals, remember, represent the difference between the observed dependent variable and the one *determined* by the explanatory variables.) So to my mind, there is no separate regression choice problem, only a choice of causal relationship. But that does not mean I see no difference in status between the theoretical equation and the regression equation. This may have been the case in the past, when we all used to think you could simply go out, find the nearest data, and measure demand curves. Now, we are a little more sophisticated and can see some of the difficulties involved. My defence above should have made it clear that I see the measured regression equation as having the status of a statistical or empirical relationship. This may provide a good approximation to the theoretical relationship, but it is not the same thing.

This has been a rather long letter and I hope it answers your questions. You may feel my approach has been developed on a rather ad hoc basis, but it has produced a viable way of relating theory to data. I must say that I am still puzzled about the limited role that economic theory plays in your approach. Does your method rely on you knowing and using the full set of variables involved in the theoretical relationship or do you omit variables as well? How do you choose the variables in the regression equation? I have great admiration for the way you have tackled the problems of measurement errors, but I have not found your model very useful because we do not generally have enough information about the measurement errors. May I ask whether you now have a practical solution to the problem of measurement errors in all the variables?

Yours Beta

This letter reflects a number of views: those of Schultz (1928) on omitted variables and the general methodology of simple to general modelling, and those of Gilboy (1930) and Ezekiel (1928) on the idea of measuring a statistical law rather than an economic law. These views were more generally held amongst the applied workers of the 1930s according to Koopmans (1945) who also confirms that the choice of dependent variable and errors-in-equations versus errors-in-variables were issues for debate in the 1930s. (The fact that Schultz's views figure in both this and the preceding letter does not necessarily make him inconsistent in his views; he liked to cover every aspect of the topic, and tended to keep these ideas in separate boxes.).

7.2   Errors and interdependent relationships

Letter 8   From Alpha to Beta and Gamma

Dear Beta and Gamma,

I found the arguments of your previous letters very compelling, yet I fear that you both may have overlooked an important dimension to the regression choice problem. The point I want to make concerns the interdependence of economic variables and relationships. Am I not correct in thinking that most economic theory is concerned with variables which are jointly dependent in some sense, or with relationships which are interdependent within a system as a whole? Surely most economists would argue, for example, that the price and quantity demanded of a good are both determined by the conditions of supply and demand for that good. Does not this interdependency interfere with the regression choice? Suppose that you wanted to measure the supply elasticity of a good, as well as its demand elasticity. How would you set about doing that, when the same two variables, quantity and price, are concerned in both relationships?

I look forward to having these further mysteries explained to me!

Regards Alpha

That there was difficulty in unravelling supply and demand was evident in the early work on demand by Lehfeldt (1914), Lenoir (1913) and Moore (1914), but work of this early period concentrated on isolating single relationships. As we shall see, estimating interdependent systems did not properly begin until the 1920s, and the problem of several relationships holding together in the data began to be tackled in the 1930s. The statistical issues of joint dependency as such were only sorted out in the 1940s.

Letter 9   From Beta to Alpha

Dear Alpha,

Your point about the interdependency of economic variables is well made and I assure you, well taken. However, I do not think it is necessary to abandon my previous arguments in the face of this criticism.

The problem of interdependent relationships can be solved for measurement purposes as follows. In our demand example, I suggested that you choose the regression equation on the basis of your belief in economic theory. Similarly, the choice of supply equation depends on your theoretical views. For example, suppose we consider the market for some annual crop such as wheat: I believe that the quantity supplied each year will depend on the previous year's price (in other words a high price last year will cause increased production this year) while the price will depend on the quantity demanded in the same year (excess demand this year will force this year's price up). This can be represented in equation form:

(1) supply equation $\quad Q_t^S = b_0 + b_1 P_{t-1}$
(2) demand equation $P_t \quad = A_0 + A_1 Q_t^D$

and where $\qquad\qquad\qquad Q_t^S \equiv Q_t^D$

In this way I can estimate both demand and supply parameters from only two data series, prices and quantities. Of course, such a model will not always be applicable; it will depend on the nature of the commodity concerned. I think it is a good model for a number of annual crops, though a longer lag length might be appropriate for crops such as sugarcane.

I hope this answers your query satisfactorily.

Regards Beta

Moore began experimenting with two-equation systems in 1919 when he fitted two interesting models in both of which he used different data for the supply quantity than for the demand quantity. One model was designed to be a perfect competition model and used acreage data for supply and production data for demand. The other was an imperfect competition alternative in which the supply curve was derived from cross-section sample survey data. In 1925 Moore used the joint model discussed in this letter and fitted both curves to the same data set. This recursive model was popularised by Schultz's discussion of 1928 (though Schultz himself used a measurement errors approach in his estimation). A much more sophisticated version of this model dealing with the interdependent lagged relationships between the 'corn cycle' and the 'hog cycle' was developed in agricultural econometrics by S. Wright (1925). (His method of path analysis made little impact on econometrics, though it was influential in genetics and sociology.) The theory choice decision rule in interdependent systems was given by Ezekiel (1928).

Letter 10   From Alpha to Beta

Dear Beta

You suggested a method of estimating two different relationships for the same two-variable data set by using a lagged term in one of the equations. I have been thinking about this and wondering whether it would be possible to estimate two relationships from the data without lagging. The demand and

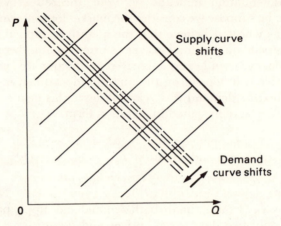

P

Supply curve
shifts

Demand
curve shifts

0   Q

Figure 16   Demand and supply curve shifts

supply model you suggested seems very reasonable for an agricultural good like wheat, but how about an industrial or consumer good? Prices and quantities in these markets might not be determined exactly together, but they may well be determined within the same time span as one unit of the data. Surely it would be better to model these as an interdependent system?

Typically, we think of supply and demand curves shifting backwards and forwards over time due to disturbing factors in the conditions of supply and demand. This variability is caused by factors such as population growth or changes in the income of consumers, which affect the demand for a good, and other factors affecting the supply of a good. We try to allow for these effects by adjusting our data before carrying out the regression but there are always some factors which we have not allowed for. It is these omitted factors which cause the observed variability in our data. We could model the problem like this:

(1) demand equation $Q_t^D = a_1 P_t + u_{1t}$
(2) supply equation $Q_t^S = b_1 P_t + u_{2t}$

where u_{1t} and u_{2t} are the disturbing factors.

If the disturbance u_{2t} causes much greater variability in the supply curve than is present in the demand curve due to u_{1t}, then we can estimate the demand curve (equation (1)). You can see that this is so by looking at the diagram [Figure 16] where the movement in the supply curve traces out a virtually stable demand curve. Presumably we could also model these disturbing variables directly in the demand and supply system by adding in the omitted variables causing the shifting of each curve to the relevant equation. Our example then becomes:

(3) demand equation $\quad Q_t^D = a_1 P_t + a_2 Y_t$
(4) supply equation $\quad\;\; Q_t^S = b_1 P_t + b_2 X_t$

where Y_t is income and X_t is a cost variable. We could then estimate both sets of parameters, a_i and b_i, provided that the two 'disturbance' variables, Y_t and X_t, are independent of each other in the sense that their movements are uncorrelated.

What do you think of this idea, do you think it is sound?

Regards Alpha

P.S. I hear that Gamma is working on some scheme to incorporate interdependent relationships within his framework; as usual he wants to call them something else, namely 'confluent relations'.

Frisch (1933) was the first to investigate formally the two-equation demand and supply model in its errors-in-equation format (equations (1) and (2)), as part of a critique of statistical work on demand. But the idea of estimating both demand and supply equations from the same data was put forward by E. J. Working (1927), who typically used graphs like the one here to show what was happening. He suggested the pre-adjustment of each data set to exclude the disturbing variables (the variables which caused the errors in the curve: the u_{it}) from each equation before estimation. His views were influential and provided the lead in estimating the two equations separately. P. G. Wright (1928) incorporated the information on the disturbing variables into the estimation process using an early instrumental variables estimator (recently discussed by Goldberger (1972)). Tinbergen (1930) was the first to set up a two-equation system (like equations (3) and (4)) which incorporated the omitted variables directly into the estimated equation. He estimated the model and he derived and estimated its reduced form. We see here also the beginnings of discussion on a more technically advanced level as theoretical econometrics began to develop.

Letter 11   From Gamma to Alpha and Beta

Dear Alpha and Beta,

After considerable thought I have come up with a way of dealing with more than one relationship holding at one time between a set of variables. This additional problem compounds the original one, not only are we unable to measure directly the relationship of interest because of the measurement errors, but we also have to deal with the complicating presence of other relationships, which might themselves be hidden by the measurement errors. I have called my method of analysis for discovering and measuring these relationships 'confluence analysis'.

These difficulties can be formally stated in the following two statements: first, that, as before, all variables are measured with error; and second, that there exists more than one exact linear relationship in the true variables (although not all the relationships necessarily involve all the variables). That said, it will be easier to explain confluence analysis with a practical example than to take you through the mathematical analysis. Let us take the case of the demand for butter, where the observed variable X_1 is the quantity demanded, the variable X_2 is the price and the variable X_3 is income. Suppose that the usual exact relationship holds between the true variables, ξ_i:

$$(1) \quad \xi_{1t} = B_{12}\xi_{2t} + B_{13}\xi_{3t}$$

Using the observed data (X_{it}), we can estimate the demand parameter B_{12} in three different ways, assuming in each case that the errors of measurement (to be minimised by the least squares method) occur in only one of the variables. So we have three different elementary regression equations:

$$(2) \quad X_{1t} = b_{12}^1 X_{2t} + b_{13}^1 X_{3t}$$
$$(3) \quad X_{1t} = b_{12}^2 X_{2t} + b_{13}^2 X_{3t}$$
$$(4) \quad X_{1t} = b_{12}^3 X_{2t} + b_{13}^3 X_{3t}$$

where b_{12}^i is the ordinary least squares estimator of B_{12} and the superscript denotes the direction of minimisation. In the case of two variables, we know that the true coefficient lies between the two elementary regression coefficients. Generalising this suggests that the true coefficient B_{12} lies within the limits fixed by the three elementary coefficients, which given the data for our demand example are:

$$b_{12}^1 = -1.074, \quad b_{12}^2 = -1.349, \quad b_{12}^3 = -1.690$$

This demonstrates the first use of confluence analysis: it gives the limits on the coefficient of the true relationship.

The next step is to look at how these coefficients behave when other variables are added to the equation. This requires the calculation of all possible elementary regression coefficients (meaning all the coefficients in any two-variable relationship, all those between two variables in any three-variable relationship,

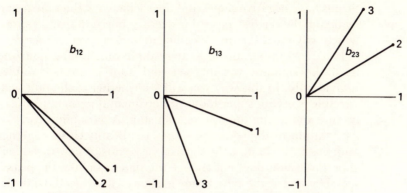

Figure 17   Bunch maps for the two-variable regressions

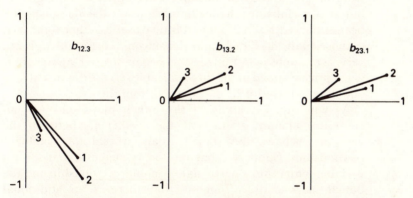

Figure 18   Bunch maps for the three-variable regressions

etc.) which are then mapped onto 'bunch maps'. Each bunch map shows the measurements of one coefficient between two variables and each beam on the map represents the slope of the coefficient when a different direction of minimisation is used (the beam being labelled with the direction). The closer together the beams on a map, the more precisely the coefficient is determined. The bunch maps for our demand example are shown in two diagrams: the first [Figure 17] shows the coefficients of the two-variable relationships; the second [Figure 18] shows the coefficients for the three-variable relationships. The bunch maps are 'read' as follows, taking the left hand case in the three-variable map as the example: all the beams have negative slopes and the coefficient values are found by taking the vertical axis value over the horizontal axis value – which will equal the three coefficient values given earlier.

It is most important to analyse these bunch maps starting from the smallest variable set and adding more variables individually. In this way you will see whether each additional variable is useful, superfluous or detrimental to the purpose of finding and fitting the true relationship. A variable is useful if its addition to the equation draws the beams closer together and, possibly, changes the signs of the beams. A new variable is superfluous if it does not change the sign or tighten the beams together and if the new beam is shorter and lies outside the original beams indicating no improvement in fit. You can see from these maps that the b_{12} coefficient is quite well determined because the beams are close together. Adding the income variable (X_3) to the relationship between price and quantity of butter is useful since the leading beams on the $b_{12.3}$ map (the beams marked 1 and 2) move a little closer together compared to those on the b_{12} bunch map. The income coefficient b_{13} is not very accurately determined (the beams are far apart), but, when price is added in the three-variable set, the coefficient $b_{13.2}$ does have the positive sign expected from theory.

As you can see, study of the bunch maps tells you an enormous amount about how the coefficients between the variables behave, but they will also reveal the confluent relationships. Suppose economic theory suggests that several variables enter into a particular economic relationship and the bunch map analysis suggests that there is an additional well-defined linear relationship between two of the variables. This could occur either because of a previously neglected theoretical relationship involving the two variables or because of the characteristics of the particular sample of data being used. For example, theory suggests that the price of butter will be affected by the prices of other goods, in particular by the price of its substitute, margarine. Suppose that in fact the prices of margarine and butter are very highly correlated. This will cause collinearity in the data set since the bunch maps have shown that we already have a well-defined relationship between the variables:

$$X_1 = b_{12.3}X_2 + b_{13.2}X_3.$$

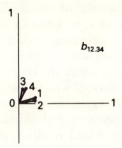

Figure 19   Exploding bunch map

and now we also have:

$$X_1 = b_{14}X_4$$

In this case, as you can see in my third diagram [Figure 19], adding the variable X_4 to the set causes the bunch map for the coefficient for $b_{12.34}$ to explode: this is the danger signal indicating the presence of confluent relations. The variable X_4 is therefore considered to be a 'detrimental' variable for the set.

The presence of a supply as well as the demand relationship in a data set provides another good example of the meaning and effect of confluent relationships. The demand and supply relationships will form two intersecting planes in the same scatter of data, but the confluence of the two relationships causes the observed relationship to collapse into a smaller dimension: we can only observe a line where the planes intersect instead of the two planes. This particular aspect of confluent relations, the reduction of the dimension of the relationship of interest, is called 'multicollinearity'. Multicollinearity, due to confluent relations in the data, in theory causes the data matrix X of size $(n \times n)$ to become singular (that is, rank $(X'X) = n-1$). In practice, the presence of measurement errors prevents the matrix ˙becoming singular and we do observe some scatter for each plane; the coefficients of both relationships are therefore determinate, though probably nonsense. These nonsense coefficients are represented by the short, widely spaced beams of the exploded bunch map. This explains why it is essential to map out and examine all the possible bunch maps in order to determine which relationships between the variables are well defined and can be measured by regression equations, and which are nonsense.

The great advantage of my confluence analysis over the usual methods is that, as you can see, it makes no assumptions about the structural relationships (the theoretical relationships between the true variables) that are not thoroughly investigated in the data. The bunch map method enables you to decide which variables suggested by the theory do actually occur in the relationship and which can be omitted (in answer to a criticism made by Beta). It also enables you to see which relationships are identified (which ones can be found) and which other relationships hold at the same time (in answer to your query, Alpha). By treating the variables symmetrically, the method also takes into account measurement errors in every variable and helps you to choose a well-fitting equation closest to the true relationship.

I have to admit that confluence analysis is rather difficult to understand for one brought up on elementary regressions, but I am sure it will repay the effort required. Interpreting the results will also take some experience, so I hope that you will both try it out in your work, for the more we can learn about the way such confluent relations behave, the better.

Yours Gamma

Confluence analysis represents Frisch's work on the joint problem of errors-in-variables and multicollinearity. His approach also treated the issues of identification, inference and model choice. Confluence analysis (1934) was an extension of earlier work, see Frisch (1929) and Frisch and Mudgett (1931). (Once again we have an econometrician's ideas represented in two consecutive letters. Frisch worked on many different problems at the same time. As well as his work on errors-in-equations models, he was also working on time-series problems (discussed in Chapter 3). The latter work was similar to confluence analysis in that both addressed the problems of how to unravel and find the hidden and intertwined relationships or components in the observed data. In both he used determinants to find the maximum linearly independent set of variables. Confluence analysis is also linked with his later paper (1938) on autonomy (discussed in Chapter 4).) Confluence analysis, which came to be synonymous with bunch maps and the investigation of multicollinearity, was used in econometrics into the 1950s. The numerical example and graphs used are adapted from a mimeographed paper by Staehle and Haavelmo (1941) explaining confluence analysis. The example is fully analysed (and the data matrices are given) in an extended discussion of the history of confluence analysis and its difficulties in Hendry and Morgan (1989). See Griliches (1974) for a more general assessment. The errors-in-variables story continues in Chapter 7.3.

Letter 12   From Beta to Alpha

Dear Alpha,

I think I disagree with your model of demand and supply in which both relationships are determined within the same time period. In your models [Letter 10], both quantity demanded and quantity supplied are determined by price, but there is no way in which price is determined. An alternative model could have price determine the quantity demanded in the demand equation and quantity supplied determine the price in the supply equation:

(1) demand equation $Q_t^D = a_1 P_t + a_2 Y_t$
(2) supply equation $P_t = b_1 Q_t^S + b_2 X_t$

But at least in the measurement equations, where the same quantity data are usually used in both, this seems to have the difficulty of two-way causality: the model implies that quantity determines price and price determines quantity at the same time. I find it difficult to believe that in reality the economic system is determined simultaneously. Causal forces surely only work in one direction at any one time and these forces should be reflected in the models we build.

It is easy to see if the variables in a demand and supply model are arranged in a logical causal sequence, like the lagged demand and supply model which I discussed in my last letter to you [Letter 9]:

(3) supply equation $Q_t^S = b_0 + b_1 P_{t-1}$
(4) demand equation $P_t = A_0 + A_1 Q_t^D$

In macrodynamic models (such as those of the business cycle), each dependent variable in a causal relationship usually depends indirectly on some variables in other equations. If these models are large, it is not so easy to see if they form causal chains in which the variables are determined sequentially. To build a determinate causal model, we need to know the dynamic interrelations of all the variables in terms of the time lapse between causes and effects. (This may require experimenting with different lagged values to establish the correct time lapse between cause and effect appropriate for each particular relationship.) Once we have constructed the causal sequence depicting how the economy works, we are in a better position to find out how changes in the economy occur and how economic activity would be affected by different policies. Further, we can reduce the system of dynamic causal relations to one 'final form' equation (that is, one variable expressed as a function of its own lagged terms), which can be solved to show us the dynamic path of the economy. This is only possible if the equations in the system involve no simultaneously determined equations of the type that you suggest.

Another advantage of the causal chain model is that it is associated with a particularly neat explanation of the fact that business cycle data show jagged and irregular cycles, whereas our theory models suggest smooth and symmetric cycles. This is known as the 'shock' theory of business cycles; small shocks to the macrosystem are carried along in time by the causal chain of relationships, with the result that the disturbance of economic activity continues to be felt through several time periods. Disturbances which only influence the system at one time point cannot account for the time-series data we see.

I suspect that large systems which do not have a causal sequence will also be more liable to the sort of problems outlined in Gamma's letter on confluence analysis which I have just received. What do you think of his ideas?

Regards Beta

Causal chain models were proposed and used in Tinbergen's early macroeconometric models, both in his model of the Dutch economy (1937) and his work for the League of Nations (1939). He represented his causal chain models with 'arrow schemes'. These models were discussed further and labelled 'recursive systems' by Wold in Bentzel and Wold (1946) (and for further discussion, Morgan (1987a)). Accidental or random shocks were recognised as a component of economic time-series data in the analysis of business cycles (at least from the work of Persons (1919)), but were not recognised in the regression relations used in other economic work. Error terms did not appear explicitly in Tinbergen's equations even though he was working with a 'shock' model of the type proposed by Frisch (1933).

Letter 13   From Alpha to Gamma

Dear Gamma,

Thank you for your very long letter and explanation of 'confluence analysis' [Letter 11]. I found the discussion of confluent relations in general very helpful. As I understand your terminology: structural relationships are the theoretical relationships you are trying to measure and which should be matched by equivalent empirical relationships, but these structural relationships are not necessarily empirically determinable because of the presence of other simultaneously holding relations (which may also be structural or may be due to characteristics of the data). I found your bunch map technique quite difficult to understand and use, although the maps do appear to be quite good at uncovering unsuspected confluent relations.

One of the problems is that, like Beta, I disagree with your formulation of structural equations as exact laws; in my view they are not exact but in some sense 'average' with an unexplained scatter. Suppose we think of a small macrodynamic model with n variables and with n independent structural relationships (involving lagged variables) between them, for example:

$$(1) \quad X_{it} = \sum_{j \neq i} a_{ij} X_{jt} + \sum_j b_{ij} X_{jt-1} + \ldots$$
$$\text{for } i, j = 1, \ldots, n$$

In order for these equations to be satisfied at each point in time by the data, we could view the parameters (a_{ij}, b_{ij}) as being variable rather than constant. In other words, each coefficient consists of an average value $(\bar{a}_{ij}, \bar{b}_{ij})$ plus a random term which is different in each time period:

$$(2) \quad a_{ijt} = \bar{a}_{ij} + \alpha_{ijt} \quad \text{and} \quad b_{ijt} = \bar{b}_{ij} + \beta_{ijt}$$

(where α and β are the random terms in each parameter). So now the underlying structural equations are in fact stochastic equations.

In the way you have set up the problem, these structural equations will not be empirically determinable, not because of the presence of measurement errors, but because they all hold at the same time. But, by a process of substitution and elimination, we can obtain the empirically determinable confluent relations, each relation involving only one of the n variables. This is somewhat similar to the method used by Beta for his causal chain approach to systems of equations, and the confluent relations will be of the same form as his 'final form' equations:

$$(3) \quad X_{it} = A_1 X_{it-1} + A_2 X_{it-2} + \ldots$$

There are two differences: Beta estimates the individual elementary equations first and then solves for the final form, whereas your analysis of the problem suggests that it is only worthwhile to estimate the final or confluent relations.

Secondly, in my set up, the coefficients of the final confluent relationship (3) will also involve random elements E_i (dependent on t):

$$(4) \quad A_{it} = \bar{A}_i + E_{it}$$

This gives us an alternative formulation for the empirically determinable equations of the dynamic 'shock' theory of the business cycle.

It seems to me that this sort of 'confluence analysis' is more appropriate than your bunch map method for business cycle work. Cycle models are highly likely to suffer from multicollinearity, for they include a number of economic relationships involving the same variables holding in the same time period.

I look forward to discussing all this with you, perhaps at the next meeting of the Econometric Society: shall you be there?

Yours Alpha

The idea of varying parameter models was suggested by Sasuly in 1930 in conjunction with an errors-in-equations model. Haavelmo in 1938 developed a version of confluence analysis with errors-in-parameters but neither model became popular. The idea of solving the structural relations to get to final form confluent relations which were empirically determinable represented a twist in the meaning of confluent relationships and in the basic bunch map method as outlined by Frisch in 1934. This change appears to have had Frisch's support as can be seen from his comments on Haavelmo's presentation of these ideas to the Oxford Meeting of the Econometric Society in 1936, and on Tinbergen's work at the same meeting (both are to be found in *Econometrica* for 1937). See Aldrich (1989) and Hendry and Morgan (1989) for further discussion. Some of Haavelmo's suggestions were developed further by Marschak (1942) (but written in 1940), in particular the variable parameter model and identification in interdependent systems. Macrodynamic models of the 'shock' theory type were discussed by Hurwicz (1944) in which the system is solved before estimation.

Letter 14   From Alpha to Beta

Dear Beta,

I read your discussion of causal chain models [Letter 12] with great interest. It seems to me that a variable is defined as causal only in relation to another variable, it is a relative not an absolute notion. A variable within a given sector of a large model can be causal in relation to one dependent variable, but when you get to the full macromodel that same causal variable may be a dependent variable in some other equation. This system of mutually dependent relations may incorporate both simultaneous relationships and causal chains of the type you suggest.

There are several reasons why I prefer to model systems of relations as simultaneous systems. In the first place, as I mentioned in my last letter, most of our data is in the form of annual observations and many of the relationships of interest will be determined within the time span of one observation and thus should be treated as if they were simultaneous. There are also clear cases where there may be no appreciable time delay between cause and effect, for example, think of the speed with which exogenous shocks are transmitted through the economic system. The most important reason to my mind is that the simple relationships which we use for measurement will in turn be dependent on a more fundamental set of unobserved relationships which reflect the simultaneous behaviour of economic agents reacting to circumstances. In this sense our observed phenomena are the result of simultaneously determined relationships. This might account for the fact that simple causal models work well in some periods but break down in others. In the same way, confluent relations are empirically observable but may be derived from a number of other more fundamental or autonomous relationships. We need to know these deeper simultaneous relationships from which the causal chain or confluent relationships have been derived in order to understand what will happen if there is a change in behaviour at the deeper level.

You seem to suggest in your discussion that a random error or stochastic term should be an explicit part of our econometric models. I fully agree with you. It seems to me that observed economic laws are far from exact. They are the result of aggregation of individual behavioural relationships and incorporate the effects of extraneous shocks, both reasons why the observed relationship should be stochastic even before taking account of the problems of omitted variables and measurement errors. But, I do think it is important that the errors should be explicit in the relationship, not an ad hoc rationalisation of the regression residuals. If we are dealing with probabilistic or stochastic relationships and if we explicitly recognise that fact, we should also abide by the rigour of statistical theory and adopt a full-scale probability approach in econometrics.

Suppose we consider a demand and supply system which we already know will be an identified model. The model is written in its true variable form (capital Roman letters represent the true variables, Greek letters the true parameters) and the model has errors in the equations:

(1) demand equation $Q_t^D + \alpha_1 P_t + \alpha_2 Y_t = u_{1t}$
(2) supply equation $\quad Q_t^S + \alpha_3 P_t + \alpha_4 X_t = u_{2t}$

and where the u_i are independently and normally distributed variables representing the errors in each equation. The usual way of estimating these as two single equations supposes that P_t, Y_t, and X_t are fixed in repeated samples and that Q_t reflects the sampling fluctuation of u_{1t} in the demand equation and of u_{2t} in the supply equation. Now we have made the errors u_{it} explicit, we can see that this is only possible in repeated samples if the random elements, u_{1t} and u_{2t}, are perfectly correlated. This implication of the choice of fixed factors is inconsistent with our model in which u_{1t} represents neglected disturbance factors in the demand equation and u_{2t} neglected factors in the supply equation. These will necessarily be different from each other and therefore not perfectly correlated, though there may be some degree of correlation. On the other hand, if we select Q_t as the dependent variable in equation (1) and assume that all three other variables are fixed if repeated samples of Q were drawn – then this precludes us from using P_t as the dependent variable in equation (2) where it would need to vary from sample to sample.

If we assume that only the 'other' (or exogenous) factors, Y_t and X_t, are fixed, then we can solve the system of equations to give the reduced form as follows:

(3) $Q_t = \pi_1 Y_t + \pi_2 X_t + e_{1t}$
(4) $P_t = \pi_3 Y_t + \pi_4 X_t + e_{2t}$

where

$$\pi_1 = \frac{-\alpha_2\alpha_3}{\alpha_3 - \alpha_1}, \quad \pi_2 = \frac{\alpha_1\alpha_4}{\alpha_3 - \alpha_1}, \quad \pi_3 = \frac{\alpha_2}{\alpha_3 - \alpha_1}, \quad \pi_4 = \frac{-\alpha_4}{\alpha_3 - \alpha_1}$$

$$e_{1t} = \frac{\alpha_3 u_{1t} - \alpha_1 u_{2t}}{\alpha_3 - \alpha_1}, \quad e_{2t} = \frac{u_{2t} - u_{1t}}{\alpha_3 - \alpha_1}$$

This way of looking at the model shows how the two dependent (or endogenous) variables are determined simultaneously since Q_t and P_t are now jointly dependent on the two fixed variables,

Y_t and X_t, and the two random error terms, u_{1t} and u_{2t}. If u_{1t} and u_{2t} are jointly normally distributed, so therefore are Q_t and P_t. This gives us a consistent statistical model for the estimation of the parameters of the two equations and a model which is also consistent with the economic theory of the joint determination of quantity and price. That is, both price and quantity change because of shifts in supply and demand conditions caused by changes in the values of the exogenous variables, Y_t and X_t (which we assumed fixed but which we could have assumed were also random variables), and in the errors or disturbances (u_{1t} and u_{2t}).

There is no reason why this probability model should not also incorporate Gamma's measurement errors, as well as errors in the equations. Suppose the quantity variable is measured with error but all the other variables are measured accurately:

$$(5) \quad q_t = Q_t + \varepsilon_t, \ p_t = P_t, \ y_t = Y_t, \ x_t = X_t$$

where ε_t is independently and normally distributed. (Capital Roman letters represent true variables as before, small letters the observed variables.) The reduced form model with the observed variables then becomes:

$$(6) \quad q_t = \pi_1 y_t + \pi_2 x_t + e_{1t} + \varepsilon_t$$
$$(7) \quad p_t = \pi_3 y_t + \pi_4 x_t + e_{2t}$$

The dependent variables, q_t and p_t are still jointly normal because they are linear functions of u_{1t}, u_{2t}, and ε_t.

We can best estimate the parameters of the original system of equations ((1) and (2) above) by the method of maximum likelihood (which chooses as estimates of the parameters those values of the true parameters for which the observed sample is most probable). If we estimate the confluent relations ((3) and (4), or (6) and (7)) separately by ordinary least squares and solved back to find the structural parameters, we would reach the same results in this case because of the particular characteristics of the model. But it would be incorrect (and would produce biased estimates) for the reasons I outlined above to estimate our original structural model by least squares.

A simple adjustment to our initial equations to incorporate a lagged value of P_t in our supply equation gives the following model:

$$(8) \text{ supply } \quad Q_t = \alpha_3 P_{t-1} + \alpha_4 X_t + u_{1t}$$
$$(9) \text{ demand } \quad P_t = \alpha_1 Q_t \quad + \alpha_2 Y_t + u_{2t}$$

This is now a causal chain or recursive model of the type you mentioned in your letter. In the supply equation the disturbance u_{1t} cannot affect past prices, so Q_t must be the dependent variable. In the demand equation, Q_t is already determined, and the sampling fluctuations of the disturbance u_{2t} are therefore reflected only in P_t. Assuming that the disturbance terms are uncorrelated, we would be correct in estimating this model directly by least squares since there is no inconsistency in the sampling assumptions which would lead to bias in the results.

The examples here have shown that if the model is not made up of independent relationships – but you treat it as if it were – then the usual least squares method of measuring the parameters will be inappropriate, and will lead to biased measurements. More important, I have demonstrated that my probability approach has the advantage of being very general for it can cope both with your causal chain model as well as Gamma's measurement error model.

Regards Alpha

The idea of a full-scale probability approach to econometrics was the work of Haavelmo. It was published in 1944 but had already received wide circulation in mimeo form in 1941. Haavelmo recognised the debt to his teacher, Frisch, for many of the ideas he proposed in this paper (for example for the ideas on identification and structure, put forward in Frisch's critique of Tinbergen's work in 1938), but Frisch's severe doubts about the use of probability theory in econometrics were well known, and in this respect Haavelmo was probably influenced by Wald and Neyman. The genesis of the simultaneous equations model is less clear. Popular versions of that model, and the probability approach, were produced by Haavelmo in 1943 and Koopmans in 1945. The approach also formed the basis of the influential Cowles Commission research programme of the period 1943–7. Their basic programme dealt with a simultaneous equations model with errors-in-equations, although some work on joint 'shock-error' models (errors-in-equations and errors-in-variables) was undertaken by Anderson and Hurwicz (1946) and found its way into L. R. Klein's textbook (1953).

7.3   Postscript: measurement errors and the method of instrumental variables

Letter 15   From Delta to Gamma

Dear Gamma,

Forgive me for writing to you out of the blue, but I am interested in the measurement error problem and Beta has kindly shown me your interesting letter on confluence analysis

[Letter 11]. I was very impressed by your treatment of multicollinearity and related matters, but I would like to concentrate on the other contribution of your paper, namely, the attempt to solve the errors-in-variables problem.

To start with, let me restate the model: the data set consists of k variables each of which is measured with error:

(1) $x_{it} = \xi_{it} + \varepsilon_{it}$ $i = 1, \ldots, k$
or $\mathbf{x}_t = \boldsymbol{\xi}_t + \boldsymbol{\varepsilon}_t$

(where x_{it} are the observed data, ξ_{it} the true or systematic variables and ε_{it} the errors of measurement all given here in mean deviation form; in the alternative vector notation, $\mathbf{x}_t$ for example is a $(k \times 1)$ vector at time t). The exact linear relation holds between the true variables:

(2) $\boldsymbol{\gamma}' \boldsymbol{\xi}_t = 0$ for each t

(where γ_i are the true coefficients of the relationship). The usual assumptions about the measurement errors are that they are uncorrelated with each other and with the true variables:

(3) $E(\varepsilon_{it}\varepsilon_{jt}) = 0$ for all $i \neq j$
(4) $E(\varepsilon_{it}\xi_{jt}) = 0$ for all i, j.

Now let me review the solutions suggested so far. The first solution proposed, when all the variables in an equation are measured with error, was the orthogonal regression or 'line of best fit'. This led to the attempt to find regressions which were invariant to general linear transformations, such as changes in scale of the variables, and produced the diagonal mean regression and other variations on ordinary least squares measurements. Unfortunately, all these suffer from the same problems of scale dependency and the search for invariant regressions in economics seems to have died out.

The second solution to the problem of measurement errors is contained in your own work on confluence analysis. This consists in working out all the elementary regression equations to provide the bounds or limits to the true relationship; each elementary regression being equivalent to an extreme assumption about the relative weights (that is, the size or importance) of the measurement errors. You are therefore concerned only with the error in measuring the relationship which is due to the wrong choice of weights.

I am concerned that there will also be errors of sampling which your method neglects. Let me explain this. You have assumed that the measurement errors are uncorrelated, both mutually and with the true or systematic parts of the variables. These characteristics may be true of the population (treating the measurement errors as random variables with a particular distribution) but it is unlikely to be fulfilled in any particular sample of measurement errors you are faced with. I know that you are opposed to use of the probability approach in econometrics but I believe it has much to offer. In the classical system, as you know, the explanatory variables are error-free; the only errors involved are attached to the dependent variable. The regression coefficients change when a different sample of observations is used because a different sample of errors is involved. So the regression coefficients have their own sampling error, dependent on the population distribution of the errors.

My own proposal for the errors-in-variables problem shows how to incorporate known information on the measurement errors into the estimation of the regression parameters. Suppose to begin with that we know the error variances; we can use this information in a method closely akin to that of your orthogonal regression. Estimates for the exact relationship parameters (γ_i) in equation (2) can be obtained by minimising the usual sum of squares for orthogonal regression:

(5) $S^2 = \gamma' X' X \gamma$

where X is now the $(T \times k)$ matrix of $\mathbf{x}_t'$ observations but subject to the restriction that $\gamma' \Omega \gamma = 1$ (where Ω is the known error variance matrix) instead of the usual orthogonal regression restriction that $\gamma' \gamma = 1$.

Of course this method is only useful if we know the variance matrix (Ω) of the measurement errors. If we guess this information and guess it wrongly – then the coefficients will be biased. It seems to me that we should try to work out some way of estimating the unknown matrix (Ω), so that we can use the estimate $\hat{\Omega}$ in the method presented above. Do you have any suggestions as to how this might be done?

Yours Delta

The search for invariant regressions was only briefly followed in econometrics after Frisch's work on the problem in 1928. The critique of the ideas of confluence analysis and the attempt to integrate the ideas of Frisch into the sampling approach was the subject of Koopmans' thesis (1937), in turn discussed by Tinbergen (1939, I). The idea of using information on the errors was not new, but

Koopmans analysed the method and used it to extend Frisch's confluence analysis results on the limits to the true regression to take account of sampling errors. (The idea that in some cases only the relative error variances need to be known was proposed by Allen (1939). No immediate progress was made in estimating Ω, except that Tintner (1944 and 1950) suggested using the variate difference method (developed earlier in time-series analysis) for the purpose.)

Letter 16   From Delta to Gamma

Dear Gamma,

I have just come across another idea for dealing with the errors-in-variables problem besides the three I mentioned in my last letter. The unusual feature of this idea is that it by-passes the unknown error covariance matrix Ω and assumes only that the matrix is diagonal and that, as usual, the errors are uncorrelated with the true variables. The method uses the estimation techniques of group averages, rather than a least squares fitting device, as follows:

(i)   divide the sample of observations into two groups such that the subdivision is defined independently of the measurement errors;

(ii)   estimate the coefficients of the model: $y = \alpha + \beta x$ (where y and x are observed random variables measured with error) by using the group means of the divided data set:

$$\hat{\beta} = \frac{\bar{y}_1 - \bar{y}_2}{\bar{x}_1 - \bar{x}_2}, \quad \hat{\alpha} = \bar{y} - \hat{\beta}\bar{x}$$

(where $\bar{y}_1, \bar{y}_2, \bar{x}_1$ and $\bar{x}_2$ are the means of the two groups of data and $\bar{y}$ and $\bar{x}$ are means from the total sample).

This provides consistent estimates of the parameters but they may not be very efficient. The most efficient estimate we could find would be to rank the true values of x and partition the set in the centre of the ranking. The true values of x are, of course, unknown, but if the error is small relative to the value of the variable, then the ranking of the observed variable will be the same as the ranking of the true variable. Even though the errors are correlated with the corresponding observed values, the subdivision will be independent of the measurement errors in y and in x.

This method seems to work by replacing the information that we have, namely the observed values which are correlated with the measurement errors, with information which is free of contamination by those same errors. Maybe this idea can be adapted in some way to be used with the least squares fitting method?

Yours Delta

P.S. Incidentally, the method also gives consistent estimates of the unknown Ω based on the sample moments of the observed variables and the already estimated $\hat{\beta}$.

This idea was proposed by Wald in 1940 as a solution to the errors-in-variables problem. It was widely read and referenced and seemed to present a breakthrough in the treatment of the measurement error problem.

Letter 17   From Gamma to Delta

Dear Delta,

Thank you for your two letters regarding the errors-in-variables problem. Despite your enthusiasm, I find neither of the two new methods that you suggest very appealing. To begin with the error variance matrix Ω is so rarely known that your first method will almost never be applicable to economic data. Your second method of by-passing the matrix appears to rely on the method of group averages (surely a somewhat outdated and unsophisticated method) which as you point out is of doubtful efficiency. I still think that my confluence analysis has much to offer and I present two alternative methods developed from it, both allow for a symmetric treatment of the variables and by-pass the unknown Ω matrix.

Alternative 1   This is based on the assumption that the measurement errors are uncorrelated over time. If this is true, then it turns out that certain equations involving the data moments between the observed data at time t, and at a lagged period, $t - s$, are zero and can be used to estimate the parameters of the true relationship.

We know that the true variables in the exact underlying relationship are equal to the observed values minus the measurement errors (using the notation of your first letter) [Letter 15]:

$$(1) \quad \boldsymbol{\gamma}' \boldsymbol{\xi}_t = \boldsymbol{\gamma}' (\mathbf{x}_t - \boldsymbol{\varepsilon}_t) = 0$$

which can be rewritten:

$$(2) \quad \boldsymbol{\gamma}' \mathbf{x}_t = \boldsymbol{\gamma}' \boldsymbol{\varepsilon}_t$$

When in addition to the normal assumptions that the errors are uncorrelated with each other (equation (3) of your letter), we also have that the errors at different time periods are uncorrelated, then:

(3) $E(\varepsilon_{it}\varepsilon_{jt-s}) = 0$ for all $s \neq 0$

and the following equation of the expected lagged moments of the observed data is also zero:

(4) $E(\boldsymbol{\gamma}'\mathbf{x}_t\mathbf{x}'_{t-s}\boldsymbol{\gamma}) = \boldsymbol{\gamma}'E(\boldsymbol{\varepsilon}_t\boldsymbol{\varepsilon}'_{t-s})\boldsymbol{\gamma} = 0$

By taking a sufficient number of these equations involving lagged terms (by choosing different values of s), and replacing the expected values by the observed data covariances for the relevant time periods, we can estimate the structural coefficients γ from:

(5) $\boldsymbol{\gamma}'(\mathbf{X}_t'\mathbf{X}_{t-s})\boldsymbol{\gamma} = 0$

(where $\mathbf{X}_t$ is the $(T \times k)$ data matrix, $t = 1, \ldots, T$, and $\mathbf{X}_{t-s}$ is the $(T \times k)$ data matrix, $t = 1 - s, \ldots, T - s$).

Alternative 2 This method depends on the use of an additional set of observed variables (z_{jt}), which are uncorrelated with the measurement errors of the original variable set. That is, in addition to the normal assumptions (numbered (1) to (4) of your first letter), we have:

(6) $E(\varepsilon_{it}z_{jt}) = 0$ for all i, j

We can then use this information in a similar way to that of the previous alternative:

$$\begin{aligned} (7) \quad E(\boldsymbol{\gamma}'\mathbf{x}_t z_{jt}) &= E\{\boldsymbol{\gamma}'(\boldsymbol{\xi}_t + \boldsymbol{\varepsilon}_t)z_{jt}\} \\ &= E\{(\boldsymbol{\gamma}'\boldsymbol{\xi}_t\, z_{jt}\} = 0 \\ &\quad \text{for all } j = 1, \ldots, k \end{aligned}$$

We can then use the sample moments (computed over the whole time period) to estimate the coefficients (γ_i) of the true relationship:

(8) $\boldsymbol{\gamma}'\text{cov}(\mathbf{X}_t'\mathbf{z}_j) = 0$ for $j = 1, \ldots, k$

(and where $\mathbf{z}_j$ is the $(T \times 1)$ vector of observations z_{jt}).

What do you think? I look forward to hearing your views on these two methods of estimating errors-in-variables models.

Yours Gamma

These two suggestions for by-passing Ω were hidden in amongst a number of extensions to Frisch's confluence analysis model in an article by Reiersøl in 1941. Reiersøl credited Frisch with the first alternative and Frisch's influence is apparent in other parts of the article. The second alternative was also suggested by Geary (1942 and 1943) though he apparently arrived at the idea independently of Reiersøl's work (see Qin (1988)).

Letter 18   From Delta to Gamma

Dear Gamma,

I have been rereading our correspondence on errors-in-variables models and it suddenly struck me, while reading your last alternative, that really all these ideas for by-passing the error covariance matrix can be seen as special cases of one general type which I will call the 'instrumental variables' method. It will be helpful, first, to reformulate the model as follows:

$$(1) \qquad \xi_1 = \xi'\gamma$$

(where ξ and γ are now vectors of length $k - 1$). Replacing the true values by the observed variables minus their measurement errors, and with T observations, we get:

$$(2) \quad (\mathbf{x}_1 - \boldsymbol{\varepsilon}_1) = (X - V)\gamma$$

or

$$(3) \qquad \mathbf{x}_1 = (X - V)\gamma + \boldsymbol{\varepsilon}_1$$

(where X and V are now $(T \times (k - 1))$ matrices, X is $(x_2, \ldots, x_k)$, V is $(\boldsymbol{\varepsilon}_2, \ldots, \boldsymbol{\varepsilon}_k)$ and each $\mathbf{x}_i$, $\boldsymbol{\varepsilon}_i$ is a vector of length $(T \times 1)$). I know this looks like an errors-in-equations model, but do not stop reading here – the reformulation is merely designed to make the problem easier!

Suppose you then pick a set of $k - 1$ variables, z_{it} (in matrix form $\mathbf{Z}$ is of dimension $(T \times (k - 1))$), which I call the instrumental variables. These instrumental variables should have the following properties:

(i)   they should be independent of $\boldsymbol{\varepsilon}_1$: $E(\mathbf{Z}'\boldsymbol{\varepsilon}_1) = 0$;

(ii)   there should be some natural correspondence or connection between each z_{it} and its corresponding x_{it} (i.e. they should be highly correlated);

(iii)   they should be uncorrelated with the measurement errors of $\mathbf{X}$: $E(\mathbf{Z}'\mathbf{V}) = 0$.

Now if we pre-multiply the new model (3) by the instruments and take the expectations we obtain:

$$(4) \quad E(\mathbf{Z}' \mathbf{x}_i) = E[\mathbf{Z}'(\mathbf{X} - \mathbf{V})\boldsymbol{\gamma} + \mathbf{Z}'\boldsymbol{\varepsilon}_1]$$
$$= E(\mathbf{Z}'\mathbf{X}\boldsymbol{\gamma} - \mathbf{Z}'\mathbf{V}\boldsymbol{\gamma} + \mathbf{Z}'\boldsymbol{\varepsilon}_1)$$
$$= E(\mathbf{Z}'\mathbf{X}\boldsymbol{\gamma})$$

and so we can estimate $\boldsymbol{\gamma}$ from a formula which resembles the least squares one:

$$(5) \qquad \hat{\boldsymbol{\gamma}} = (\mathbf{Z}'\mathbf{X})^{-1}\mathbf{Z}'\mathbf{x}_1$$

I know this procedure seems peculiar at first sight. The intuitive reasoning goes as follows: the problem with errors-in-variables models is that we do not have enough independent information to estimate all the parameters. If we bring in some more information (the instrumental variables) then we are in a position to find at least the parameters we are most interested in, though not to estimate the error variance matrix.

In case you remain unconvinced, suppose we look at a couple of examples. First, your own suggestion of using lagged variables (Alternative 1 in your last letter). Let me take a simple two-variable model rewritten:

$$(6) \quad x_{1t} = \beta\xi_{2t} + \varepsilon_{1t} = \beta x_{2t} + \beta\varepsilon_{2t} + \varepsilon_{1t}$$

Take x_{1t-1} as the instrument (for it is reasonable to assume that x_{1t-1} is correlated with x_{2t}, but uncorrelated with ε_{1t} and ε_{2t}). Then multiply by the instrumental variable and taking expectations we have:

$$(7) \quad E(x_{1t-1}x_{1t}) = E(\beta x_{1t-1}x_{2t}) + E(\beta x_{1t-1}\varepsilon_{2t})$$
$$+ E(x_{1t-1}\varepsilon_{1t})$$
$$= \beta\{E(x_{1t-1}x_{2t})\}$$

and you can estimate β by using the sample moments in place of the expected value terms as in formula (5):

$$(8) \qquad \hat{\beta} = \frac{\displaystyle\sum_{t=2}^{T} x_{1t-1}x_{1t}}{\displaystyle\sum_{t=2}^{T} x_{1t-1}x_{2t}}$$

Consider another example, the ranking method using group averages which I discussed previously [Letter 16]. In this case the data were ranked and split into two sets. The parameter estimate of β (in $y = \alpha + \beta x$) was:

$$(9) \quad \hat{\beta} = \frac{\bar{y}_1 - \bar{y}_2}{\bar{x}_1 - \bar{x}_2}$$

If we define our instrumental variable such that:

$$(10) \quad z = +1 \text{ for } x > x_m$$

and

$$z = -1 \text{ for } x < x_m$$

(where x_m is the median value of the n observations). Then the z variable is correlated with x but is uncorrelated with both errors in x and in y. Taking (5) as our estimator, we get:

$$(11) \quad \hat{\beta} = \frac{\sum zy}{\sum zx} = \frac{\sum_{i=1}^{m-1} (+1)y_i + \sum_{i=m}^{n} (-1)y_i}{\sum_{i=1}^{m-1} (+1)x_i + \sum_{i=m}^{n} (-1)x_i}$$

which equals the estimator in (9). So here our instrumental variable is simply a dummy variable taking the value $(+1)$ or (-1) depending on the value of x_i.

In fact I can think of a number of other instrumental variable sets that would be appropriate in having a natural correspondence with certain data sets besides lagged values or dummy variables. For example, the moving averages of the data for a time series, the deviations from the trend for a cyclical series, the nominal values for real x values, etc.

How do you feel about this generalisation? I hope you think it makes sense because it seems to me to be a method which could be used in many different circumstances.

Yours Delta

Reiersøl realised this generalisation for the errors-in-variables cases and should be credited with the 'idea' of instrumental variables (but he claimed in an interview on 17 June 1982 that Frisch coined the term). The idea formed the basis of Reiersøl's thesis (1945): 'Confluence Analysis by Means of Instrumental Sets of Variables'. (Confluence analysis soon became outmoded, but the use of instrumental variables in other models was extended, primarily by Sargan's classic paper (1958).)

CHAPTER 8

Haavelmo's probability model

A 'probabilistic revolution' occurred in econometrics with the publication of Trygve Haavelmo's 'The Probability Approach in Econometrics' in 1944.[1] It may seem strange that this 'revolution' should have been delayed until mid-century for, from the early days of the twentieth century, economists had been using statistical methods to measure and verify the relationships of economic theory. But, even though these early econometricians used statistical methods, they believed that probability theory was not applicable to economic data. Here lies the contradiction: the theoretical basis for statistical inference lies in probability theory and economists used statistical methods, yet they rejected probability. An examination of this paradox is essential in order to understand the revolutionary aspects of Haavelmo's work in econometrics.

At the beginning of the century, applied economists believed that there were real and constant laws of economic behaviour waiting to be uncovered by the economic scientist. As we have seen, this early econometrics consisted of two sorts of activity depending on the status of the theory concerned and the type of law to be uncovered. Where a well-defined and generally agreed theory existed, as in the work on demand, the role of statistical methods was to measure the parameters or constants of the laws. This measurement function was an important one, but not one in which questions of inference arose: because the theory was not in doubt, the measured law was taken to be the 'true' law corresponding to that of theory. In other areas, such as business cycle research, where the theoretical laws were in doubt, where theorists disagreed or where empiricists reigned, statistical methods

[1] Trygve Haavelmo (born 1911): a Norwegian economist who studied economics with Frisch at Oslo. He travelled in the USA on Rockefeller Foundation and American–Scandinavian Fellowships from 1939 to 1942. From 1943 to 1946 he was in New York and Washington undertaking war work and also finding time for academic research with the Cowles Commission (then based at Chicago). He returned to Oslo University in 1947 as Professor of Economics, where he has worked since.

were to act as the midwife in bringing forth the true laws or phenomena from the data. Again the role of inference seemed to be limited, for whatever lawlike relationships emerged from the data were taken to be the correct representations of economic life. Sophisticated inference procedures – ways of comparing theoretical laws and empirical relationships, and the need to argue between these two levels – appeared to be unnecessary under either approach.

This description does not paint an entirely accurate picture of econometrics prior to Haavelmo's paper, not because the picture of underlying beliefs is untrue, but because applied results rarely came out neatly. Measured relationships did not correspond with theoretical laws for a variety of reasons that econometricians grappled with in the 1920s and 1930s. Formal inference procedures, based on probability reasoning, were not invoked to help in these difficulties because of another belief held by econometricians, namely that economic data did not constitute raw material to which probability reasoning could properly be applied. So, economists' perception of the role of probability theory in the 1920s and 1930s was that it had a narrow domain of application, which extended neither to the treatment of economic data nor to the activity of uncovering economic relationships; still less was probability seen as an element in theory itself. The attitudes of economists in using statistical methods but rejecting probability theory can best be illustrated by examples from the two fields already discussed in the earlier chapters of this book.

8.1   Statistics without probability

In the early work on demand discussed in Chapters 5 and 6, the least squares method was used as an estimation device without underpinnings from probability theory, that is, without reference to underlying probability distributions or arguments. There was no obvious reason why probability theory should have entered here since the observations were often for aggregates and rarely the result of any sampling procedure.[2] In addition, there was occasional use of standard errors of coefficients, or of the regression, to measure the significance of results; but use of these tools of inference was not by any means standard procedure. The estimated single-equation models were held to *represent* the exact theoretical relationships which investigators

---

[2] In this rejection of probability reasoning, we hear once again the echoes of nineteenth-century social statistics in which, according to Porter (1986), probability inference was seen as irrelevant because data were from complete enumerations such as the census of population.

believed were the 'true' demand curves. There were two explanations for the failure of the observations to lie exactly on the measured relationship and therefore for the lack of complete correspondence between the observed data and a theoretical demand curve formulated as a simple and exact linear relationship. The first of these explanations, omitted factors, came from economic theory considerations; and the second, measurement errors, from statistical ideas. The development of equivalent formal models to match these explanations has already been discussed in Chapter 7; here the focus is on the role of probability in these explanations.

Errors-in-equations arose in the applied work on demand because in practice the *ceteris paribus* clauses of demand theory were not fulfilled. Demand data covered a number of time periods in which the other factors in the relationship changed, thus causing disturbances in the observed demand curve. Early econometricians tried to make their econometric models match economic theory models by dealing with these changing factors, as we have seen in Chapter 5. Initially they adjusted the data to allow for these changes prior to estimating the demand elasticity and later they included the most important factors in the equation to be estimated. Perhaps the clearest representation of this view can be seen in the work of Schultz (1928), whose discussion of the alternative methods of dealing with disturbing factors concluded:

> All of these statistical devices are to be valued according to their efficacy in enabling us to lay bare the true relationship between the phenomena under consideration. An ideal method would eliminate entirely all of the disturbing factors. We should then obtain perfect correlation between changes in the quantity demanded and corresponding changes in price.
>
> (Schultz (1928), p. 33)

The remaining disturbing factors (those not accounted for, or included in the equation) were taken to be the reason for approximation in the measurement of the 'true' demand curve. These omitted factors were rarely explicitly modelled or discussed as 'errors' in the econometric relationship. Instead, discussion was focussed almost entirely on those disturbing influences which were taken into account.

The lack of correspondence between theoretical models and applied results that arose because of the inability to hold all disturbing factors constant led some econometricians to take a less sanguine view of their results. In the late 1920s Mordecai Ezekiel suggested that statistical laws have their own worth, but because of the changing conditions under which they are obtained they cannot be taken to represent fundamental laws of economic behaviour. The underlying (or fundamental) relationships might still be considered constant and exact, but it was believed that probability theory could not be applied to the statistical or measurable relationships because these represented situations which were subject to change:

> the results obtained by statistical determination of the relations are not fundamental 'laws of nature' in the same sense as is the law of gravity. They are measures of the way that particular groups of men, in the aggregate, have reacted to specific economic conditions during a specified period in the past. If the study is elaborate enough, it may even reveal the way in which the reaction has been changing during the period considered, and the direction and rate of change. But it does not tell how long the same reaction will continue to prevail, what new causes may arise to change the responses, or what the relations would be in the new situation. The theories of mathematical probability do not apply.
>
> (Ezekiel (1928), p. 223)

Lionel Robbins refused to allow that the relationships which econometricians found even held the status of 'statistical laws':

> a moment's reflection should make it plain that we are here entering upon a field of investigation *where there is no reason to suppose that uniformities are to be discovered*. The 'causes' which bring it about that the ultimate valuations prevailing at any moment are what they are, are heterogeneous in nature: there is no ground for supposing that the resultant effects should exhibit uniformity over time and space. No doubt there is a sense in which it can be argued that every random sample of the universe is the result of determinate causes. But there is no reason to suppose that the study of a random sample of random samples is likely to yield generalisations of any significance. That is not the procedure of the sciences. Yet that, or something very much like it, is the assumption underlying the expectation that the formal categories of economic analysis can be given substantial content of permanent and constant value.   (Robbins (1932), p. 99)

In order to make his point, Robbins satirised the early econometric work on demand by describing the methods of one, Dr Blank, researching the demand for herrings:

> Instead of observing the market for herrings for a few days, statistics of price changes and changes in supply and demand may be collected over a period of years and by judicious 'doctoring' for seasonal movements, population change, and so on, be used to deduce a figure representing average elasticity over the period. And within limits such computations have their uses ... But they have no claims to be regarded as 'laws' ... there is no reason to suppose that their having been so in the past is the result of the operation of homogeneous causes, nor that their changes in the future will be due to the causes which have operated in the past.

Important as such investigations may be, . . . there is no justification for claiming for their results the status of the so-called 'statistical' laws of the natural sciences. (Robbins (1932), p. 101)

Robbins ended with a final criticism of econometric and quantitative economics in all its guises, and here his denial of the use of statistics was supported by direct reference to probability theory:

The theory of probability on which modern mathematical statistics is based affords no justification for averaging where conditions are obviously not such as to warrant the belief that homogeneous causes of different kinds are operating. (Robbins (1932), p. 102)

As we shall see, econometricians mostly agreed with Robbins that the conditions required for the application of probability theory were not fulfilled by economic data, but they did not see this as undermining their use of statistical methods.

The presence of measurement errors in the price and quantity data used in demand studies provided a second, and sometimes concurrent, rationalisation for the lack of exact fit in the estimated relationship. This statistical explanation (the errors-in-variables model) found favour with a number of econometricians, perhaps because it threw the onus of failure onto the quality of the data rather than implying that the statistical 'experiment' had failed to replicate the economic theory due to the presence of uncontrolled disturbing factors. The application of least squares as a measurement method in the case of errors had a respectable pedigree in other scientific fields, such as astronomy, in the nineteenth century. Yet there were only cursory references in the econometrics literature to an underlying probabilistic model for these errors, and again they were not explicitly modelled as part of the relationship.

The agricultural economist, Holbrook Working, in 1925 defined the problem of measurement errors and other 'extraneous' (i.e. non-economic factors) as follows:

There is but one true relationship and one line describing it; if all the extraneous disturbing factors could be eliminated the actual observations would all fall on this single line. (H. Working (1925), p. 530)

He went further towards accepting probability ideas than most, in linking his statistical techniques to sampling theory with the admission that,

If the *form* of the relationship is properly judged, a statistical determination should give the true theoretical relationship, subject to the fluctuations of sampling, whenever the significant effects of errors and of extraneous forces are reflected only in the dependent variable.

(H. Working (1925), p. 539)

But such references to the sampling aspect were rare, for the data used in demand studies were not samples and the theoretical discussion of measurement errors in econometrics developed in a specifically anti-probability (or anti-sampling) framework set by Frisch.

Frisch was not against probability theory as such, only against its unthinking application in economics:

> Of course, this contains no reflection on the value of sampling theory in general. In problems of the kind encountered when the data are the result of *experiments* which the investigator can control, the sampling theory may render very valuable services. Witness the eminent works of R. A. Fisher and Wishart on problems of agricultural experimentation.
>
> (Frisch (1934), p. 6)

Whereas the standard method of regression assumed errors only in the dependent variable, it seemed to Frisch (as it did to others) much more likely that all variables were measured with error. Frisch's (1934) work on confluence analysis dealt with the compound problem of measurement errors in all variables *and* several relationships existing between the variables. Frisch described his data-analytic approach to this complicated problem as follows:

> if the sampling aspect of the problem should be studied from a sufficiently general set of assumptions, I found that it would lead to such complicated mathematics that I doubted whether anything useful would come out of it. And, on the other hand, if the sampling aspect should be studied under simple assumptions, for instance, of not collinear and normally distributed basic variates, the essence of the confluence problem would not be laid bare ... I decided therefore first to attack the problem more from the experimental side, working out numerically - on actual economic data as well as on constructed examples - various other types of criteria which intuitively and heuristically may suggest themselves.
>
> (Frisch (1934), pp. 7–8)

In Frisch's model, all variables were made up of a systematic part plus a measurement error, and an exact relationship was believed to hold between the systematic ('true') variables. Frisch had not specified the full distribution of these measurement errors, but had assumed that the errors in different variables were uncorrelated with each other and with the systematic components. The solution to the problem of measurement errors, Frisch decided, lay in the choice of weights for each variable in the relationship. These weights were to be chosen in accordance with the relative size of the variance of the measurement errors in each case. The correct choice of weights would enable the 'true' relationship of interest to be found. In the absence of knowledge about the relative size of errors he believed it would be possible to place limits on the 'true' relationship by taking the least squares measurements under different assumptions.[3] Though this measurement error approach began in the demand literature, theoretical discussions of the problem (like Frisch's) made the issue general.

Econometric work of this early period was primarily concerned with *measuring* the elasticity of demand. There remains the question of inference, but this was not an important part of econometric work. If the measured value seemed unreasonable, then it was usually assumed that the data were no good; doubt was rarely cast on the theory. These attitudes limited the role of statistical inference and appeared to obviate the need for probability theory. Probability played little part in econometric demand analysis in the 1920s and 1930s, and in many instances probability theory was actually rejected.

If probability was not part of demand analysis, did it enter other strands of applied research? Chapters 1 and 2 discussed the different approaches to the statistical study of the business cycle. These involved the use of least squares to fit trend lines and correlation analysis to determine lagged relationships between different variables. The methods were also used to decompose time-series data into trends, seasonal and cyclical components. The left-over elements in the data were thought to be the result of accidental or random causes but of no intrinsic interest. These uses of statistical techniques in business cycle analysis were accompanied by clear denials of a positive role for probability theory, and of the reasons why.

For example Warren Persons, founder of the influential Harvard Business Barometer, in his 1923 presidential address to the American Statistical Association was vehement in his rejection of probability:

> The view that the mathematical theory of probability provides a method of statistical induction or aids in the specific problem of forecasting economic conditions, I believe, is wholly untenable.   (Persons (1924), p. 6)

Persons' reason for rejecting the use of probability theory was that economic data are time-related; that is each observation is related to the previous observation.[4] In his essay version of the speech, Persons went on to explain why he rejected probability reasoning (and in the process confused the notions of randomness and independence):

> the actual statistical data utilized as a basis for forecasting economic conditions, such, as a given time series of statistics for a selected period in the past, cannot be considered a random sample except in an unreal,

[3] For further discussion of confluence analysis see Chapter 7 Letter 11, and Hendry and Morgan (1989).

[4] Yule's (1926) paper on nonsense correlations, by illuminating the dangers of using correlations analysis on data which did not satisfy the classical rules of sampling, reinforced this view.

hypothetical sense; that is to say, unless assumptions be made concerning our material which cannot be retained in actual practice. Any past period that we select for study is ... not 'random' with respect to the present ... If the theory of probability is to apply to our data, not merely the series but the individual items of the series must be a random selection ... Since the individual items are not independent, the probable errors of the constants of a time series, computed according to the usual formulas, do not have their usual mathematical meaning ...

Granting, as he [the statistician] must, that consecutive items of a statistical time series are, in fact, related, he admits that the mathematical theory of probability is inapplicable.   (Persons (1924a), pp. 9–11)

Though he rejected the mathematical theory of probability in business cycle analysis and forecasting, Persons believed that probability as a measure of rational belief did have a role in social science and drew on J. M. Keynes' *Treatise on Probability* (1921) (a work rarely cited in econometrics) in support of his views:

It is obviously impossible to state, in terms of numerical probability, a forecast or an inference based upon both qualitative and quantitative evidence; and even if all the evidence were quantitative, we have seen that it does not express a numerical measure of rational belief for the future. So when we say that 'the conclusions of the social scientist are expressed in terms of probabilities' we mean merely that his conclusions do not have the certainty of those of the natural scientist. The probabilities of the economic statistician are not the numerical probabilities which arise from the application of the theorems of Bernoulli and Bayes; they are, rather, non-numerical statements of the conclusions of inductive arguments.

(Persons (1924a), p. 12)

More specific reasons for the rejection of probability theory were given by Oskar Morgenstern (1928) who was later to become director of the Institut für Konjunkturforschung in Vienna.[5] He defined the problems as the lack of homogeneity of underlying conditions, the non-independence of time-series observations and the limited availability of data. Marget wrote a beautifully rhetorical reply to Morgenstern's criticisms, in which he agreed with Morgenstern on only one point, namely:

whatever may be the case in the other sciences, the formal technique of probability analysis can only rarely, if ever, be applied to economic data with any hope of obtaining reasonably significant results.

(Marget (1929), p. 315)

[5] Oskar Morgenstern (1902–77) criticised business cycle forecasting in his habilitation thesis (1928). He was director of the Institute from 1931 to 1938. His second critique of econometrics dealt with the accuracy of economic data; he is, of course, better known for his development, with von Neumann, of game theory.

Yet, even on this point, Marget sought to rob Morgenstern of any real victory:

> One has only to try to recall concrete instances of formal attempts to employ the technique of probability analysis to the problem of business forecasting to be convinced that our author is, after all, fighting with a shadow. (Marget (1929), p. 316)

The statistical methods used in isolating the business cycle were similar to those used in demand, but in cycle analysis the rejection of probability theory was more clearly articulated and seen to be particularly associated with forecasting. Probability theory was believed to be inapplicable to economic data because economic data did not behave according to the laws of probability: data observations were not independent of each other (they were related through time) and underlying conditions were not homogeneous throughout the time period. In practice, in demand work and in cycle analysis, econometricians rejected data from obviously non-homogeneous time periods (such as the war years, 1914–18) and removed some time-related elements in the data (for example, the removal of trends or trending factors). But the ostensible reason for these data control procedures was to fulfil the *ceteris paribus* clauses of economic theory (in order to reveal the underlying 'true' demand relationship or business cycle) not to fulfil the data demands of probability theory. Econometricians did not cite data control procedures to justify their use of statistical methods because they did not believe that they needed to do so. They rarely stated why they believed statistical methods could be used to measure the past but not be used to make inferences about the future, for they did not regard their statistical measurement methods as dependent on the probability calculus.

Their position is defensible, for devices such as least squares and correlation operate as measurement methods independently of probability theory and reasoning; the latter enters only in order to justify the quality (or goodness) of the measurements taken. (For example, the relationship between two variables can be measured by a least squares line but inferences about whether it is a good measure will depend on the distributions of the variables.) The history of statistics is also on the side of the econometricians. As Porter (1986) shows, nineteenth-century social statistics arose largely independently of probability theory, and S. M. Stigler (1986) points out that although the least squares method was developed in the eighteenth century, it only received justification from the law of errors in the nineteenth century. The use of the same method in the field of the biological and social sciences was a relatively recent occurrence (late nineteenth century) while full understanding of inference procedures and justification in such situations was delayed until the work of R. A. Fisher, and the advances of J. Neyman and E. S. Pearson in the 1920s and 1930s.

Prior to the 1930s, then, a strong current in econometric thought rejected the application of mathematical theories of probability to economic data on the grounds that the data did not fulfil the necessary conditions. At the same time, there was widespread use of statistical methods, which did not seem to econometricians to be tainted with probabilistic ideas.

8.2   Signs of change

The 1930s saw early signs of the 'revolution' to come. These stirrings were visible in the desire to develop better ways of measuring relationships and better methods of testing competing economic theories, and even in economic theory itself.

One of the most notable of Haavelmo's forerunners in developing the probability approach to *measurement* was Tjalling Koopmans whose thesis of 1936 extended Ragnar Frisch's work on measurement errors.[6] Koopmans' main argument with Frisch was that he had concerned himself only with one type of error, the measurement error, to the neglect of the sampling error:

> if all variables contain an erratic component, an estimated regression equation is subject to two quite different kinds of error, ... Only one of them is considered by Frisch, and is due to absence of knowledge on the ratio's [*sic*] of the variances of the errors in the individual variables. The other one is the usual sampling error, ... It arises from the fact that the errors in the variables, even if being uncorrelated, mutually and to the systematic components, in the parent distribution, will in general fail to be so in a sample. Therefore, the assumptions [those of mutual uncorrelatedness etc.] are tantamount to the complete neglect of this sampling error.   (Koopmans (1937), p. 45)

Koopmans wanted to reset Frisch's confluence analysis model into the classical probability scheme because be believed:

> The loss in generality imposed by the assumptions involved in the construction of a parent distribution is then to some extent compensated by a gain in mathematical rigour in this respect, that by the sampling approach to the

---

[6] Tjalling C. Koopmans (1910–85) studied physics in the Netherlands and soon switched to econometrics, writing his thesis (1936, published in 1937) on the application of advanced mathematical statistics to economic data. He joined the Cowles Commission in 1944 and was its director 1948–54.

problem it is possible to attach definite risks of error to the test criteria reached, though of course on the hypothesis that the parent distribution was rightly specified. (Koopmans (1937), p. 30)

But it was not, at first sight, clear to Koopmans what the sampling framework should be in economics, because of the lack of repeatable experiments or controlled variability (compared with work on the design of agricultural experiments), and because the data on economic variables were time-related:

> variables are developing in time in cyclical oscillation, apparently to a large extent governed by some internal causal mechanism, and only besides that influenced, more or less, according to the nature of the variable, by erratic shocks due to technical inventions, variations in crop yields, etc. At any rate, they are far from being random drawings from any distribution whatever. (Koopmans (1937), p. 5)

Koopmans kept to the standard econometric model of the period, which was both causal and exact:

> the distinction has been drawn between a regression coefficient conceived as a quantitative measure of a causal relationship and a regression coefficient conceived as a quantity descriptive for a multivariate distribution . . . here the former sense is adopted . . . It is assumed that there is a 'true regression equation' which would be exactly satisfied by the 'true values' of the variables. (Koopmans (1937), p. 6)

The sampling framework was described as:

> The observations constituting one sample, a repeated sample consists of a set of values which the variables would have assumed if in these years the systematic components had been the same and the erratic components had been other independent random drawings from the distribution they are supposed to have. (Koopmans (1937), p. 7)

Koopmans believed that both economic data and econometric models were compatible with the general 'classical' method (as propounded by R. A. Fisher) in which the dependent variable (X_1) contained both measurement error and omitted variable error and the independent variables ($X_2, X_3, \ldots, X_k$) were without error. He claimed that:

> A conspicuous advantage is that this specification does not imply any assumption as to the distribution of $X_2, \ldots, X_k, \ldots$ these observational variables need not be a random sample drawn from any probability distribution, but may as well be the values assumed by variables which develop in time by an, [sic] possibly unknown, causal mechanism; or they may be, as an intermediate case between these extremes, drawings from a series of distributions ordered in time, the next of which depends on the

values drawn in the preceding ones, ... This generality of Fisher's specification is a point strongly in favour of its use in economic regression analysis.   (Koopmans (1937), pp. 29–30)

Working in this classical framework, Koopmans showed how taking account of sampling error would affect Frisch's results on measurement error, but his treatment was theoretical, highly technical in nature and probably understood by relatively few econometricians. Certainly, Frisch's bunch map (or confluence) analysis continued to be used in applied work, and there were very few cases of Koopmans' tests being used.[7] There were one or two other statisticians associated with the econometrics group who also tried to initiate a more rigorous probability approach during the 1930s. Hotelling is one (see, for example, his (1934)), but like Koopmans, his exhortations to the econometricians made little impact.

The 1930s also saw developments that involved probability ideas in both *theory construction* and in *testing* models. As discussed in Chapters 3 and 4, statistical business cycle analysis was overtaken during that decade by the development of macrodynamic model building. For a long time, accidental or random events from outside the economy had been thought to precipitate crises or turning points in the cycle. Frisch's 'rocking horse' model of 1933 made these random shocks an integral part of the model in order to bridge the gap between theory and data: the shocks were responsible for maintaining oscillations in the economic system and producing irregular-looking data. Such models, by formally incorporating random errors also provided a theoretical counterpart to the regression residuals of statistical work. Jan Tinbergen's econometric business cycle research of the period 1936–9 was much more ambitious than the earlier applied work either on demand or on business cycles. In particular, in his work for the League of Nations in 1937–8 he was effectively the first to use statistical techniques to try to test, as well as to measure, the macroeconomic relationships of the business cycle. As discussed in Chapter 4, Tinbergen used both statistical and economic criteria to test his results because he feared that sampling considerations and omitted variables (amongst a host of other difficulties) might make the results unreliable. He used a variety of statistical methods and tests including Fisher's method (the standard application of ordinary least squares) and Frisch's method of confluence analysis (and even Koopmans' additional tests). He also tested to see if the residuals (the empirical equivalent of Frisch's shocks) were normally distributed. Tinbergen clearly had

[7] Indeed, I have succeeded in finding only one example: Tinbergen, see Chapter 4.2.

some awareness of the role of probability ideas in his testing programme, but his decisions about which theories to reject and which to explore further were not formally based on the probability scheme; there was no framework for comparing economic theories and deciding which was best.

Another area of work, this time in the microeconomic field, also gave early warning of the 'revolution'. Once again this was a result of econometricians trying to build more adequate (realistic) models of economic behaviour. The problem was how to incorporate into econometric models the uncertainty in an individual consumer's or firm's behaviour resulting from unfulfilled plans and forecasts. Both Tinbergen (1933) and Tintner (1938) wrote on this question during the 1930s. Tinbergen attempted to establish planning horizons by modelling plans and their corrections when new information became known. Such ideas provided another channel for a natural application of probability in the theory models used by econometricians, rather than through purely statistical devices for measurement of economic relationships.

The literature discussed so far has been concerned primarily with errors: errors in relationships and errors in variables. This was because economic life was thought of as a largely deterministic exercise, with the unknown, unknowable or immeasurable bits dealt with as something outside the concerns of economic theory.[8] In this setting, probability theory could not be part of economic models until economists thought that economic life itself involved elements of chance. By the end of the 1930s there had been some movement towards the integration of 'chance' into theory both at the macroeconomic level (as in Frisch's model of the cycle) and at the microeconomic level (as in Tinbergen's models of unfulfilled plans). Despite these signs of change, economic theories were still formulated as exact rather than as probabilistic models.

The role of probability theory in measurement and inference was still restricted, although this too was beginning to change. In the early days, probability theory was not thought to be applicable to economic data and econometricians had been naive about inference. But, because of the lack of correspondence between applied results and economic theory and because of the growing desire to test theories rather than be content with measurement, econometricians in the 1930s were gradually becoming more sophisticated about matters of inference.

---

[8] There were a few outlyers such as Bowley (1933), and perhaps Mills (1936), who were interested in analysing the frequency distributions of economic variables but not in applying probability thinking to economic relationships.

8.3　　Haavelmo's probabilistic revolution in econometrics

Given the attitudes of econometricians in the 1920s and 1930s, it is not surprising that a slightly defensive tone is evident in the published presentation of Trygve Haavelmo's 'The Probability Approach in Econometrics' in 1944.[9] The paper also bore signs of the evangelicism of the newly converted. Haavelmo had been a student of Frisch and later his research assistant and Frisch, while not totally against probability theory, believed that there were many situations in economics where it was not applicable. Haavelmo by his own admission owed much to Frisch and several sections of the probability paper develop ideas initiated by Frisch. Despite Frisch's influence, Haavelmo was converted to the usefulness of probability ideas by Jerzy Neyman and he was also influenced by Abraham Wald, a brilliant statistician whom he credited as the source of his understanding about statistical theory.[10]

Haavelmo recognised that the bulk of econometricians thought probability theory had nothing to offer, though they made use of statistical methods. He argued that since probability theory was the body of theory behind statistical methods, it was not legitimate to use the latter without adopting the former:

> The method of econometric research aims, essentially, at a conjunction of economic theory and actual measurements, using the theory and technique of statistical inference as a bridge pier. But the bridge itself was never completely built. So far, the common procedure has been, first to construct an economic theory involving exact functional relationships, then to compare this theory with some actual measurements, and, finally, 'to judge' whether the correspondence is 'good' or 'bad'. Tools of statistical inference have been introduced, in some degree, to support such judgements, e.g., the calculation of a few standard errors and multiple-correlation coefficients. The application of such simple 'statistics' has been considered legitimate, while, at the same time, the

[9] Haavelmo's paper was written while he was visiting Harvard in 1941 and circulated in mimeographed form. The 1944 version was similar throughout (apart from a few alterations in wording) except for the addition of a final section on forecasting. Haavelmo also published one section – on simultaneous relationships – on its own, in 1943 (see (1943a)). His 1944 paper gained him a doctorate degree from Oslo in 1946.

[10] It was apparently while trying to convert Jerzy Neyman to confluence analysis that Haavelmo's conversion to probability reasoning occurred. (This emerged during discussions on the history of econometrics in Oslo in 1987 – I thank David Hendry for the information.) J. Neyman and E. S. Pearson were responsible for a statistical testing procedure which Haavelmo adopted. Abraham Wald (1902–50) studied as a mathematician in Rumania and joined the business cycle research institute in Vienna (1932–8). He worked at Columbia University from 1938 until his death. He exerted a considerable influence on the econometric work of the Cowles group in the 1940s. He is renowned for his work in statistical decision theory.

adoption of definite probability models has been deemed a crime in economic research, a violation of the very nature of economic data. That is to say, it has been considered legitimate to use some of the *tools* developed in statistical theory *without* accepting the very *foundation* upon which statistical theory is built. For *no tool developed in the theory of statistics has any meaning* - except, perhaps, for descriptive purposes - *without being referred to some stochastic scheme.*   (Haavelmo (1944), Preface, p. iii)

The problems of non-independence of observations and of non-homogeneous time periods (over which economic relationships were unlikely to remain stable) were the stong arguments of the anti-probability lobby. Haavelmo argued to the contrary: that these features did not prevent probability theory being applied to economic data:

> The reluctance among economists to accept probability models as a basis for economic research has, it seems, been founded upon a very narrow concept of probability and random variables. Probability schemes, it is held, apply only to such phenomena as lottery drawings, or, at best, to those series of observations where each observation may be considered as an independent drawing from one and the same 'population'. From this point of view it has been argued, e.g., that most economic time series do not conform well to any probability model, 'because the successive observations are not independent'. But it is *not* necessary that the observations should be independent and that they should all follow the same one-dimensional probability law. It is sufficient to assume that the *whole set* of, say n, observations may be considered as *one* observation of n variables (or a 'sample point') following an n–dimensional *joint* probability law, the 'existence' of which may be purely hypothetical. Then, one can test hypotheses regarding this joint probability law, and draw inference as to its possible form, by means of *one* sample point (in n dimensions).   (Haavelmo (1944), Preface, p. iii)

This reversal of the usual argument - that far from having a narrow domain of application, the probability approach is very generally applicable - was the basis of Haavelmo's revolutionary scheme for econometrics.

By adopting probability theory, Haavelmo suggested that economists would be providing themselves with an adequate framework for conducting economic research and rigorous testing of theories in place of their present vague notions:

> if we want to apply statistical inference to testing the hypotheses of economic theory, it *implies* such a formulation of economic theories that they represent *statistical* hypotheses, i.e., statements - perhaps very broad ones - regarding certain probability distributions. The belief that we can make use of statistical inference without this link can only be based upon lack of precision in formulating the problems. (Haavelmo (1944), Preface, p. iv)

These were Haavelmo's major points as set out in the Preface to his 1944 paper. The arguments of the succeeding 115 pages, which constituted the paper, involved a discussion of many issues in econometrics, in all of which he made use of probability ideas to provide an integrated treatment of the subject and practice of econometrics. For example, Haavelmo covered such difficult questions as the permanence of economic laws, the autonomy of relationships (on which, see Aldrich (1989)) and the question of prediction. Only the more important strands in Haavelmo's arguments relating to how and why the probability approach should be implemented are discussed here.

8.3.1   Theory and data

The first problem was that of comparing an economic theory to data. Haavelmo's argument took the following line:

> The facts will usually disagree, in some respects, with any *accurate* a priori statement we derive from a theoretical model . . .

therefore:

> it is practically impossible to maintain any theory that *implies* a nontrivial statement about certain facts, because sooner or later the facts will, usually, contradict any such statement . . .

and so:

> What we want are theories that, without involving us in direct logical contradictions, state that the observations will *as a rule* cluster in a limited subset of the set of all conceivable observations, while it is still consistent with the theory that an observation falls outside this subset 'now and then'.
>
>   As far as is known, the scheme of probability and random variables is, at least for the time being, the only scheme suitable for formulating such theories.   (Haavelmo (1944), pp. 1, 2 and 40)

Haavelmo gave a simple example of what he meant in his 1943 paper in defence of Tinbergen; I mentioned this example in Chapter 4, but it is worth recalling here. No economist, Haavelmo said, would want to work with an economic theory that predicted that national income would be exactly $X million next year, because it would almost certainly be contradicted by fact. Instead, applied economists prefer to work with the type of theory that predicts that the level of national income next year will be close to $X million. So, though they might not admit to it, Haavelmo considered that econometricians already worked with an informal probability scheme and he argued that probability theory merely provides a formal way of specifying such theories.

Economic theories must therefore be formulated as probabilistic statements. But what did this mean and how would it help in relating theory to data? In order to compare theory and data, it is normally necessary to specify the experimental conditions under which the theory is expected to hold. Haavelmo believed the same was true for economics. He argued that a theoretical economic model:

> will have an economic meaning only when associated with a design of actual experiments that describes - and indicates how to measure - a system of 'true' variables (or objects) $X_1, X_2, \ldots, X_n$ that are to be identified with the corresponding variables in the theory ...
>
> The model thereby becomes *an a priori hypothesis* about real phenomena, stating that every system of values that we might observe of the 'true' variables will be one that belongs to the set of value-systems that is admissible within the model. The idea behind this is, one could say, that Nature has a way of selecting joint value-systems of the 'true' variables such that these systems are as if the selection had been made by the rule defining our theoretical model. Hypotheses in the above sense are thus the joint implications - and the only testable implications, as far as *observations* are concerned – of a theory *and* a design of experiments.
>
> (Haavelmo (1944), pp. 8–9)

There were problems with this definition that a hypothesis equals a theory plus a design of experiments. To begin with, economists are rarely explicit about their experimental design. Haavelmo recognised this nettle and grasped it firmly. He began by grouping experiments into two classes:

> (1) experiments that *we should like to make* to see if certain real economic phenomena - when *artificially isolated* from 'other influences' - would verify certain hypotheses, and (2) the stream of experiments that Nature is steadily turning out from her own enormous laboratory, and which we merely watch as passive observers ...
>
> In the first case we can make the agreement or disagreement between theory and facts depend upon *two* things; the facts we choose to consider, as well as our theory about them ...
>
> In the second case we can only try to adjust our theories to reality as it appears before us. And what is the meaning of a design of experiments in this case? It is this: We try to choose a theory and a design of experiments to go with it, in such a way that the resulting data *would be* those which we get by passive observation of reality. And to the extent that we succeed in doing so, we become master of reality – by passive agreement.
>
> Now, if we examine current economic theories, we see that a great many of them, in particular the more profound ones, require experiments of the first type mentioned above. On the other hand, the kind of economic data that we actually have belong mostly to the second type.
>
> (Haavelmo (1944), pp. 14–15)

Haavelmo reached to the heart of the fundamental problem of econometrics. Economists are not in a position to isolate, control and manipulate economic conditions: they cannot undertake experiments. Instead, they have to make do with passive observations (those from Nature's experiments) which are influenced by a great many factors not accounted for by the theory. Of course, Haavelmo was aware that this problem was not confined to economics. His solution was simple:

> If we cannot clear the data of such 'other influences', we have to try to introduce these influences in the theory, in order to bring about more agreement between theory and facts.   (Haavelmo (1944), p. 18)

In practical terms, there did not seem to be anything revolutionary about this solution: indeed it provides a good description of the ad hoc statistical practices of the early econometricians.

Yet the old problem still remained: how could theories be reformulated as probabilistic statements if these 'passive observations of reality' resulted in data that were from non-constant circumstances. Haavelmo insisted that this was not a real problem, and that probability theory was general enough to cope with the vagaries of economic data. He argued that qualities of independence and randomness could be associated not only with individual observations on individual variables but also with a system or a set of variables $X_1, \ldots, X_r$. For example, if this were the set of variables which influenced the consumption decisions of individuals in a population, then observations on each person's set of variables would be represented by one point in r-dimensional space and the Xs would be subject to a joint probability law. A sample of size s taken from all consumers would give a set of information of dimension r by s, which could be regarded either as a sample of size s on an r-dimensional population, or a sample of size s on one system of values $(X_1, \ldots, X_r)$ or even one observation of dimension r by s. In other words, economic data could be dealt with in a number of different ways in probability theory. Usually, random sampling would denote that the s different points in the r space were independently chosen and that the dependence within the system (the relationship between the r different Xs) was 'given by Nature'.

Haavelmo's idea was that the relationship which existed between the population and the sample in probability theory provided a model for the correspondence relationship between economic theory and passive economic data ('a sample selected by Nature'). This probabilistic formulation of economic theory imposed a formal relationship between non-experimentally obtained data and the theory. He inserted an example to explain how such statements were formulated in practice.

His case was the consumption of a commodity by individuals (Y_i) to be explained by a number of factors ($X_1, \ldots, X_n$):

$$Y_i = f(X_1, \ldots, X_n)$$

Haavelmo defined the statistical population as all possible values of each Y, that is, as the

> infinity of possible *decisions* which might be taken with respect to the value of Y,   (Haavelmo (1944), p. 51)

which formed an acceptable economic theory definition of Y. Then, the observed values of Y (the data), described as:

> all the decisions taken by all the individuals who were present during one year,   (Haavelmo (1944), p. 51)

constituted one sample of data from the population, the decisions in the next year a second sample, and so on. Economists could then, if they wished, select a subsample from the observed data using some random selection procedure.

The economic factors (the Xs) could be treated either as having a joint probability distribution or as fixed at their observed values. In a sample of individuals with the same set of X values, the Y values naturally differed, so Haavelmo argued that an additional explanatory factor should be included – the shift factor, S – to represent the factors specific to the individual:

$$Y = f(X_1, \ldots, X_n) + S$$

This factor, S, was also subject to a probability law:

> When we assume that S has, for each fixed set of values of the variables X, a certain probability distribution, we accept the *parameters* (or some more general properties) of these distributions as certain additional character-istics of the theoretical model itself. These parameters (or properties) describe the *structure* of the model just as much as do systematic influences of $X_1, X_2, \ldots, X_n$ upon Y. Such elements are not merely some superficial additions 'for statistical purposes'.   (Haavelmo (1944), p. 51)

Haavelmo justified the stochastic scheme in his example by a specific appeal to the variability in individuals' behaviour:

> It is on purpose that we have used as an illustration an example of individual economic behaviour, rather than an average market relation. For it seems rational to intoduce the assumptions about the stochastical elements of our economic theories already in the 'laws' of behaviour for

the single individuals, firms, etc., as a characteristic of their behaviour, and then derive the average market relations or relations for the whole society, from these individual 'laws'. (Haavelmo (1944), pp. 51–2)

Haavelmo argued further that even those who believed in exact theory and only allowed for the presence of measurement error should also accept his stochastic scheme. This was because the exact equations which characterised such models could only be satisfied approximately in real life. It was necessary to bridge the gap between the exact theory and the facts with stochastic measurement errors, that is, measurement errors specified as probability laws.

8.3.2   Testing theories

Haavelmo's revolution was concerned with changing both approach and practice: from an unchallengeable belief in theory plus the use of data adjustment processes which aimed to make the data correct for the given theory, to a new approach which aimed to find the correct choice of model for the observed data by using statistical tests. The returns to the probability approach lay in its ability to test theories and thus aid in the correct choice of model. Haavelmo argued that a properly formulated stochastic model (with a design of experiment) is an hypothesis which states which set of values are admissible. Observations may sometimes fall outside this set of admissible values without leading to a rejection of the theory since the probabilistic model

> does not exclude any system of values of the variables, but merely gives different weights or probabilities to the various value-systems.
> (Haavelmo (1944), p. 9)

The hypothesis states which sets of values are highly likely and which are almost impossible. It is this feature, according to Haavelmo, which provides the power to compare theories and demonstrates the true value of the probability approach:

> For the purpose of *testing* the theory against some other alternative theories we might then agree to deem the hypothesis tested false whenever we observe a certain number of such 'almost impossible' value-systems.
> (Haavelmo (1944), p. 9)

If the problem of economic theory were essentially

> to construct hypothetical probability models from which it is possible, by random drawings, to reproduce samples of the type given by 'Nature',
> (Haavelmo (1944), p. 52)

then the problem of testing the theory using these samples was one of statistical theory and technique. This brought Haavelmo round to his last major point, the advances in statistical testing theory particularly due to Neyman and Pearson. Following an outline of the Neyman–Pearson procedure, Haavelmo set out the way in which the economist should formulate theories for testing purposes. First of all, Haavelmo proposed that the theoretical models to be compared to the data should involve systems of theoretical random variables corresponding to the observed variables. The observed data (nN values: X_{1t}, X_{2t}, . . . , X_{nt}, $t = 1, . . . , N$) were to be considered as a sample point in an nN-dimensional sample space of nN random variables with a certain joint probability distribution.

> It is indeed difficult to conceive of any case which would be contradictory to this assumption. For the purpose of testing hypotheses it is not even necessary to assume that the sample could actually be repeated. We make hypothetical statements before we draw the sample, and we are only concerned with whether the sample rejects or does not reject an a priori hypothesis.   (Haavelmo (1944), p. 70)

Autonomous (exogenous) elements could be considered constant (fixed with probability equal to one). In addition to the nN set of theoretical variables, he also required a set of 'auxiliary random parameters' (e_{1t}, e_{2t}, . . . , e_{nt}; $t = 1, . . . , N$) with a specified joint distribution. These auxiliary variables might be 'counterparts to some real phenomenon' such as measurement errors. A set of constant parameters and restrictions completed Haavelmo's model. The assumptions made about the es and the Xs would restrict the class of probability laws to which the model belonged. But, despite these restrictions, Haavelmo argued, different models might lead to the same set of probability laws and therefore the models would be indistinguishable from the point of view of the observations.

As Haavelmo pointed out, a well-fitting model (a theory which fits the data well) may produce useful restrictions upon the class of prior theoretical models, but there is no guarantee that it is the 'true' model. This is because many different probability schemes might be capable of producing the same observed data:

> Since the assignment of a certain probability law to a system of observable variables is a trick of our own, invented for analytical purposes, and since the same observable results may be produced under a great variety of different probability schemes, the question arises as to which probability law should be chosen, in any given case, to represent the 'true' mechanism under which the data considered are being produced. To make this a

rational problem of statistical inference we have to start out by an axiom, postulating that every set of observable variables has associated with it one particular 'true', but unknown, probability law.

(Haavelmo (1944), p. 49)

The problem of choosing the correct model remained a practical problem, precisely because the 'true' probability law remained unknown.

Early in his paper, Haavelmo had warned economists to be sceptical about their theories, for

whatever be the 'explanations' [of economic phenomena] we prefer, it is not to be forgotten that they are all our own artificial inventions in a search for an understanding of real life; they are not hidden truths to be 'discovered'.   (Haavelmo (1944), p. 3)

Haavelmo himself seemed to 'prefer an explanation' based on the realism of probabilities in economics.[11] But he argued that other economists did not have to share this belief; they need only treat economic variables 'as if' they were governed by probability laws in order to adopt the probability approach. For Haavelmo, the important message was that economists should adopt his approach because it was the best scientific practice available, and in order to get this across he made occasional concessions to those who did not share his views on the nature of economic variables:

Purely empirical investigations have taught us that certain things in the real world happen only very rarely, they are 'miracles' while others are 'usual events'. The probability calculus has developed out of a desire to have a formal logical apparatus for dealing with such phenomena of real life. The question is not whether probabilities *exist* or not, but whether – if we proceed *as if* they existed – we are able to make statements about real phenomena that are 'correct for practical purposes'.

(Haavelmo (1944), p. 43)

Perhaps Haavelmo was also aware that the philosophical, theoretical and polemical character of much of his paper would be off-putting to those economists he was most anxious to convert for he concluded his paper in an entirely different style: his final down-to-earth statements laid stress on the usefulness, reliability and fruitfulness of the probability approach in solving practical econometric problems.

---

[11] The nature of Haavelmo's own belief in probability is discussed further in the original version of this paper (see Morgan (1987), pp. 188–9).

8.4   The new consensus

The most immediate, and probably most important, effect of Haavelmo's paper was its influence on the work of the Cowles Commission for
Research in Economics (by then based at the University of Chicago).
Haavelmo's paper had been circulated amongst econometricians in an
unpublished form in 1941 and formed the basis of a new research
programme initiated at Cowles by Jacob Marschak in 1943.[12] He
involved a talented group of young statisticians, mathematicians and
economists including T. W. Anderson, L. Hurwicz, T. C. Koopmans as
well as Haavelmo himself. Inspired by Haavelmo's methodological
blueprint for econometrics, their aim was to continue in the tradition of
Tinbergen's pioneering work on business cycles but to improve on his
work by implementing the working practices of the 'Probability
Approach'. They saw themselves as armed with very powerful, pre-
cision-engineered tools based on the probability approach (in comparison with the previous tools of econometrics fashioned in the bronze
age) which they believed would solve a host of econometric problems.

Having adopted Haavelmo's blueprint, the researchers at the Cowles
Commission devoted a great deal of energy to developing the statistical
technology to go with the framework laid down by Haavelmo. They
attacked these problems with considerable technical expertise, statistical insight and rigour and involved others around them, such as
Abraham Wald and Herbert Simon. Applied work was not omitted
from this programme, although, almost inevitably given their idealism,
its results were more disappointing than those of the theoretical work
on statistical problems. For one thing, as the Cowles Commission
archives make clear, applied work was held back by the very heavy
computational burden imposed by the use of the maximum likelihood
technique. Despite this, the latter part of the 1940s and early 1950s saw
an impressive succession of Cowles Commission Monographs and
papers.[13]

Given the content of the Cowles Commission's research programme,
opposition to Haavelmo's ideas might have turned up disguised as
opposition to the Cowles' work. This turned out not to be the case,

[12] Marschak became research director of the Commission in 1943 and adopted Haavelmo's
work as a basis for their new econometric programme of work. (See Cowles Commission
annual reports for 1943–8, and references cited in Chapter 2 n. 11 for further work on
Cowles history. On Marschak, see Chapter 5 n. 17.)

[13] These were Monographs 10 (ed. Koopmans (1950)), 11 (by L. R. Klein (1950)), and 14
(ed. Hood and Koopmans (1953)); also papers in *Econometrica* and elsewhere in the late
1940s by Cowles Commission members. See Epstein (1987), Qin (1988) and (1989) for
assessments.

although there was strong opposition to the Cowles' programme. The opposition to the Cowles approach was most clearly stated in the debate sparked off by Koopmans' 'Measurement Without Theory' review of the 1946 NBER business cycle study by Burns and Mitchell. The differences of opinion over economic theory were discussed in Chapter 2, but Koopmans' (1947) review also attacked the statistical work of the NBER volume for its inadequate treatment of the data and almost complete lack of inference procedures. Koopmans argued for a more rigorous formulation of economic hypotheses in probabilistic terms so that the most advanced statistical estimation and inference procedures could be used.

It is a measure of the extent to which the Cowles programme was perceived to have diverged from the Haavelmo blueprint that in the debate which followed, both Vining (a visiting research associate at the NBER) and Koopmans (by this time director of the Cowles Commission) called upon Haavelmo's authoritative paper in support of their conflicting positions. Koopmans had no need to cite Haavelmo, for it was obvious (as Vining recognised) that Koopmans had taken Haavelmo's paper as his text. In his reply Vining (1949) in turn accused the Cowles Commission of measuring without economic theory, citing Haavelmo's emphasis on the need to undertake economic theory research, before hypotheses could be given a statistical formulation. Vining claimed that Cowles' version of statistical economics had little or no role to play in the discovery of such economic hypotheses.

Vining did not reject probability theory as a way of investigating economic data but argued for a broader interpretation of the approach:

> Distributions of economic variates in as large groups as can be obtained should be studied and analyzed, and the older theories of the generation of frequency distributions should be brushed off, put to work, and further developed. That is to say, statistical economics is too narrow in scope if it includes just the estimation of postulated relations. Probability theory is fundamental as a guide to an understanding of the nature of the phenomena to be studied and not merely as a basis for a theory of the sampling behaviour of estimates of population parameters the characteristics of which have been postulated. In seeking for interesting hypotheses for our quantitative studies we might want to wander beyond the classic Walrasian fields and poke around the equally classic fields once cultivated by men such as Lexis, Bortkiewicz, Markov, and Kapteyn.
>
> (Vining in Vining and Koopmans (1949), p. 85)

Koopmans seemingly agreed, but maintained it was necessary to start with some prior economic theory:

> I believe that his term 'statistical theory in its broader meaning' is used in the same sense in which the econometricians speak of 'model construction'. It is the model itself, as a more or less suitable approximation to reality,

which is of primary interest. The problems of estimation of its parameters or testing of its features have a derived interest only.

> (Koopmans in Vining and Koopmans (1949), pp. 89–90)

On the other hand, Koopmans was not prepared to concede that statistical theory had nothing to do with hypothesis seeking:

> It is possible to take a formal view and argue that hypothesis-seeking and hypothesis-testing differ only in how wide a set of alternatives is taken into consideration . . . To the extent that hypothesis-seeking is an activity that can be formalized by such a (statistical) theory, there is little doubt that the concept of statistical efficiency will remain relevant . . . However, there remains scope for doubt whether all hypothesis-seeking activity can be described and formalized as a choice from a preassigned range of alternatives.   (Koopmans in Vining and Koopmans (1949), p. 90)

On closer analysis then, there seemed to be a considerable measure of agreement that probability theory had an important role to play in economics, though this was partly hidden by the desire of both parties to score points.

The debate carried on into a review in 1951 by Hastay (from the NBER) of a collection of the main statistical results of the Cowles' work of the 1940s (Cowles Commission Monograph 10, edited by Koopmans (1950)). Once again, Haavelmo's name seemed an important talisman:

> Is it the most fruitful view of economic theory that which treats it in essential analogy with mechanics and meteorology? Such is the philosophy of the econometric school . . . a stochasticized Walrasian model is arbitrarily laid down as the essence of economic reasoning, and the authors take as their text a principle of Haavelmo that every testable economic theory should provide a precise formulation of the joint probability distribution of all observable variables to which it refers. It can be argued, however, that Haavelmo's principle is sounder than the program for realizing it worked out in this book.
>
> (Hastay (1951), pp. 388–9)

Though the NBER did not adopt an econometric approach, they did use a variety of quantitative techniques, which accounts for their desire to claim Haavelmo on their side. The argument may also be seen as an exercise in propaganda, for both institutions needed to attract and retain adequate research funding. The Cowles Commission had managed to obtain some financial backing from the Rockefeller Foundation, but that same foundation had supported the NBER for many years and in 1947 had made them a very substantial grant.[14]

---

[14] The grants awarded and taken up by the two bodies can be traced in the annual reports of the Rockefeller Foundation. This Foundation also played an important role in supporting a number of individual econometricians on fellowships (see Craver (1986) and (1986a)).

Though Haavelmo's 1944 paper was dense and may have been difficult for his contemporaries to understand,[15] part of the programme he suggested had already been published in more accessible versions. Haavelmo's (1943) defence of Tinbergen against Keynes' criticisms (already discussed in Chapter 4) had been used to introduce and justify the probability approach to testing in an easily appreciated form. In another paper in that year, Haavelmo (1943a) had published a version of one of the chapters of his long paper, which marketed the probability approach as a necessary adjunct to the simultaneous equations model. Haavelmo showed economists that, if they believed this to be the correct model of the world, then they should adopt the probability approach in their applied work to avoid biased results (see Chapter 7, Letter 14). This paper was more influential because it was easier to understand than the later 'Probability Approach', the example provided a very convincing argument and as Richard Stone (1946) pointed out, it contained the essentially new result in estimation.[16] This was reinforced by Koopmans' article of 1945, written with the specified aim of popularising Haavelmo's papers. Another influential, but more difficult, paper which developed Haavelmo's approach was that by Mann and Wald, also in 1943.[17] It dealt with maximum likelihood estimation of the typical econometric model used by the Cowles

---

[15] The review of Haavelmo's 1944 paper by Allen (1946), p. 161, who was himself a mathematical economist and statistician stated: 'It is not easy reading even for a mathematician and the non-mathematical economist is likely to be scared off at a first sight of its pages. Patience is well rewarded.' On the other hand, Stone (1946) suggested that the greater part of Haavelmo's work was accessible to the non-mathematician. E. B. Wilson (on the board of *Econometrica*, but not an active econometrician) berated Haavelmo in his review (1946) for mystifying the subject by an excessively formal approach and suggested that such rigorous statistical treatment and specification of economic hypotheses was unnecessary since the lack of such rigour had not prevented progress in other sciences such as physics, engineering, biology and psychology. (It is strange to note that Wilson (and Schumpter) were also thanked for their help by Haavelmo (1944).)

[16] Neil de Marchi has suggested that the lack of references to Haavelmo's 1944 paper means that it effected a silent revolution. This is not quite the case, for the paper (published only as a long journal article) received reviews and answering articles in other journals at the time (see n. 15 above.) Further evidence of its propogation comes from oral history which confirms that those who learnt their econometrics in the late 1940s, before the Cowles Monographs became available, were given Haavelmo's paper as their prime text. It is true that the probability aspect very quickly became a standard view (i.e. to use Kuhn's notion, it became part of 'normal' econometrics, in which case there becomes no further need to refer to it). The simultaneous equations paper (1943a) remained contentious and is much more heavily referenced.

[17] The Cowles Commission originally planned to issue Haavelmo's paper with the Mann and Wald paper in a single volume. This plan fell through because of the wartime paper shortage and this is why Haavelmo's paper was printed as a Supplement to *Econometrica*. (The Cowles Commission and the journal were run from the same offices in the 1930s and 1940s.)

Commission: a linear stochastic difference equation or system of equations. Haavelmo's ideas and Cowles' work dominated the output of econometric theory in the 1940s, giving the impression that econometrics had been successfully taken over by the probabilists. Certainly, there were no notable econometricians who publicly dissented from the probability approach in the late 1940s. But some important figures did disagree with other parts of Haavelmo's programme.

One group of economists led by Herman Wold rejected the simultaneous equations model advanced by Haavelmo in favour of a recursive, causal chain, model of economic relationships.[18] Econometricians from Moore, Schultz and Frisch, to Koopmans and Tinbergen had all thought of their models as being causal models. For Wold, simultaneously determined relationships involved the contradiction of simultaneous two-way causality. Despite their rejection of the model form as an unacceptable model of reality, the probabilistic formulation and treatment of models was adopted by Wold's group with approval as can be seen from Wold (1948) and Bentzel and Wold (1946). It was only later, in the 1950s, that Wold came to question the usefulness of the probability approach in dealing with economic data.

Gerhard Tintner (1946) was another econometrician who accepted the probability aspect of Haavelmo's work, but he, like Stone (1946), believed that Haavelmo had not dealt adequately with the problem of measurement errors.[19] In fact, Haavelmo had allowed for the presence of such errors in all variables in his theoretical scheme but, in the few examples he gave, had been forced to reduce their presence (though not to ignore them entirely) in order to make the models he dealt with tractable. On the other hand, Haavelmo's research programme, as reinterpreted by the Cowles group, concentrated almost entirely on errors in the equation due to omitted variables, thus deserving Tintner's criticism.

---

[18] Herman Wold was born in 1908 in Norway and spent much of his working life in Sweden where he studied under Cramér. He is known in econometrics for his book on stationary time series and stochastic processes (1938); his championship of the recursive model and applied work on demand models in the 1940s. His recursive model has recently been reanalysed by Jang (1973) and the argument between Wold and the Cowles group is discussed in Morgan (1987a).

[19] Gerhard Tintner (1907–83) took his doctorate in economic statistics and law, and worked at the Vienna business cycle Institute during the early 1930s, and in the USA thereafter (with a brief period at the Cowles Commission in the late 1930s). He was active in the econometric movement and was best known during the 1940s for his development and application of the variate difference method of time-series analysis (forming the subject matter of a Cowles Commission Monograph). He was also influenced by the Roos–Evans developement of mathematical economics. On Richard Stone, and his work, see Gilbert (1988).

By the late 1940s, Haavelmo's ideas for a probability approach were generally accepted in econometrics. A comparison of post-Haavelmo econometrics with the pre-Haavelmo era may help to pinpoint exactly what was revolutionary about Haavelmo's 'Probability Approach'. Before Haavelmo's work, econometricians used statistical methods but for the most part ignored or rejected any role for probability theory. This was because economists had believed that certain features of economic data (non-independence of successive observations and non-homogeneity of conditions) made the theory inapplicable. At the same time, econometricians perceived little need for the framework of probability theory as an aid to inference or in theory testing. Economists were persuaded of the value of the probability approach by the example of the simultaneous equations model, where the use of the approach produced accurate estimates, while the old-style statistical methods produced biased results.[20] Having accepted the logic of the probability approach for measurement, there was less of a bar to the more gradual acceptance of its usefulness in the more difficult task of inference and testing. Post-Haavelmo, statistical methods and probability theory have not been seen as separate entities but as one and the same bag of tools used by econometricians. Haavelmo himself believed in a full-scale probability approach where all the variables are thought of as having been generated from some probabilistic process (referred to as 'Haavelmo's principle' by Hastay). Even when econometricians since the 1940s have been more half-hearted or indifferent about the probabilistic nature of economic variables, and preferred to make use of Haavelmo's 'as if' argument, they have continued to use a version of Haavelmo's programme. In this sense, then, Haavelmo did cause a revolution in thinking: subsequent econometricians did not think, as the early econometricians clearly had done, that statistical methods could be used but that probability theory should be rejected.

It is easy enough to describe the probabilistic revolution in these terms, but what was the real difference in practice? The practical difference was not in estimation techniques since, following Haavelmo and the work of the Cowles Commission, there was a reversal towards the use of least squares for various reasons (not least the computational difficulties of implementing the full-scale approach). The more important practical result of Haavelmo's paper was that probability theory provided a framework for testing economic theories. The evaluation

---

[20] Though some econometricians, notably Stone and his colleagues at the Department of Applied Economics, Cambridge, and the agricultural econometricians, believed this bias to be small compared to those biases from other problems.

aspect was important: in early econometrics, data could be rejected but not theory. This was because applied results were judged according to a given theory; if results were thought suspect, it was usually interpreted as a problem of the data (because of the presence of errors, for example), rather than something wrong with the theory.

This problem became acute when researchers wanted to compare a number of different theories as there was no obvious way of proceeding. Tinbergen had experienced considerable difficulty in executing the League of Nations' commission to test the available theories of business cycles and sort out which were correct. Faced with many, apparently conflicting, but possibly complementary, theories in a verbal form he had put many of them together to form one large econometric model. He had then compared this model with the individual theories, judging his results on criteria internal to the theory. He used some external statistical tests but lacked the framework for using these criteria to judge which was the best of the theories. The first macroeconometric model to use the probability principles was built by L. R. Klein on behalf of the Cowles Commission. A comparison of his confident statements of intent, with the quotations given earlier from Tinbergen, show the impact of Haavelmo's work:

> We want to do more than is suggested by the title to Tinbergen's work (though not by the book itself), i.e., more than mere testing of business-cycle theories. We want also to discover the best possible theory or theories which explain the fluctuations that we observe. If we know the quantitative characteristics of the economic system, we shall be able to forecast with a specified level of probability the course of certain economic magnitudes ... In the course of the search for models which are suitable for our purposes of forecasting and making policy recommendations, we shall inevitably have to consider several alternative economic theories as admissible hypotheses. The acceptance or rejection of these hypotheses in the course of our search for truth will be our contribution to the problem of testing business-cycle theories.
>
> (Klein (1950), p. 1)

Haavelmo's work marks the shift from the traditional role of econometrics in measuring the parameters of a given theory to a concern with testing those theories. He had argued that if a theory were treated as pregnable – rather than as an unchallengeable truth – it could be treated as an hypothesis about a probability distribution, and the non-experimentally obtained data could be considered a sample from this distribution. This formalisation of the problem allowed applied economists to be more flexible in their attitude to theory, since any chosen hypothesis might be incorrect and an alternative model correct. By laying out a framework in which decisions could be made about which theories are supported by data and which are not, Haavelmo provided an adequate experimental method for economics.

Conclusion

Haavelmo's 1944 paper marks the end of the formative years in econometrics and the beginning of its mature period. His treatise set out the best methods for the practice of econometrics and explained the reasoning behind these rules. His novel ideas on the role of probability pointed the future way for econometrics, but in many other respects the concepts and approach of Haavelmo's programme were firmly rooted in the past. In his hands, the individual practical solutions and insights generated by the earlier work were finally fitted together as in a completed jigsaw puzzle, showing one single econometrics applicable to all branches of economics.

The coherence of Haavelmo's blueprint derived from a deep understanding of how econometrics worked as an applied science. His paper contained the most explicit and rewarding discussion in econometrics about its most fundamental problem: the problem of non-experimental data that come from

> the stream of experiments that Nature is steadily turning out from her own enormous laboratory, and which we merely watch as passive observers.
> (Haavelmo (1944), p. 14)

Clearly, econometricians could not isolate or control such data to match their theory, as in the ideal type of experiment — and here I return to the themes of my Introduction. Haavelmo suggested an alternative form of experimental design, in which economic theory could be constructed to meet the conditions of the data. But, for practical econometrics, he recognised that elements of both design types would be required. He advised his fellow econometricians that to the extent they could not adjust their data to fit their theory, they must adjust their theory to fit their data. Both theory and data were to be flexible in the attempt to bring the two elements to a point where statistical measurement and testing could take place.

The method of adjusting both theory and data proposed by

Haavelmo was exactly that used (albeit unconsciously) by econometricians in the period prior to 1940. The field of demand showed the method at work. Econometricians were aware from the very beginning that they had to adjust their data by various means to make it fit the theory. They soon realised that theory adjustments were needed too, to bring it closer to the available data. All too soon it was clear that the adjustment method did not fully solve the problem of experiments in econometrics; for if you aim to meet in the no-man's land between theory and data, how do you know when you have got there, and what do the measured relationships represent? For the early econometricians, these problems appeared in many guises as questions of correspondence, of the interpretation of results and levels of explanation achieved, and of the purpose and nature of testing. These were not philosophical issues to be discussed far into the night, but practical everyday questions.

The most elusive of these early difficulties (at least for the historian) concerns the interpretation of econometric results. Econometrics had taken on board correlation and least squares regression as general tools of analysis from biometrics. But once these tools had been applied out of their original contexts, it was not necessarily clear how the results should be interpreted, nor what was the status of econometric relationships. Porter (1986) suggests that the advent of autonomous statistical laws (like those of regression and correlation) had the potential to free the social sciences from the determinism of nineteenth-century physical science. This is no doubt correct, but this new scientific ideal had to be brought into focus for economics, and this naturally took time. Thus, econometricians seemed to vacillate between interpretations. Sometimes they favoured the deterministic model found in nineteenth-century astronomy, with exact relations and errors of measurement, for the measured equations could readily be interpreted as the exact economic relations of economic theory. Others, at other times, adopted the newer ideas and interpreted their econometric relationships as 'statistical laws', with the suggestion that they reflected average behaviour, or that they were descriptions of covariation without causal interpretation.

Uncertainty over the new interpretation partly arose because econometricians were not always sure what kind of phenomena they were trying to explain, nor what 'statistical' meant. Early econometricians had the benefit of two exemplars of statistical interpretation and explanation. First, Quetelet's description of average behaviour (the 'average man') and individual deviancy (distributed according to the law of errors). The second exemplar was Galton's regression law, which explained the pattern of aggregate behaviour in terms of a statistical process. Neither of these interpretations of a statistical relationship exactly fitted econometrics. With Haavelmo, the profession seemed to have arrived at a consensus: a statistical model of plural economic causes and errors in the relations. But in the meantime, the old scientific ideal had also changed, from a deterministic to a probabilistic view of the way the world worked. This left the explanatory level of Haavelmo's model open to new doubts. Was it really based on underlying random behaviour of the economic variables (as in contemporary evolutionary biology and quantum mechanics), or was it, after all, only a convenient way of formally dealing with inference in the non-experimental framework?[1]

As we have seen, the early econometricians' understanding that the raw economic data did not behave in accordance with the calculus of chance delayed the introduction of probability ideas to improve inference but did not mean econometricians had no idea of statistical testing. On the contrary, their ideas on this subject were far from naive; those as diverse in their views as Mitchell and Tinbergen both claimed that statistical methods might enable you to disprove something, but not prove it. Tinbergen had a notion of statistical verification which concerned his ability to explain the past behaviour of his data and the history of the economy. There were other notions, too, for these early econometricians expressed their aims in broad terms: they wanted to find out about the real world.[2] The extent of their success in feeling a way through the fog of difficulties to get at that world can best be demonstrated by recalling again the histories of the applied fields. In the business cycle field, the first problem econometricians faced was in defining and measuring their phenomena. Further, there were many economic theories of the cycle, but they were incomplete and lacked clarity. Consequently, the gap between theory and data was ill-defined. The extent and manner of the necessary adjustments, and the relative roles of theory and data, were uncertain and the question of how to test the multiplicity of theories loomed large. In contrast, the theory of demand commanded a considerable consensus and the nature of the data-theory gap was more clearly defined than in the business cycle field. It was thus in studies of demand that issues of correspondence

---

[1] Even a cursory survey of econometrics textbooks of the 1960s and 1970s reveals the extent of confusion over just where probability enters in and how the errors (or residuals) in the relations should be interpreted.

[2] I have written elsewhere (Morgan (1988)) about the range of testing ideas and test criteria prevalent in the early econometrics. In my interpretation, the early econometricians' idea of testing was something like quality control testing. I argue that their current terminology of statistical testing pays lip service to a notion of Popperian testing, but continues many of the early traditions.

appeared most ominous. In the face of all these difficulties, econometricians set about their tasks of adjusting theory to data and data to theory.

But more was required than this, for, as observed earlier, an experiment requires the scientist both to control some variables and to vary others. By the 1930s, econometricians had come to appreciate both of these points; they had begun to understand the role of multiple regression in controlling the variable circumstances in relations, and so indirectly achieve the necessary *ceteris paribus* conditions. In the context of demand studies, they had also realised that it was only when the supply curve did vary (as, for example, when Nature manipulated the weather), that they could isolate the demand relationship of interest. In business cycle econometrics, they had begun to understand what properties were needed for their equations to represent the relevant aspects of both theory and data. In learning how to cope with the requirements of their statistical method, econometricians developed the important notion of an 'econometric model' as the mid-way point between theory and data, to which both theory and data could be compared.

Looking back, we can see a certain freedom in those early years, allowing a rich diversity of ideas, practice and interpretation. Though much had been achieved, both in the way of individual solutions and in the crucial idea of an econometric model as an intermediary between theory and data, econometricians still suffered from the fact that they had no general techniques and no general rules of design for their 'experimental method'. These rules were provided in Haavelmo's paper of 1944 (and codified by the Cowles Commission). Econometric texts of the early 1950s openly referred to these new design rules as providing an alternative to the experimental method of science.[3] With these advances, econometrics, which had already made a name for itself as the most promising and highly technical area of applied economics, now fully differentiated itself from statistical economics. The difference between the two is most clearly to be seen in their attitudes to the role of theory and inference. Statistical economists (of both institutional and time-series persuasions) believed, more or less as Quetelet had done, that the regularities and relationships they sought would emerge pristine out of the murky swirl of data. Econometricians, on the other hand, believed that data would deliver up their secrets only when faced

---

[3] Econometricians of such diverse backgrounds as Tinbergen (1951a), Tintner (1952), Wold (with Juréen (1953)) and L. R. Klein (1953) all contain somewhere in their introductory remarks a discussion of econometrics and its rules of experiment in these terms. Some of them also refer to psychometrics and biometrics as having the same logical foundations, on which see my arguments in the Introduction.

with theory (in the form of a well-designed econometric model) and probability inference.

If there was progress in settling the rules of econometrics, there were also losses, for in the period after Haavelmo, as econometrics grew into the new technology, it left behind some of the interesting ideas and concepts of its youth. For example, Aldrich (1989) has discussed Frisch's important concept of 'autonomy' which entered briefly into our history only to disappear by the 1950s. Hendry and Morgan (1989) trace the parallel history of confluent relations which also disappeared. Both notions have more recently reappeared. Dynamic models sank under the tidal wave of largely static Keynesian models (see Morgan (1987a)), general equilibrium theories (see Weintraub (1985)) and Cowles simultaneous equations systems. The variety of correspondence notions disappeared as 'the identification problem' was given precedence. This last story provides an excellent example of the wider changes underway in econometrics in the 1940s. In the earlier discussions of the 1920s and 1930s work it was clear that identification issues, in their many forms, were a problem of both data and theory.[4] Qin (1989) has shown that as the Cowles Commission formulated this into a theoretical problem in order to provide a rigorous and general solution, models at two distinct levels, the mathematical one (representing economic theory) and the statistical one (representing the data), were collapsed into one mathematical model. By the textbook treatment of the 1960s, the identification question had become one to be answered by applying arithmetical rules to the theoretical model, with no data anywhere in sight.

The nature of applied econometrics also changed with the new rules. In the early work, more was involved than just the application of simple statistical techniques to data; econometrics was a creative juggling in which theory and data came together to find out about the real world. It involved a large element of craft skill (the experimenter's art) in which successful econometricians were those who, like Tinbergen, were extremely knowledgeable about their data, its quality and its behaviour. To them, it was as great a sin to apply a theory to data without understanding the conditions of measurement (as Leontief found to his cost), as it was to undertake measurement without any theory (as Mitchell found to his). With the setting of rules of experimental design and the formality imposed by Haavelmo's approach, applied econometrics seemed to enter a less creative phase. Data were

---

[4] For example, the idea of locating a relationship in the data can be contrasted with the idea of uniquely estimating the parameters of a given mathematical model and so on. I have tried elsewhere (Morgan (1985)) to categorise and differentiate these notions.

taken less seriously as a source of ideas and information for econometric models, and the theory-development role of applied econometrics was downgraded relative to the theory-testing role. The notion of an econometric model seems to have undergone a subtle change of meaning under the pressure of these changes in econometric thought. Econometric models came to be regarded as the passive extensions of economic theory into the real world, as the 'statistical complement of pure economics' rather than as representatives of a 'synthetic economics' in which theoretical knowledge and information from the real world are combined.[5]

In the first half of the twentieth century, econometricians found themselves carrying out a wide range of tasks: from the precise mathematical formulation of economic theories to the development tasks needed to build an econometric model; from the application of statistical methods in data preparation to the measurement and testing of models. Of necessity, econometricians were deeply involved in the creative development of both mathematical economic theory and statistical theory and techniques. Between the 1920s and the 1940s, the tools of mathematics and statistics were indeed used in a productive and complementary union to forge the essential ideas of the econometric approach. But the changing nature of the econometric enterprise in the 1940s caused a return to the division of labour favoured in the late nineteenth century, with mathematical economists working on theory building and econometricians concerned with statistical work.[6] By the 1950s the founding ideal of econometrics, the union of mathematical and statistical economics into a truly synthetic economics, had collapsed.

[5] I have used Moore's phrase 'the statistical complement of pure economics.' (taken out of context from his title (1908)) because it captures the notion I have in my mind. It contrasts strongly with the 'synthetic economics' (another of Moore's titles (1929)) which I believe characterised early econometric work and models. I speculate that the post-1950s shift implied here must have made interpretation easier, for if econometric models are regarded as close to theory models (and thus far from data descriptions) their interpretation becomes less problematic. (This change may also be linked to the downgrading of Haavelmo's probability ideas and the pushing out of probabilistic aspects into the residuals in the 1960s.) It would also make theory-testing seem easier, too, for the interpretation of econometric relationships as mid-way between theory and data makes it difficult to see what inferences can be drawn about what.

[6] This redivision of labour was helped no doubt by numerous other internal and external pressures, such as increasing specialisation in a rapidly growing economics profession. Haavelmo's 1957 address (see Haavelmo (1958)) to the Econometric Society is both a final statement of the joint programme and a plea for its return.

References

Aldrich, J. (1987), 'Jevons as Statistician: The Role of Probability', *The Manchester School*, **55**, 233–56

(1989), 'Autonomy', *Oxford Economic Papers* **41**, 15–34

Allen, R. G. D. (1934), 'A Critical Examination of Professor Pigou's Method of Deriving Demand Elasticity', *Econometrica*, **2**, 249–57.

(1939), 'The Assumptions of Linear Regression', *Economica* (New Series), **6**, 191–204

(1940), review of J. Tinbergen, *Statistical Testing of Business-Cycle Theories*, Vols. I and II, *Economica*, **7** (New Series), 335–9

(1946), review of T. Haavelmo: 'The Probability Approach in Econometrics', *American Economic Review*, **36**, 161–3

(1950), 'The Work of Eugen Slutsky', *Econometrica*, **18**, 209–16

Allen, R. G. D., and Bowley, A. L. (1935), *Family Expenditure*, London: P. S. King and Son.

Ames, E. (1948), 'A Theoretical and Statistical Dilemma – The Contributions of Burns, Mitchell and Frickey to Business-Cycle Theory', *Econometrica*, **16**, 347–69

Anderson, R. L (1945), review of T. Haavelmo: 'The Probability Approach in Econometrics', *Journal of the American Statistical Association*, **40**, 393–4

Anderson, T. W. and Hurwicz, L. (1946), 'Statistical Models with Disturbances in Equations and/or Disturbances in Variables', unpublished Cowles Commission paper.

Andvig, J. C. (1978), 'Wicksell's Influence on Frisch's Macroeconomics in the Thirties', *Scandinavian Journal of Economics*, **80**, 148–67

(1981), 'Ragnar Frisch and Business Cycle Research during the Interwar Years', *History of Political Economy*, **13**, 695–725

(1985), *Ragnar Frisch and the Great Depression*, Oslo: Norsk Utenrikspolitisk Institutt.

Arrow, K.J. (1960), 'The Work of Ragnar Frisch, Econometrician', *Econometrica*, **28**, 175–192

Bean, L. H. (1929), 'A Simplified Method of Graphic Curvilinear Correlation', *Journal of the American Statistical Association*, **24**, 386–97

Benini, R. (1907), 'Sull'uso delle Formole Empiriche nell'Economia Applicata', *Giornale degli Economisti*, 2nd series, **35**, 1053–63

Bentzel, R., and Hansen, B. (1954), 'On Recursiveness and Interdependency in Economic Models', *Review of Economic Studies*, **22**, 153–68

Bentzel, R., and Wold, H. (1946), 'On Statistical Demand Analysis from the Viewpoint of Simultaneous Equations', *Skandinavisk Aktuarietidskrift*, **29**, 95–114

Bercaw, L. O. (1934), 'Price Analysis: Selected References on the Theoretical Aspects of Supply and Demand Curves and Related Subjects', *Econometrica*, **2**, 399–421

Beveridge, W. H. (1920), 'British Exports and the Barometer', *Economic Journal*, **30**, 13–25

(1921), 'Weather and Harvest Cycles', *Economic Journal*, **31**, 429–52

(1922), 'Wheat Prices and Rainfall in Western Europe', *Journal of the Royal Statistical Society*, **85**, 412–78

Blaug, M. (1968), *Economic Theory in Retrospect* (2nd edn), London: Heinemann

(1976), 'Kuhn versus Lakatos or Paradigms versus Research Programmes in the History of Economics', in S. Latsis (ed.), *Method and Appraisal in Economics*, Cambridge: Cambridge University Press.

(1980), *The Methodology of Economics*, Cambridge: Cambridge University Press

Bowley, A. L. (1901), *Elements of Statistics*, London: P. S. King and Son

(1933), 'The Action of Economic Forces in Producing Frequency Distributions of Income, Prices, and other Phenomena: A Suggestion for Study', *Econometrica*, **1**, 358–72

Bridgman, P. (1927), *The Logic of Modern Physics*, New York: Macmillan

Broster, E. J. (1937), 'A Simple Method of Deriving Demand Curves', *Journal of the Royal Statistical Society*, **100**, 625–41

Brownlie, A. D., and Prichard, M. F. L. (1963), 'Professor Fleeming Jenkin, 1833–85: Pioneer in Engineering and Political Economy', *Oxford Economic Papers*, **15**, 204–16

Bullock, C. J. (1919), 'Prefatory Statement', *Review of Economic Statistics*, **1**

Burns, A. F. (1952), *Wesley Clair Mitchell: The Economic Scientist*, New York: National Bureau of Economic Research.

Burns, A. F. and Mitchell, W. C. (1946), *Measuring Business Cycles*, New York: National Bureau of Economic Research.

Cargill, T. F. (1974), 'Early Applications of Spectral Methods to Economic Time Series', *History of Political Economy*, **6**, 1–16

Cartwright, N. (1989), *Nature's Capacities and their Measurement*, Oxford: Oxford University Press

Cassels, J. M. (1933), 'A Critical Consideration of Professor Pigou's Method of Deriving Demand Curves', *Economic Journal*, **43**, 575–86

Christ, C. F. (1952), 'History of the Cowles Commission 1932–1952', in *Economic Theory and Measurement*, Chicago: Cowles Commission for Research in Economics

(1985), 'Early Progress in Estimating Quantitative Economic Relationships in America', *American Economic Review*, **75**:6, 39–52

Clark, J. M. (1913), 'The Bullion Market and Prices: An Inductive Study of Elasticity of Demand', *American Economic Review*, **3**, 584–8

Cournot, A. A. (1838), *Researches into the Mathematical Principles of the Theory of Wealth*, English translation: 1897, New York: Macmillan

Craver, E. (1986), 'The Emigration of the Austrian Economists', *History of Political Economy*, **18**, 1–32

(1986a), 'Patronage and the Directions of Research in Economics: The Rockefeller Foundation in Europe, 1924–1938', *Minerva*, **24**, 205–22

Craver, E., and Leijonhufvud, A. (1987), 'Economics in America: The Continental Influence', *History of Political Economy*, **19**, 173–82

Crum, W. L. (1923), 'Cycles of Rates on Commercial Paper', *Review of Economic Statistics*, **5**, 17–29

Crump, N. (1924), 'The Interrelation and Distribution of Prices and their Incidence upon Price Stabilization', *Journal of the Royal Statistical Society*, **87**, 167–219

Davenant, C. (1699), *An Essay upon the Probable Methods of Making a People Gainers in the Balance of Trade*, London

Davis, H. T. (1941), *The Analysis of Economic Time Series*, Cowles Commission Monograph 6, Bloomington, Indiana: Principia Press

(1941a), *The Theory of Econometrics*, Bloomington, Indiana: Principia Press

Davis, H. T. and Nelson, W. F. C., (1935), *Elements of Statistics*, Bloomington, Indiana: Principia Press

Derksen, J. B. D., and Rombouts, A. (1937), 'The Demand for Bicycles in the Netherlands', *Econometrica*, **5**, 295–300

Dorfman, J. (1949), *The Economic Mind in American Civilization: 1865–1918*, Vol. III, New York: Viking Press

Durbin, J. (1954), 'Errors in Variables', *Review of the International Statistical Institute*, **22**, 23–32

Durkheim, E. (1895), *The Rules of Sociological Method*, translated by S. A. Solovay and J. H. Mueller, ed. G. E. G. Catlin (1964), New York: The Free Press

Edvardsen, K. (1970), 'A Survey of Ragnar Frisch's Contribution to the Science of Economics', *De Economist*, **118**, 175–96

Epstein, R. J. (1987), *A History of Econometrics*, Amsterdam: North-Holland

Evans, G. C. (1924), 'The Dynamics of Monopoly', *American Mathematical Monthly*, **31**, 77–83

(1931), 'A Simple Theory of Economic Crises', *Journal of the American Statistical Association*, **26** (Supplement), 61–8

Ezekiel, M. (1924), 'A Method of Handling Curvilinear Correlation for any Number of Variables', *Journal of the American Statistical Association*, **19**, 431–53

(1928), 'Statistical Analyses and the "Laws" of Price', *Quarterly Journal of Economics*, **42**, 199–227

(1930), *Methods of Correlation Analysis*, New York: Wiley

(1930a), 'Moore's Synthetic Economics', *Quarterly Journal of Economics*, **44**, 663–79

(1933), 'Some Considerations on the Analysis of the Prices of Competing or Substitute Commodities', *Econometrica*, **1**, 172–80

(1938), 'The Cobweb Theorem', *Quarterly Journal of Economics*, **52**, 255–80

Farquhar, A. B., and Farquhar, H. (1891), *Economic and Industrial Delusions*, New York: G. P. Putnam's Sons

Ferger, W. F. (1932), 'The Static and the Dynamic in Statistical Demand Curves', *Quarterly Journal of Economics*, **47**, 36–62

    (1932a), 'Notes on Pigou's Method of Deriving Demand Curves', *Economic Journal*, **42**, 17–26

Fisher, I. (1925), 'Our Unstable Dollar and the So-called Business Cycle', *Journal of the American Statistical Association*, **20**, 179–202

Fox, K. A. (1989), 'Agricultural Economists in the Econometric Revolution: Institutional Background, Literature and Leading Figures', *Oxford Economic Papers*, **41**, 53–70

Friedman, M. (1938), 'Mr. Broster on Demand Curves', *Journal of the Royal Statistical Society*, **101**, 450–4

    (1940), review of J. Tinbergen: *Statistical Testing of Business-Cycle Theories*, Vol. II: *Business Cycles in the United States of America 1919–1932*, *American Economic Review*, **30**, 657–60

Frisch, R. (1927), *The Analysis of Statistical Time Series*, unpublished mimeo

    (1928), 'Changing Harmonics and Other General Types of Components in Empirical Series', *Skandinavisk Aktuarietidskrift*, **11**, 220–36

    (1929), 'Correlation and Scatter in Statistical Variables', *Nordic Statistical Journal*, **8**, 36–102

    (1931), 'A Method of Decomposing an Empirical Series into its Cyclical and Progressive Components', *Journal of the American Statistical Association*, **26** (Supplement), 73–8

    (1933), 'Propagation Problems and Impulse Problems in Dynamic Economics', in *Economic Essays in Honour of Gustav Cassel*, London: Allen & Unwin

    (1933a), 'Pitfalls in the Statistical Construction of Demand and Supply Curves', *Veröffentlichungen der Frankfurter Gesellschaft für Konjunkturforschung*, New Series, Vol. V, Leipzig: Hans Buske

    (1933b), 'Editorial', *Econometrica*, **1**, 1–4

    (1934), *Statistical Confluence Analysis by Means of Complete Regression Systems*, Oslo: Universitetets Økonomiske Institutt

    (1934a), 'More Pitfalls in Demand and Supply Curve Analysis', *Quarterly Journal of Economics*, **48**, 749–55

    (1936), 'Note on the Term "Econometrics"', *Econometrica*, **4**, 95

    (1938), 'Statistical versus Theoretical Relations in Economic Macrodynamics', *League of Nations Memorandum* (reproduced in 1948, with Tinbergen's comments, in *Autonomy of Economic Relations*, Memorandum, Oslo: Universitetets Sosialøkonomiske Institutt)

    (1939), 'A Note on Errors in Time Series', *Quarterly Journal of Economics*, **53**, 639–40.

    (1970), 'Econometrics in the World of Today', in W. A. Eltis, M. F. G. Scott and J. N. Wolfe (eds.), *Induction, Growth and Trade: Essays in Honour of Sir Roy Harrod*, Oxford: Clarendon Press

Frisch, R., and Holme, H. (1935), 'The Characteristic Solutions of a Mixed

Difference and Differential Equation Occurring in Economic Dynamics', *Econometrica*, **3**, 225–39

Frisch, R., and Mudgett, B. D. (1931), 'Statistical Correlation and the Theory of Cluster Types', *Journal of the American Statistical Association*, **26**, 376–92

Frisch, R. and Waugh, F. V. (1933), 'Partial Time Regressions as Compared with Individual Trends', *Econometrica*, **1**, 387–401

Funkhouser, H. G. (1938), 'Historical Development of the Graphical Representation of Statistical Data', *Osiris*, **3**, 269–404

Garcia-Mata, C., and Shaffner, F. I. (1934), 'Solar and Economic Relationships: A Preliminary Report', *Quarterly Journal of Economics*, **49**, 1–51

Garvy, G. (1943), 'Kondratieff's Theory of Long Cycles', *Review of Economic Statistics*, **25**, 203–20

Geary, R. C. (1942), 'Inherent Relations between Random Variables', *Proceedings of the Royal Irish Academy* (Section A), **47**, 63–76

  (1943), 'Relations between Statistics: The General and the Sampling Problem when the Samples are Large', *Proceedings of the Royal Irish Academy* (Section A), **49**, 177–96

Gilbert, C. L. (1988), 'The Development of Econometrics in Britain since 1945', D. Phil. Thesis, University of Oxford

Gilboy, E. W. (1930), 'Demand Curves in Theory and in Practice', *Quarterly Journal of Economics*, **44**, 601–20

  (1931), 'The Leontief and Schultz Methods of Deriving "Demand" Curves', *Quarterly Journal of Economics*, **45**, 218–61

  (1932), 'Studies in Demand: Milk and Butter', *Quarterly Journal of Economics*, **46**, 671–97

  (1932a), 'Demand Curves by Personal Estimate', *Quarterly Journal of Economics*, **46**, 376–84

  (1934), 'Time Series and the Derivation of Demand and Supply Curves: A Study of Coffee and Tea: 1850–1930', *Quarterly Journal of Economics*, **48**, 667–85

Gini, C. (1910), 'Prezzi e Consumi', *Giornale degli Economisti*, 3rd series, **40**, 99–114, 235–49

  (1921), 'Sull'interpolazione di una Retta quando i Valori della Variabile Independente sono Affetti da Errori Accidentali', *Metron*, **1**, 63–82

Goldberger, A. S. (1972), 'Structural Equation Methods in the Social Sciences', *Econometrica*, **40**, 979–1001

Gordon, R. A. (1949), 'Business Cycles in the Interwar Period: The "Quantitative-Historical" Approach', *American Economic Review* (Papers and Proceedings), **39**:3, 47–63

Granger, C. W. J. (1961), 'First Report of the Princeton Economic Time Series Project', *L'Industria* 194–206

Greenstein, B. (1935), 'Periodogram Analysis with Special Application to Business Failures in the United States, 1867–1932', *Econometrica*, **3**, 170–98

Griliches, Z. (1974), 'Errors in Variables and Other Unobservables', *Econometrica*, **42**, 971–98

Haavelmo, T. (1938), 'The Method of Supplementary Confluent Relations, Illustrated by a Study of Stock Prices', *Econometrica*, **6**, 203–18 (for earlier report see *Econometrica* **5**, 373–4)

(1940), 'The Inadequacy of Testing Dynamic Theory by Comparing the Theoretical Solutions and Observed Cycles', *Econometrica*, **8**, 312–21

(1941), 'On the Theory and Measurement of Economic Relations', mimeo., Cambridge, Mass. (published as Haavelmo (1944))

(1943), 'Statistical Testing of Business-Cycle Theories', *Review of Economic Statistics*, **25**, 13–18

(1943a), 'The Statistical Implications of a System of Simultaneous Equations', *Econometrica*, **11**, 1–12

(1944), 'The Probability Approach in Econometrics', Supplement to *Econometrica*, **12**

(1958), 'The Role of the Econometrician in the Advancement of Economic Theory', *Econometrica*, **26**, 351–7

Haberler, G. (1937), *Prosperity and Depression*, Geneva: League of Nations

Hacking, I. (1983), *Representing and Intervening: Introductory Topics in the Philosophy of Natural Science*, Cambridge: Cambridge University Press

(1983a), 'The Autonomy of Statistical Law', in N. Rescher (ed.), *Scientific Explanation and Understanding*, Lanham: University Press of America

Hastay, M. (1951), review of T. C. Koopmans (ed.): *Statistical Inference in Dynamic Economic Models*, *Journal of the American Statistical Association*, **46**, 388–90

Hendry, D. F. (1980), 'Econometrics – Alchemy or Science', *Economica*, **47**, 387–406

Hendry, D. F., and Morgan M. S. (1989), 'A Re-Analysis of Confluence Analysis', *Oxford Economic Papers*, **41**, 35–52

(forthcoming) (eds.), *The Foundations of Econometric Analysis*, Cambridge: Cambridge University Press

Hicks, J. R. (1937), 'Mr. Keynes and the "Classics": A Suggested Interpretation', *Econometrica*, **5**, 147–59

Hicks, J. R., and Allen, R. G. D. (1934), 'A Reconsideration of the Theory of Value', *Economica* (New Series), **1**, 52–76

Hildreth, C. (1986), *The Cowles Commission in Chicago, 1939–1955*, Berlin: Springer-Verlag

Hood, W. C. and Koopmans T. C. (1953) (eds.), *Studies in Econometric Method*, Cowles Commission Monograph 14, New York: Wiley.

Hooker, R. H. (1900), 'Farm Prices of Wheat and Maize in America, 1870–1899', *Journal of the Royal Statistical Society*, **63**, 648–57

(1901), 'Correlation of the Marriage Rate with Trade', *Journal of the Royal Statistical Society*, **64**, 485–92

(1905), 'On the Correlation of Successive Observations Illustrated by Corn Prices', *Journal of the Royal Statistical Society*, **68**, 696–703

Hotelling, H. (1927), 'Differential Equations Subject to Error, and Population Estimates', *Journal of the American Statistical Association*, **22**, 283–314

(1932), 'Edgeworth's Taxation Paradox and the Nature of Demand and Supply Functions', *Journal of Political Economy*, **40**, 577–616

(1934), 'Analysis and Correlation of Time Series' (Abstract), *Econometrica*, **2**, 211

(1935), 'Demand Functions with Limited Budgets', *Econometrica*, **3**, 66–78

(1939), 'The Work of Henry Schultz', *Econometrica*, **7**, 97–103

Hull, G. H. (1926), *Industrial Depressions*, New York: Codex Book Co.

Hurwicz, L. (1944), 'Stochastic Models of Economic Fluctuations', *Econometrica*, **12**, 114–24

Hutchison, T. W. (1953), *A Review of Economic Doctrines 1870–1929*, Oxford: Clarendon Press

Ingraham, M. H. (1923), 'On Professor H. L. Moore's Mathematical Analysis of the Business Cycle', *Journal of the American Statistical Association*, **18**, 759–65

International Encyclopedia of the Social Sciences, Vols. I–XVIII (1968), Vol. XVIII (1979), ed. D. Sills, New York: The Free Press

Jang, Y. S. (1973), *Econometric Model Building: A Comparative Study of Simultaneous Equation Systems*, Yonsei University Press, South Korea.

Jenkin, H. C. Fleeming (1887), *Papers Literary, Scientific, etc. by the Late Fleeming Jenkin F.R.S., LL.D.*, ed. S. Colvin and J. A. Ewing (2 vols.), London: Longmans, Green

Jevons, H. S. (1910), *The Sun's Heat and Trade Activity*, London: P. S. King and Son

Jevons, W. S. (1871), *The Theory of Political Economy*, London: Macmillan

(1874), *The Principles of Science*, London: Macmillan

(1884), *Investigations in Currency and Finance*, London: Macmillan

(1977 and 1981), *Papers and Correspondence of W. S. Jevons*, Vol. IV & V: 1977, Vol. VII: 1981, ed. R. D. Collison Black, London: Macmillan

Juglar, C. (1862), *Des crises commerciales et de leur retour périodique en France, en Angleterre et aux Etats-Unis* (2nd edn 1889), Paris: Guillaumin

Kærgaard, N. (1984), 'The Earliest History of Econometrics: Some Neglected Danish Contributions', *History of Political Economy*, **16**, 437–44

Kendall, M. G. (1945), 'On the Analysis of Oscillatory Time-Series', *Journal of the Royal Statistical Society*, **108**, 93–141

Kendrick, J. W. (1970), 'The Historical Development of National-Income Accounts', *History of Political Economy*, **2**, 284–315

Keynes, J. M. (1921), *A Treatise on Probability*, London: Macmillan

(1936), 'William Stanley Jevons 1835–1882. A Centenary Allocution on his Life and Work as an Economist and Statistician', *Journal of the Royal Statistical Society*, **99**, 516–55

(1973), *The Collected Writings of John Maynard Keynes*, Vol. XIV, ed. D. Moggridge, London: Macmillan

Keynes, J. M., and Tinbergen, J. (1939 and 1940), 'Professor Tinbergen's Method', *Economic Journal*, **49**, 558–68 (review of Tinbergen (1939), I); 'A Reply', by J. Tinbergen, and 'Comment' by J. M. Keynes, *Economic Journal*, **50**, 141–56.

Keynes, J. N. (1891), *The Scope and Method of Political Economy*, London: Macmillan

Kindleberger, C. P. (1978), *Manias, Panics and Crashes: a History of Financial Crises*, New York: Basic Books

King, W. I. (1917), 'The Correlation of Historical Economic Variables and Misuse of Coefficients in this Connection', *Journal of the American Statistical Association*, **15**, 847–53

(1939), 'Can Production of Automobiles be Stabilized by Making their Prices Flexible?', *Journal of the American Statistical Association*, **34**, 641–51

Klein, J. L. (1986), 'The Conceptual Development of Population and Variation as Foundations of Econometric Analysis', PhD Thesis, City of London Polytechnic

(1987), 'Perceptions and Problems of Time in the Early Interactions of Economics and Statistics', unpublished paper, Mary Baldwin College

(1987a), 'Early Developments in Graphic Representation of Economic Thought', unpublished paper, Mary Baldwin College

Klein, L. R. (1950), *Economic Fluctuations in the United States 1921–1941*, Cowles Commission Monograph 11, New York: Wiley

(1953), *A Textbook of Econometrics*, Evanston, Illinois: Row, Peterson & Co.

Klein, L. R., and Goldberger, A. S. (1955), *An Econometric Model of the United States 1929–1952*, Amsterdam: North-Holland

Kondratieff, N. D. (1935), 'The Long Waves in Economic Life', *Review of Economic Statistics*, **17**, 105–15

Koopmans, T. C. (1937), *Linear Regression Analysis of Economic Time Series*, Netherlands Economic Institute, Publication No. 20, Haarlem: F. Bohn

(1945), 'Statistical Estimation of Simultaneous Economic Relations', *Journal of the American Statistical Association*, **40**, 448–66

(1947), 'Measurement Without Theory', *Review of Economic Statistics*, **29**, 161–72

(1949), 'Identification Problems in Economic Model Construction', *Econometrica*, **17**, 125–44

(1950) (ed.), *Statistical Inference in Dynamic Economic Models*, Cowles Commission Monograph 10, New York: Wiley

Krüger, L., *et al.* (1987), *The Probabilistic Revolution*, Vol. I: *Ideas in History*, ed. L. Krüger, L. J. Daston and M. Heidelberger; Vol. II: *Ideas in the Sciences*, ed. L. Krüger, G. Gigerenzer and M. S. Morgan, Cambridge: MIT Press

Kuhn, T. S. (1970), *The Structure of Scientific Revolutions* (2nd edn), Chicago: University of Chicago Press

Kuznets, S. (1929), 'Random Events and Cyclical Oscillations', *Journal of the American Statistical Association*, **24**, 258–75

Lakatos, I. (1976), *Proofs and Refutations: The Logic of Mathematical Discovery*, ed. J. Worrall and E. Zahar, Cambridge: Cambridge University Press

(1978), *The Methodology of Scientific Research Programmes*, ed. J. Worrall and G. Currie, Cambridge: Cambridge University Press

Lehfeldt, R. A. (1914), 'The Elasticity of Demand for Wheat', *Economic Journal*, **24**, 212–17

(1915), review of H. L. Moore: *Economic Cycles: Their Law and Cause*, *Economic Journal*, **25**, 409–11

Lenoir, M. (1913), *Etudes sur la formation et le mouvement des prix*, Paris: M. Giard et E. Brière

Leontief, W. W. (1929), 'Ein Versuch zur statistischen Analyse von Angebot und Nachfrage', *Weltwirtschaftliches Archiv*, **30**, 1–53

(1934), 'Pitfalls in the Construction of Demand and Supply Curves: A Reply', *Quarterly Journal of Economics*, **48**, 355–61

(1934a), 'More Pitfalls ... – A Final Word', *Quarterly Journal of Economics*, **48**, 755–9.

(1948), 'Econometrics', in *A Survey of Contemporary Economics*, ed. H. S. Ellis, Homewood, Illinois: R. D. Irwin, for American Economic Association

Lewis, E. E. (1939), 'Intercommodity Relationships in Stable Demand', *Econometrica*, **6**, 130–42

Lucas, R. E., Jnr (1980), 'Methods and Problems in Business Cycle Theory', *Journal of Money, Credit and Banking*, **12**, 696–715

Mackenzie, D. A. (1981), *Statistics in Britain: 1865–1930*, Edinburgh: Edinburgh University Press

Mackeprang, E. P. (1906), *Pristeorier*, Copenhagen: Bugge

Magnus, J. R., and Morgan, M. S. (1987), 'The ET Interview: Professor J. Tinbergen', *Econometric Theory*, **3**, 117–42

Mann, H. B., and Wald, A. (1943), 'On the Statistical Treatment of Linear Stochastic Difference Equations', *Econometrica*, **11**, 173–220

Marchal, A. (1952), *Méthode scientifique et science économique*, Paris: M. T. Genin

Marget, A. W. (1929), 'Morgenstern on the Methodology of Economic Forecasting', *Journal of Political Economy*, **37**, 312–39

Marschak, J. (1931), *Elastizität der Nachfrage*, Tübingen: J. C. B. Mohr

(1934), 'More Pitfalls ... – Some Comments', *Quarterly Journal of Economics*, **48**, 759–66

(1939), 'On Combining Market and Budget Data in Demand Studies – A Suggestion', *Econometrica*, **7**, 332–5

(1942), 'Economic Interdependence and Statistical Analysis', in *Studies in Mathematical Economics and Econometrics – In Memory of Henry Schultz*, ed. O. Lange, F. McIntyre and T. O. Yntema, Chicago: University of Chicago Press

Marschak, J., and Lange, O. (1940), 'Mr. Keynes on the Statistical Verification of Business Cycle Theories', unpublished paper

Ménard, C. (1980), 'Three Forms of Resistance to Statistics: Say, Cournot, Walras', *History of Political Economy*, **12**, 524–41

Merlin, S. D. (1950), *The Theory of Fluctuations in Contemporary Economic Thought*, New York: Columbia University Press

Metzler, L. (1940), 'The Assumptions Implied in Least Squares Demand Technique', *Review of Economic Statistics*, **22**, 138–49

Mill, J. S. (1872), *A System of Logic Ratiocinative and Inductive* (8th edn), London: Longmans, Green, Reader, and Dyer

Mills, F. C. (1924), *Statistical Methods*, New York: Henry Holt and Co.

(1936), 'Price Data and the Problems of Price Research', *Econometrica*, **4**, 289–309

Mitchell, W. C. (1913), *Business Cycles and their Causes*, Berkeley: California University Memoirs, Vol. III

 (1927), *Business Cycles: The Problem and its Setting*, New York: National Bureau of Economic Research

Moore, H. L. (1908), 'The Statistical Complement of Pure Economics', *Quarterly Journal of Economics*, **23**, 1–33

 (1911), *Laws of Wages*, New York: Macmillan

 (1914), *Economic Cycles – Their Law and Cause*, New York: Macmillan

 (1917), *Forecasting the Yield and Price of Cotton*, New York: Macmillan

 (1919), 'Empirical Laws of Demand and Supply and the Flexibility of Prices', *Political Science Quarterly*, **34**, 546–67

 (1922), 'Elasticity of Demand and Flexibility of Prices', *Journal of the American Statistical Association*, **18**, 8–19

 (1923), *Generating Economic Cycles*, New York: Macmillan

 (1925), 'A Moving Equilibrium of Demand and Supply', *Quarterly Journal of Economics*, **39**, 357–71

 (1926), 'A Theory of Economic Oscillations', *Quarterly Journal of Economics*, **41**, 1–29

 (1929), *Synthetic Economics*, New York: Macmillan

Morgan, M. S. (1984), 'The History of Econometric Thought: Analysis of the Main Problems of Relating Economic Theory to Data in the First Half of the Twentieth Century', PhD Thesis, University of London

 (1985), 'Correspondence Problems and the History of Econometrics', unpublished paper, University of York

 (1987), 'Statistics without Probability and Haavelmo's Revolution in Econometrics', in *The Probabilistic Revolution*, Vol. II: *Ideas in the Sciences*, ed. L. Krüger, G. Gigerenzer and M. S. Morgan, Cambridge: MIT Press

 (1987a), 'The Stamping out of Process Analysis from Econometrics', prepared for a Symposium on the History and Philosophy of Econometrics, Duke University, November 1987

 (1988), 'Finding a Satisfactory Empirical Model', in *The Popperian Legacy in Economics*, ed. N. de Marchi, Cambridge: Cambridge University Press

Morgenstern, O. (1928), *Wirtschaftsprognose: eine Untersuchung ihrer Voraussetzungen und Möglichkeiten*, Vienna: Julius Springer

 (1961), 'A New Look at Economic Time Series Analysis', in *Money, Growth and Methodology*, ed. H. Hegeland, Lund: C. W. K. Gleerup

Norton, J. P. (1902), *Statistical Studies in the New York Money-Market*, New York: Macmillan

Orcutt, G. H. (1948), 'A Study of the Autoregressive Nature of the Times Series used for Tinbergen's Model of the Economic System of the United States, 1919–1932', *Journal of the Royal Statistical Society*, Series B, **10**, 1–53

Palgrave, R. H. I. (1894–8), *Dictionary of Political Economy* (3 Vols.), London: Macmillan

Patinkin, D. (1976), 'Keynes and Econometrics: On the Interaction between the Macroeconomic Revolutions of the Interwar period', *Econometrica*, **44**, 1091–123

Persons, W. M. (1910), 'The Correlation of Economic Statistics', *Journal of the American Statistical Association*, **12**, 287–322

(1914), review of W. C. Mitchell: *Business Cycles and their Causes*, *Quarterly Journal of Economics*, **28**, 795–810

(1915), review of H. L. Moore: *Economic Cycles*, *American Economic Review*, **5**, 645–8

(1916), 'Construction of a Business Barometer Based upon Annual Data', *American Economic Review*, **6**, 739–69

(1919), 'Indices of Business Conditions', *Review of Economic Statistics*, **1**, 5–110

(1919a), 'An Index of General Business Conditions', *Review of Economic Statistics*, **1**, 111–205

(1924), 'Some Fundamental Concepts of Statistics', *Journal of the American Statistical Association*, **19**, 1–8

(1924a), 'The Problem of Business Forecasting', in *The Problem of Business Forecasting*, Pollak Foundation for Economic Research Publications, No.6, London: Pitman

(1925), 'Statistics and Economic Theory', *Review of Economic Statistics*, **7**, 179–97

Pesaran, H., and Smith, R. (1985), 'Keynes on Econometrics', in *Keynes' Economics: Methodological Issues*, eds. T. Lawson and H. Pesaran, London: Croom-Helm

Pigou, A. C. (1910), 'A Method of Determining the Numerical Value of Elasticities of Demand', *Economic Journal*, **20**, 636–40

(1914), review of W. C. Mitchell: *Business Cycles and their Causes*, *Economic Journal*, **24**, 78–81

(1930), 'The Statistical Derivation of Demand Curves', *Economic Journal*, **40**, 384–400

Porter, T. M. (1986), *The Rise of Statistical Thinking 1820–1900*, Princeton: Princeton University Press

Qin, D. (1988), 'Formalization of Estimation Theory', unpublished paper, University of Oxford

(1989), 'Formalization of Identification Theory', *Oxford Economic Papers*, **41**, 73–93

Reiersøl, O. (1941), 'Confluence Analysis by Means of Lag Moments and Other Methods of Confluence Analysis', *Econometrica*, **9**, 1–24

(1945), 'Confluence Analysis by Means of Instrumental Sets of Variables', *Arkiv för Matematik, Astronomi och Fysik*, **32a**:4, 1–119

Rietz, H. L (1924) (ed.), *Handbook of Mathematical Statistics*, Cambridge, Mass.: Houghton Mifflin Co.

Robbins, L. (1932), *An Essay on the Nature and Significance of Economic Science*, London: Macmillan

Robertson, D. H. (1915), *A Study of Industrial Fluctuations*, London: P. S. King & Son.

Rockefeller Foundation (1947–9), *President's Review and Annual Report*, New York

Rogers, J. E. Thorold (1866), *A History of Agriculture and Prices in England*, Oxford: Clarendon Press

Roos, C. F. (1927), 'A Dynamical Theory of Economics', *Journal of Political Economy*, **35**, 632–56

(1933), 'Contributions of the Mathematician to Economics' (Abstract), *Econometrica*, **1**, 438–9

(1934), 'Theoretical Studies of Demand', *Econometrica*, **2**, 73–90

(1934a), *Dynamic Economics*, Cowles Commission Monograph 1, Bloomington, Indiana: Principia Press

Roos, C. F., and Szeliski, V. von (1939), 'The Concept of Demand and Price Elasticity – the Dynamics of Automobile Demand', *Journal of the American Statistical Association*, **34**, 652–64

Röpke, W. (1936), *Crises and Cycles* (adapted from the German and revised by Vera C. Smith), London: William Hodge & Co.

Samuelson, P. A. (1947), *Foundations of Economic Analysis*, Cambridge: Harvard University Press

Sargan, J. D. (1958), 'The Estimation of Economic Relationships Using Instrumental Variables', *Econometrica*, **26**, 393–415

Sasuly, M. (1930), 'Generalized Multiple Correlation Analysis of Economic Statistical Series', *Journal of the American Statistical Association*, **25** (Supplement), 146–52

Schabas, M. (1984), 'The "Wordly Philosophy" of William Stanley Jevons', *Victorian Studies*, **28**, 130–47

(1989), 'Alfred Marshall, W. Stanley Jevons, and the Mathematization of Economics', *Isis*, **80**, 60–73

Schultz, H. (1925), 'The Statistical Law of Demand', *Journal of Political Economy*, **33**, 481–504 and 577–637

(1927), 'Mathematical Economics and the Quantitative Method', *Journal of Political Economy*, **35**, 702–6

(1928), *Statistical Laws of Demand and Supply with Special Application to Sugar*, Chicago: University of Chicago Press

(1930), 'The Standard Error of a Forecast from a Curve', *Journal of the American Statistical Association*, **25**, 139–85

(1933), 'A Comparison of Elasticities of Demand Obtained by Different Methods', *Econometrica*, **1**, 274–308

(1933a), 'Interrelations of Demand', *Journal of Political Economy*, **41**, 468–512

(1938), *The Theory and Measurement of Demand*, Chicago: University of Chicago Press

Schumpeter, J. (1933), 'The Common Sense of Econometrics', *Econometrica*, **1**, 5–12

(1939), *Business Cycles* (2 vols.), New York: McGraw-Hill

(1954), *History of Economic Analysis*, New York: Oxford University Press

Seckler, D. (1975), *Thorstein Veblen and the Institutionalists*, London: Macmillan

Slutsky, E. E. (1927), 'The Summation of Random Causes as the Source of Cyclic Processes', *The Problems of Economic Conditions*, ed. by the Conjuncture Institute, Moscow, **3**:1, 34–64 (English summary, 156–61)

(1937), 'The Summation of Random Causes as the Source of Cyclic Processes', *Econometrica*, **5**, 105–46

Smith, B. B. (1925), 'The Error in Eliminating Secular Trend and Seasonal Variation before Correlating Time Series', *Journal of the American Statistical Association*, **20**, 543–5

Snyder, C. (1927), *Business Cycles and Business Measurements*, New York: Macmillan

Solo, R. (1939), 'The Demand for Passenger Cars in the U.S.: A Reply', *Econometrica*, **7**, 271–6

Spengler, J. J. (1961), 'Quantification in Economics: Its History', in *Quantity and Quality*, ed. D. Lerner, New York: The Free Press of Glencoe

Staehle, H. (1934), 'Annual Survey of Statistical Information: Family Budgets', *Econometrica*, **2**, 349–62

(1934a), 'The Reaction of Consumers to Changes in Prices and Income: A Quantitative Study in Immigrants' Behavior', *Econometrica*, **2**, 59–72

(1935), 'Family Budgets', *Econometrica*, **3**, 106–18

Staehle, H., and Haavelmo, T. (1941), *The Elements of Frisch's Confluence Analysis*, mimeograph

Stigler, G. J. (1939), 'The Limitations of Statistical Demand Curves', *Journal of the American Statistical Association*, **34**, 469–81

(1950), 'The Development of Utility Theory', *Journal of Political Economy*, **58**, 307–27 and 373–96

(1954), 'The Early History of Empirical Studies of Consumer Behavior', *Journal of Political Economy*, **62**, 95–113

(1962), Henry L. Moore and Statistical Economics', *Econometrica*, **30**, 1–21

(1965), 'Statistical Studies in the History of Economic Thought', in *Essays in the History of Economics*, Chicago: University of Chicago Press

Stigler, S. M. (1982), 'Jevons as Statistician', in *The Manchester School*, **50**, 354–65

(1986), *The History of Statistics: The Measurement of Uncertainty before 1900*, Cambridge: Belknap/Harvard University Press

Stone, J. R. N. (1946), review of T. Haavelmo: 'The Probability Approach in Econometrics', *Economic Journal*, **56**, 265–9

(1954), *The Measurement of Consumers' Expenditure and Behaviour in the United Kingdom, 1920–1938*, Cambridge: Cambridge University Press

(1978), 'Keynes, Political Arithmetic and Econometrics', *Proceedings of the British Academy*, **64**, 55–92

Szeliski, V. von, and Paradiso, L. J. (1936), 'Demand for Boots and Shoes as Affected by Price Levels and National Income', *Econometrica*, **4**, 338–55

Tinbergen, J. (1930), 'Bestimmung und Deutung von Angebotskurven', *Zeitschrift für Nationalökonomie*, **1**, 669–79 (English summary, 798–9)

(1933), 'The Notion of Horizon and Expectancy in Dynamic Economics', *Econometrica*, **1**, 247–64

(1935), 'Annual Survey: Suggestions on Quantitative Business Cycle Theory', *Econometrica*, **3**, 241–308

(1936), *Grondproblemen der Theoretische Statistiek*, Haarlem: F. Bohn

(1937), *An Econometric Approach to Business Cycle Problems*, Paris; Hermann & Cie

(1939), *Statistical Testing of Business-Cycle Theories*, Vol. I: *A Method and its Application to Investment Activity*; Vol. II: *Business Cycles in the United States of America, 1919–1932*, Geneva: League of Nations.

(1940), 'Econometric Business Cycle Research', *Review of Economic Studies*, **7**, 73–90

(1942), 'Critical Remarks on Some Business-Cycle Theories', *Econometrica*, **10**, 129–46

(1951), *Business Cycles in the United Kingdom 1870–1914*, Amsterdam: North-Holland

(1951a), *Econometrics*, London: Allen & Unwin

(1959), *Jan Tinbergen: Selected Papers*, ed. L. H. Klaassen, L. M. Koyck and H. J. Witteveen, Amsterdam: North-Holland

(1974), 'Ragnar Frisch's Role in Econometrics: A Sketch', *European Economic Review*, **5**, 3–6

(1979), 'Recollections of Professional Experiences', *Banca Nazionale del Lavoro Quarterly Review*, **32**, 331–60

Tintner, G. (1938), 'A Note on Economic Aspects of the Theory of Errors in Time Series', *Quarterly Journal of Economics*, **53**, 141–9

(1938a), 'The Theoretical Derivation of Dynamic Demand Curves', *Econometrica*, **6**, 375–80

(1944), 'An Application of the Variate Difference Method to Multiple Regression', *Econometrica*, **12**, 97–113

(1946), 'Multiple Regression for Systems of Equations', *Econometrica*, **14**, 5–36

(1950), 'Static Econometric Models and their Empirical Verification, Illustrated by a Study of the American Meat Market', *Metroeconomica*, **2**, 172–81

(1952), *Econometrics*, New York: Wiley

Vining, R., and Koopmans, T. C. (1949), 'Methodological Issues in Quantitative Economics', *Review of Economics and Statistics*, **31**, 77–94

Wagemann, E. (1930), *Economic Rhythm*, New York: McGraw-Hill

Wald, A. (1936), *Berechnung und Ausschaltung von Saisonschwankungen*, Vienna: Julius Springer

(1940), 'The Fitting of Straight Lines if Both Variables are Subject to Error', *Annals of Mathematical Statistics*, **11**, 284–300

Warming, J. (1906), review of E. P. Mackeprang's *Pristeorier*, *Nationaløkonomisk Tidsskrift*, **44**, 513–18

Weintraub, E. R. (1985), *General Equilibrium Analysis: Studies in Appraisal*, Cambridge: Cambridge University Press

Whitman, R. H. (1934), 'The Problem of Statistical Demand Techniques for Producers' Goods: An Application to Steel', *Journal of Political Economy*, **42**, 577–94

(1936), 'The Statistical Law of Demand for a Producer's Good as Illustrated by the Demand for Steel', *Econometrica*, **4**, 138–52

Wicksteed, P. H. (1889), 'On Certain Passages in Jevons' *Theory of Political Economy*', *Quarterly Journal of Economics*, **3**, 293–314

(1914), 'The Scope and Method of Political Economy in the Light of the "Marginal" Theory of Value', *Economic Journal*, **24**, 1–23

Wilson, E. B. (1934), 'The Periodogram of American Business Activity', *Quarterly Journal of Economics*, **48**, 375–417

(1946), review of T. Haavelmo: 'The Probability Approach in Econometrics', *Review of Economic Statistics*, **28**, 173–4

Wold, H. (1938), *A Study in the Analysis of Stationary Time Series*, Uppsala: Almqvist & Wiksells

(1948), 'Estimation of Economic Relationships', *Econometrica*, **16**, 33–6.

(1951), review of T. C. Koopmans (ed.): *Statistical Inference in Dynamic Economic Models*, *Econometrica*, **19**, 475–7

(1969), 'Econometrics as Pioneering in Nonexperimental Model Building', *Econometrica*, **37**, 369–81

(1969a), 'E. P. Mackeprang's Question Concerning the Choice of Regression – A Key Problem in the Evolution of Econometrics', in *Economic Models, Estimation and Risk Programming: Essays in Honour of G. Tintner*, ed. M. Beckmann, K. A. Fox, J. K. Sengupta and G. U. L. Narasimham, Berlin: Springer-Verlag

Wold, H., and Juréen, L. (1953), *Demand Analysis*, New York: Wiley

de Wolff, P. (1938), 'The Demand for Passenger Cars in the U.S.', *Econometrica*, **6**, 113–29

(1939), 'The Demand for Passenger Cars in the U.S.: A Rejoinder', *Econometrica*, **7**, 277–82

Working, E. J. (1927), 'What do Statistical "Demand Curves" Show?', *Quarterly Journal of Economics*, **41**, 212–35

(1934), 'Demand Studies during Times of Rapid Economic Change', *Econometrica*, **2**, 140–51

Working, H. (1925), 'The Statistical Determination of Demand Curves', *Quarterly Journal of Economics*, **39**, 503–43

(1928), review of W. C. Mitchell: *Business Cycles: The Problem and its Setting*, *Journal of the American Statistical Association*, **23**, 89–94

(1934), 'A Random Difference Series for Use in the Analysis of Time Series', *Journal of the American Statistical Association*, **29**, 11–24

(1935), 'Differential Price Behavior as a Subject for Commodity Price Analysis', *Econometrica*, **3**, 416–27

Wright, P. G. (1915), review of H. L. Moore: *Economic Cycles – Their Law and Cause*, *Quarterly Journal of Economics*, **29**, 631–41

(1922), 'Moore's Work in Cycles: A Review', *Quarterly Journal of Economics*, **36**, 691–704

(1924), review of H. L. Moore: *Generating Economic Cycles*, *Journal of the American Statistical Association*, **19**, 103–8

(1928), *The Tariff on Animal and Vegetable Oils*, New York: Macmillan

(1929), review of H. Schultz: *Statistical Laws of Demand and Supply*, *Journal of the American Statistical Association*, **24**, 207–15

(1930), review of H. L. Moore: *Synthetic Economics, Journal of Political Economy*, **38**, 328–44

Wright, S. (1921), 'Correlation and Causation', *Journal of Agricultural Research*, **20**, 557–85

(1925), 'Corn and Hog Correlations', *U.S. Department of Agriculture, Bulletin No. 1300*, Washington DC

Yule, G. U. (1895), 'On the Correlation of Total Pauperism with Proportion of Out-Relief', *Economic Journal*, **5**, 603–11, and (1896) **6**, 613–23

(1897), 'On the Theory of Correlation', *Journal of the Royal Statistical Society*, **60**, 812–54

(1911), *An Introduction to the Theory of Statistics*, London: Charles Griffin & Co.

(1915), review of H. L. Moore: *Economic cycles – Their Law and Cause, Journal of the Royal Statistical Society*, **78**, 302–5

(1921), 'On the Time-Correlation Problem, with Especial Reference to the Variate-Difference Correlation Method', *Journal of the Royal Statistical Society*, **84**, 497–526

(1926), 'Why Do We Sometimes Get Nonsense Correlations Between Time-Series? – A Study in Sampling and the Nature of Time-Series', *Journal of the Royal Statistical Society*, **89**, 1–64

(1927), 'On a Method of Investigating Periodicities in Disturbed Series, with Special Reference to Wolfer's Sunspot Numbers', *Philosophical Transactions of the Royal Society of London*, Series A, **226**, 267–98.

(1971), *Statistical Papers of George Udny Yule*, selected by A. Stuart and M. G. Kendall, London: Charles Griffin & Co.

Index